Unsettling the City

Unsettling the City
Urban Land and the Politics of Property

Nicholas Blomley

ROUTLEDGE
NEW YORK AND LONDON

Published in 2004 by
Routledge
29 West 35th Street
New York, NY 10001
www.routledge-ny.com

Published in Great Britain by
Routledge
11 New Fetter Lane
London EC4P 4EE
www.routledge.co.uk

Routledge is an imprint of the Taylor & Francis Group.

Printed in the United States of America on acid-free paper.

10 9 8 7 6 5 4 3 2 1

Library of Congress Cataloging-in-Publication Data

Blomley, Nicholas K.
   Unsettling the city: urban land and the politics of property / Nicholas Blomley.
      p. cm.
Includes bibliographical references and index.
   ISBN 0–415–93315–3 (hardcover: alk. paper) — ISBN 0–415–93316–1
(pbk. : alk. paper)
   1. Land use, Urban.   2. City planning.   3. Real property.   4. Gentrification.
I. Title.
   HD1391.B58 2003
   333.33'7—dc21

                                                                2003010528

Table of Contents

List of Illustrations

A farmer touches the earth in his fields. He thinks, This land is mine. A person in the city too, they walk their favorite streets, they visit their favorite parks. . . . Others are homeless, unrooted by choice or force," the Professor continued. "I know a man without a home who lives in a place where people park their cars. He knows the city like no other person, from the inside out and at all hours. But he cannot let himself attach to any square foot of it more than any other. . . . I am interested in these different connections. . . . The connections between people and the places they call their own. I am interested in how these connections are forged and broken. And how, for some, the connection refuses to break.
—Timothy Taylor, *Stanley Park*

Acknowledgements

Although I have an intellectual property in this book, it was collectively made. First and foremost, I wish to thank those Downtown Eastsiders who gave up their valuable time to talk to me. I am thankful for their friendship and amazed by their creativity, stamina, and political courage. I would like to thank Tom Laviolette, Jeff Sommers, Muggs Sigurgeirson, Jim Green, Don Larson, Marg Green, John Shayler, Bob Sarti, Joanne Hochu, Darren Kitchen, Barb Daniel, and Bud Osborn, amongst others. I have also been lucky to work with a wonderful group of graduate students over the past few years. In various ways, they offered guidance, help, and critique. Thanks to Aurian Haller, Adrienne Burk, Damian Collins, Wendy Mendes, Jeff Sommers, and Lorraine Gibson. Wendy and Jeff also provided invaluable research advice. Colleagues in various fields looked over sections of the book and offered advice. Joe Singer, whose analysis of property I draw on, Cole Harris, who knows so much about colonial geographies, and Adrienne Burk, who contributed a sensitive editorial eye and humane sensibilities, were all immensely helpful. Because of the respect in which I hold them, I was delighted that Gerry Pratt and Don Mitchell agreed to comment on the entire manuscript. Colleagues at Simon Fraser University have been supportive and comradely: my thanks to Mike Hayes, Jennifer Hyndman, Alex Clapp, Bev Pitman, Jerry Zaslove, Evelyn Pinkerton, Dara Culhane, Debbie Bell, and Paige Raibmon, amongst others. In addition to my colleagues at SFU, I would like to thank David Delaney, Terry Simmons, Peter Fitzpatrick, Edgar Hachivi Heap of Birds, Neil Smith, Kevin Gould, Nathan Edelson, Kris Olds, and David Ley. I am also in the debt of others, including Carol Rose, Crawford Macpherson, Jennifer Nedelsky, and Joseph Sax. Some of this material is reworked from earlier publications: my thanks to the editors of *Public Culture,* the *Canadian Journal of Law and Society,* and the *Law and Society Review.* Dave McBride at Routledge has been a fine editor. I would like to thank him for encouraging me to write this book in the first place.

I would also like to thank Jessie Hill. With her, I became a resident of the Downtown Eastside, a parent, and a property owner. During the writing of this book, my mother, Rikke, died. With her commitment to justice and creativity, I hope she would have liked this book.

I dedicate the book to my three daughters Caja, Elina, and Imogen. May they always be brave, smart, and beautiful.

Nicholas Kjølsen Blomley
Hammond, British Columbia
Mayday, 2003

Preface

I grew up in a small village (in the Royal County of Berkshire), deep in the English countryside a few miles from the border with Hampshire (now rebranded Jane Austen Country). With its half-timbered cottages, rustic pubs, and rolling countryside, the surrounding landscape appears the epitome of domestication and tranquillity. The coppices, bridle paths, and fields that I roamed over as a child are bit-players in a firmly English story of order, intimacy, and settlement. These are, after all, the "Home Counties." But, as any rural historian will tell you, this apparently "old" landscape was in fact recently forged through complex and often violent political struggles and legal remakings. Enclosures in the seventeenth and eighteenth centuries swept away many traditional commoners' rights in the name of improvement and monetarization. This was fiercely contested: Edward Thompson's classic treatise on the conflict over traditional property rights in the eighteenth century describes events that were partly fought out in the woods, fields, and villages around my childhood home.[1] Mythologies of rural quiescence and deferential community are belied by hierarchies of power and privilege.[2] Much of the land in the village continues to be owned by a modern-day squire, whose wealth derives from merchant banking in London. Given its proximity to London and the booming M4 corridor, the area has now been caught up in the English real estate bubble. Quaint barns and farmhouses have been gussied up and sold to those in pursuit of the rural idyll. This rural gentrification has meant that many of my former schoolmates, some of them children of tenant farmers, are unable to live in the place of their birth.

In 1988, I moved to Vancouver, retracing the route of millions of European settlers before me (some of them, no doubt, displaced by earlier rural dispossessions). I lived for several years in Vancouver's inner city, in a neighborhood known as the Downtown Eastside, participating in community affairs and politics. I went on to do research in the area. My work, which I report on here, concerned the ways in which conceptions and practices relating to real property entered into the conflict over gentrification. My hunch was that these conceptions and practices were critical to this struggle, even if they were not always acknowledged as such by analysts. Yet if land was at issue in the Downtown Eastside, it was also of obvious and pressing importance to provincial politics. Native grievances relating to aboriginal title have been unresolved since colonial settlement. Periodically, these flare up in acts of protest, such as the irruption of native protest blockades in 1990. While the issue of native title was easy to imagine as something outside the city, the visible presence of many native people in the city seemed to complicate things in important ways.

This is a book, then, about urban property and its politics. My title is a play on the word *settlement* and its multiple valences. One meaning of the infinitive *to settle* is the definitive fixing of the unstable. *Settle* is defined, variously, as "to put in order, arrange," "to make stable or permanent, establish," to fix definitely," or "to become more stable or composed, stop fluctuating or changing."[3] In this sense, we shall see that the meaning of property also appears settled. What has been termed the "ownership model" presumes clarity and determinacy in the definition of what property is, and tells us which relationships between people and scarce resources are to be valued as such, and which are not. There is a lot at stake here. The ownership model encourages us to think of property in a particular way, neatly summarized long ago by Felix Cohen: "That is property to which the following can be attached: To the world: Keep off X unless you have my permission, which I may grant or withhold. Signed: Private citizen. Endorsed: The state."[4] Property is imagined here as *private* property, with the solitary owner exercising exclusionary rights over a bounded space. While property may be public (that is, held by a state), it is rarely imagined as collective. The ownership model, I shall suggest, is hegemonic, shaping our understandings and practices relating to property. It affects legal deliberations, social discourse, and governmental interventions.

Settlement has a second meaning: "to free from disturbance; calm or quiet," "to prevent from creating a disturbance or interfering," and "to end." Thus, we talk of "settling" a dispute.[5] And the definitional clarity of the ownership model is deemed valuable, in part, because it "quiets" title, promising secure and uncontested relations with others with respect to the use and disposition of things. The enactment of property not only presumes a definitional certainty (*this* is property, *that* isn't), but also invites us to imagine that property and settlement are synonymous. The unitary owner at the center of the model is imagined as secure in her entitlements, and the institution of property is rendered a means for preventing discord. The clear markers of ownership and the "established expectations" of property are supposed to work to ensure the "quiet enjoyment" of the land. Property brings certainty. Certainty brings peace and prosperity.

The degree to which property is, indeed, "settled" is consequential, affecting the ways in which power, subjectivity, and political relations are conceived. It encourages a view of property as nonsocial; that is, as concerned with relations between people and things, thus obscuring property's affect on social relations of power. It underwrites the public/private divide, so central to capitalist institutions and ideology. In acknowledging only certain relations as "property," the ownership model ignores the claims and aspirations of many. But I suspect that the definitional "settlements" of property also affect scholarship. We tend not to reflect on the ways in which the first world city is a propertied space. Although there is a literature on the social and political dimensions of property, it tends not to focus on the metropolitan West.[6] This is, in one sense, for a good reason. Globalization and neoliberalism have wrought profound changes on property relations in the developing world. However, within the West, and more particularly within the city, urban processes and conflicts are not often framed in a similar language. Although there is a small, though important body of literature that takes property seriously, urban scholars have tended to underplay the importance of property as a set of political and legal relations to urban social relations.[7] Not only does this essentialize private property (which is, as we shall see, a good deal more complicated, cultural, and uncertain than might at first appear), it ignores the possibilities that property in the urban heartland may be differentiated and diverse. Gentrification, for example, is often theorized in relation to the economics of property, whether in relation to the dynamics of supply or demand. Although this is clearly important, I shall suggest that a focus on real estate can usefully be supplemented by an attention to real property, especially if one recognizes the importance not only of private and state property, but also of claims to property that are neither. Urban land, in other words, needs to be recognized as land over which a legal regime of real property is operative. I will try and unpack the implications of this claim for an analysis of the city more generally, arguing that spatial conflicts, urban development, urban planning, urban political identities, postcoloniality, and the construction of place are all partly shaped by and constitutive of property relations.

In calling this book *Unsettling the City,* my goal is to challenge these dominant settlements of property. On several counts, it may be that property is more definitionally, politically, and empirically heterogeneous than the ownership model supposes. For if we look more closely, we can find a striking diversity of relationships between people and land that appear property-like, even if they do not fit within the prevailing definitions of property. Although many of these relationships are collective, it also appears that private property itself may be a good deal more complicated. Property claims can also overlap; thus it is, for example, that supposedly private or state property can be claimed in the name of a community. I want to take these appropriations seriously. Perhaps because of these multiple claims, property emerges as a site for conflict. State–sanctioned property claims are challenged; alternative claims to land are articulated that are neither public nor private, but something in between. If property appears settled, perhaps this is more a "reality effect" of the ownership model, than an accurate mapping of property in the world.

But *settle* has a third meaning that I wish to challenge in relation to property. To settle can also denote stability after a period of flux. Thus, we talk of settlers as those who, like me, migrate and then "settle down." Similarly, dominant treatments of property assume that ownership rights are created at one moment in time and immutable thereafter. However, it seems useful to recognize that property is not a static, pregiven entity, but depends on a continual, active "doing." As *settle* is a verb, so property is an enactment. This enactment can include what has been termed *persuasion,* that is, communicative claims to others.[8] This can include story telling, such as Locke's influential "creation-myth" of property. But property is also enacted in more material and corporeal ways. Bodies, technologies, and things must be enrolled and mobilized into organized and disciplined practices. Real property, more generally, must be enacted upon material spaces and real people, including owners and those who are to be excluded. Police officers must enforce the law. Legal contracts must be inscribed, signed, and witnessed. Citizens must physically respect the spatial markers of property. Similarly, I shall suggest, the definitional boundaries of property must also be policed. Thus it is that certain types of property relation (almost exclusively private) are acknowledged and sanctioned, while others (almost exclusively state or communal) are derided. Property, in that sense, must be continually "settled." But as we shall see, more informal property claims (that is, not legible to the ownership model) are also enacted. That these are not always acknowledged as property perhaps speaks more to the prevalence of a certain definition of property than the degree to which these informal claims constitute viable forms of entitlement.

These enactments of property, I want to argue here, have an important geography. In recognizing this, I hope to contribute to the emergent scholarly interest in the geographies of law.[9] Not only does the making of property entail the making of space (for example, through the cadastral survey), but property's enactments are also caught up in the creation of particular landscapes that are simultaneously material and representational. The city is a particularly interesting space for these reasons. On the one hand, I shall suggest, its symbolic value as a site of civilization and settled prosperity has often been yoked to its role as a propertied space. However, the very creation of the city, and its continued remaking seems all too often to be associated with acts of dispossession and eviction. Within the West, the creation of the urban working class, Marx argued, was based on the expropriation of the rural peasantry, such as those of my rural home, in acts of "reckless terrorism."[10] In contemporary "settler societies" the inauguration of urban space has often entailed the dispossession of indigenous populations. Contemporary processes of gentrification also threaten and deliver other dispossessions. Yet these dispossessions are often evicted from urban history, despite their continued contestation by those affected.

In exploring the political geographies of urban property, I aim to make a broader argument about the analytical and political insights that come from recognizing urban spaces as propertied spaces. Property here is understood in largely political and legal terms, characterized by a particular and potent mix of rights, jural relations, ideologies, and exclusions. To invoke property is to summon up both formally prescribed rights as well as nonjusticiable, yet still powerful, understandings of ownership and entitlement. It is to recognize that property is deeply social and political, structuring immediate relations between people as well as larger liberal architectures, such as the division between public and private spheres. Property, moreover, implies diverse and often contradictory social beliefs and representations (relating to masculine citizenship, race, visions of the economy, claims to community, and so on). Property is also predicated on physical, material practices; notably the state-enforced right to expel.

To say that property is "political" is to say several things. Most obviously, it is to say that property in all its manifestations has a relation to the state. Even with the abolition of property ownership as a basis for enfranchisement, the "good" citizen is still one who enjoys a particular relation to land. The day-to-day operation and enforcement of a regime of private property, moreover, is clearly dependent on state practices, whether through cadastral mapping or policing. However, it also reminds us of the ethical dimensions of property, especially when packaged as a "right." Our "enjoyment" of property frequently depends upon the dispossession of others, whether now or in the past, for example. More generally, spatial conflicts and struggles over urban development, I suggest, frequently turn on contests over the meaning, moralities, and politics of property. Property's ethics have tended to be viewed in either a negative or positive light.

My argument will be that property can be both, depending on the particular social contexts within which it is put to work. The politics of rights, such as property, depend.

I offer an exploration of one urban place—the Downtown Eastside, in inner-city Vancouver, Canada—in an attempt at unsettling the geographies of property more generally. I do so with reference to some specific moments when the conditionality and politics of urban property in Vancouver have been forced to the surface. A "new" city, colonially speaking, Vancouver's past is still powerfully present in its contemporary landscapes. The inner city, in particular, is an intensely disputed space: local antipoverty activists have long fought gentrification and redevelopment, increasingly driven by the city's quest for a place in the globalizing order of the Pacific Rim. However, other struggles and displacements are also at issue. Although some have their roots in old injustices—including the dispossession of Native peoples, who have used these lands for millennia—they continue to resonate in this place. Although this struggle is fought over many issues, I argue that the symbolic and material dimensions of real property are central. The politics of property, I argue, turn out to be diverse.

But this book is also about much more than Vancouver. Although there is an important specificity to Vancouver, its struggles over urban space and urban property are, of course, far from unique. More immediately, while struggles over real property have long been important to many cities, they have reached a new intensity of late, given wider shifts in the social geography of the city. As cities strive for world-class status, inner-city populations have experienced intensifying displacement. The "enclosure" of the urban commons has also been a site for conflict. But for cities in settler societies, such as North America or Australasia, such "global" developments can confront "a very specific local politics deeply marked by the historical legacy of the colonial dispossession of indigenous peoples."[11] The interplay between these related dispossessions creates, I think, a particular and rarely acknowledged politics.

And in recognizing this politics I aim for other goals. Increasingly, perhaps, cities are the site for a variety of spatial struggles, many of which turn on the geographies of property, including state attempts at regulating homelessness and panhandling, in combination with a variety of development-driven displacements, such as gentrification. Such initiatives, it has been said, are sustained by an increasingly "revanchist" approach to marginalized urban populations, as well as "common-sense" assumptions about property, such as the "naturalness" of displacement, or the beneficial effects of middle-class ownership in poor neighborhoods. Consequently, there seems an urgent need to do two related things. First,

I aim to acknowledge those ongoing attempts to *contest* these dispossessions, in both their material and representational forms. Struggles over the spaces of the city can be understood as part of the long-standing struggle to resist the enclosure of the commons, and carve out a right to place. I see such struggles as an integral part of a long-standing contestation of certain configurations of property rights. But this is not simply a politics of opposition. It also relies upon the enactment of alternative claims to land, often communal in nature. Enclosure is bad, in that sense, to the extent that it threatens a valued commons. The political purchase—and endurance—of the latter needs to be acknowledged in making sense of the former. Second, in so doing, I hope to speak to the political possibilities and spaces of contemporary urban citizenship in relation to property. Although property's discourses and practices are the means by which poor and racialized city dwellers are dispossessed, such discourses and practices are also a crucial political resource in challenging these dispossessions. Property comes freighted with an array of historically layered and often contradictory possibilities. Property, as Marx insisted, is not reducible to private property.[12] Moreover, as C. B. Macpherson argued, the necessary concomitant of property's "right to exclude" is the "right *not* to be excluded."[13]

The first chapter, therefore, begins by asking the question: What is property? Although this may, as noted, appear a settled question, I shall suggest that the answer is far from obvious. The ownership model, central to legal liberalism, identifies property as essentially private, with state property as the anomalous exception. Property is imagined (and spatialized) in a particular way, moreover, with important political consequences, including a reluctance to acknowledge claims to land that do not easily fit within the model as "property." The imagined certainty to property encourages a view of property relations as settled. Property's "established expectations," as Bentham puts it, offers us a world of clarity and concord. I begin to challenge both these claims, suggesting that people in cities, as elsewhere, articulate many property-like claims that fall outside or complicate the ownership model. In part because these claims conflict, urban property itself can be a site for struggle.

Chapter 2 moves to a discussion of gentrification, with particular reference to inner-city Vancouver, arguing for the existence of a continued and complicated struggle about property. Low-income residents and activists not only challenge the exclusions of private property, they articulate a localized collective claim to certain valued spaces and buildings that are collective in their reach. Property, in other words, is both challenged and defended. I draw on the concept of landscape to try and tease out the enactments of this claim. Landscape is particularly helpful here, given its double meaning as a material site and mode of spatial representation. Both seem as important to opposition to gentrification, as they are to dominant enactments of property. Within the Downtown Eastside, the material co-production and physical occupation of the neighborhood, as well as forms of visual appropriation and mapping, play a powerful role in sustaining and reproducing a collective informal claim to space. Gentrification-induced displacement compromises this claim. Yet a collective entitlement serves, in turn, as a powerful basis for opposition.

Since chapter 2 focuses on the arguments made by low-income activists, chapter 3 includes the claims of private property owners. The moral frontier so prevalent in inner-city gentrification, I suggest, is partly forged through opposing claims and understandings related to the ethics of property. Different readings of rights, property, time, and space combine to create opposing constellations of moral claims related to gentrification and residency. These claims about residential change seek to answer a series of important framing questions, such as: What is a place like prior to gentrification? How should change occur? What are the broader dynamics of change itself? Drawing again on the Downtown Eastside, I shall focus in particular on three polarities that roughly coincide with these questions. First, a characterization of an inner-city population as mobile and transient is counterposed with a claim on behalf of the urban poor to residency and citizenship. Calls to increase "social mix" to revitalize a neighborhood are answered by the argument that "mix," in the context of prevailing property arrangements, will translate into social exclusion. Finally, a dynamic concept of "highest and best use" is countered by the concept of "community use." Such concepts rely, in turn, on particular histories and geographies of a space.

Characterizations of the residents of the inner city as mobile and unfixed bear a striking resemblance to many representations of native people. In both cases, the effect is to force a separation between a population and the space it occupies, rendering a collective claim to this space void, even invisible. My fourth chapter, then, turns to a discussion of the creation of the settler-city, and its relationship to prior indigenous claims. The beginnings of property, it seems, all too often entailed the denial of these entitlements. This denial, however, endures: there seems an enduring blindness towards both historic dispossessions and the continuation of indigenous claims to urban land. This is reflected, perhaps, in the relative paucity of scholarship on the contemporary city as an aboriginal space. I distinguish between foundational acts of *dispossession,* and continuing processes of *displacement* that present the settler-city as a necessarily and naturally nonnative space. Displacement, I suggest, is sustained through narrative, material settlement and mapping, all of which rely, in various ways, on representations of landed property. Set in motion many years ago, this process and its politics persist. Yet native people have always challenged both dispossession and displacement. The last few decades, perhaps, have seen an intensification of these challenges that have begun to implicate the settler-city. Again, the enactment of this counterclaim occurs through the creative material and representational reworking of urban space, such as public art, material occupation, and remapping. The settler-city, ground zero in the colonial imagination, is an increasingly unsettled space. While I refer to Vancouver, I also speak more generally of Australasia, Canada, and the United States.

Although the issues I cover in this book are nothing new, I have found relatively little scholarship on them. This seems surprising, as property surely matters to urban politics. If nothing else, I trust that the book makes this point. One consequence, however, is that I open up many issues without bringing them to closure. This is also a problem of my own making: it would have been easier to focus only on the politics of property in relation to gentrification. However, to then overlook the colonial land nexus as it relates to the city seems inappropriate, especially in the city I now occupy. My concluding chapter, then, tries tentatively to connect gentrification and colonial displacement. I do so by drawing upon a remarkable anonymous art installation in the Downtown Eastside. The installation alerts us to the complicated and often agonistic politics associated with the forging of the urban frontier, whether driven by capitalism, colonialism, or patriarchy. The enactment of property can erase and efface in ways that are both symbolic and ineluctably corporeal. Yet property can also serve as a site for creative remembering and reinscription. It is with these multiple possibilities that I conclude. Like the Professor in Timothy Taylor's novel, cited above, "I am interested in . . . the connections between people and the places they call their own. I am interested in how these connections are forged and broken. And how, for some, the connection refuses to break."

CHAPTER 1

Welcome to the Hotel California

It's a comfortable feeling to know that you stand on your own ground. Land is about the only thing that can't fly away.

—Anthony Trollope, *The Last Chronicle of Barset*

[T]here is not only argument about what the institution of property ought to be, there is also dispute about what it is.

—C. B. Macpherson, "The Meaning of Property"

What Is Property?

In October 1997, Wade Luciak, the owner of the Hotel California in Vancouver's Downtown South neighborhood, evicted fifty long-term tenants, and gave notice to fifty more. Rents were increased from the near-welfare rate of four hundred dollars a month that long-term residents paid to a nightly rate of sixty dollars (or eighteen hundred a month). The owner ordered the evictions to make room for higher paying tourists, and because of his concern with a proposed city bylaw designed to discourage the demolition of lower-priced units. Luciak reportedly saw this as an unjustified limitation on his profits and his abilities to run his business as he saw fit. In a media interview he claimed to regret the evictions: "I really think the world of them [his tenants] and they think the world of me."[1]

The story of the Hotel California appears quite obviously to be a story about property. From the brief description, it is easy for any observer to assign and name property's basic categories. Thus, Wade Luciak is an owner. He owns a building, the Hotel California. As such, we expect him to enjoy certain rights. The building is occupied by tenants. Though they may enjoy certain limited rights, these tenants are ultimately subject to the rights of Luciak to expel them from his property. The city of Vancouver has interests

1

that are seen as external from, and ultimately secondary to, the rights of the owner. "Economic" imperatives (an entrepreneur's need to earn a profit) are juxtaposed in this story with "political" interventions (the city's desire to curtail homelessness). In response to this threat, the owner exercises his right to dispose of his property as he sees fit. He has nothing against the tenants; in fact, they are his friends. Blame is fixed squarely with the interventions of the city.

But what is the property at the center of this, and so many other urban stories? For property more generally is far from a self-evident category. It is, claims one eminent theorist, a "social relation that defines the property holder with respect to something of value . . . against all others."[2] To an anthropologist, it is a "network of social relations that governs the conduct of people with respect to the use and disposition of things."[3] Marx pointed to "the relations of individuals to one another with reference to the material, instrument and product of labor."[4] Relations and networks, individuals and societies, things of value—these are all ambiguous and slippery concepts.

Yet, despite the potential slipperiness of property, the categories and assignments I used in discussing the Hotel California are familiar for a good reason. They exemplify a pervasive set of conceptions of what property *is*, conceptions that Joseph Singer terms the ownership model:

> What is property? One might think this was a simple question. Property is about rights over things and the people who have those rights are called owners. What powers do owners have over the things they own? Owners are free to use the property as they wish. They have the right to exclude others from it or grant them access over it. They have the power to transfer title—to pass the powers of ownership to someone else. They are also immune from having the property taken away from them without their consent, or they must be adequately compensated if the property is taken by the state for public purposes.[5]

Property, according to this model, is almost exclusively *private* property. A bright line is drawn between the owner and the state: although the state may intervene to limit the rights of the owner if they threaten harm to others, such interventions are seen as secondary to the core rights of the owner. Property rights are negative rights, in that sense. The ownership model also assumes a unitary, solitary, and identifiable owner, separated from others by boundaries that protect him or her from nonowners and grant the owner the power to exclude. The actions of the owner are imagined as self-regarding: they concern only him or her and the things owned. Mr. Luciak's property relation thus appears to rest in his right to control the occupation of his hotel rooms: the eviction of the occupants of those rooms (who think the world of him, as he does of them) appears almost as a secondary and unwanted by-product of that relationship.[6]

The ownership model, it has been said, "remains powerful and exerts substantial determinative force in adjudicating and developing the rules of property law."[7] As I note below, it shapes understandings of the possibilities of social life, the ethics of human relations, and the ordering of economic life. It also, I will argue, shapes our understanding of what property in the city actually *is* and how it *ought* to be structured.

Were we to draw a map of property in the city using the ownership model, the majority of land would appear as privately held. Similarly, private property appears as central to discussions of property more generally, as I shall note below, even to the extent that the two appear synonymous. Second, private property would be distinguished from "public" property, such as streets, parks, and schools. All land appears neatly assigned to either public or private forms of ownership. Such a mapping accords to the ownership model's categorization of property. Categorization, of course, is central to legal reasoning, providing a basis for determining whether a certain legal rule applies to a particular situation. Legal categorization, it has been argued, is definitional, grouping objects together on the basis of what are assumed to be their inherent and objective properties.[8]

That property is reducible to private property seems commonplace.[9] Charles Donahue documents a tendency within Western property law to agglomerate "in a single legal person . . . the exclusive right to possess, privilege to use, and power to convey a thing."[10] Private property has dominated debates on property, of course, since the very beginnings of political theory.[11] Macpherson argues that the centrality of private property to dominant maps reflects the particular moral controversies that it generates. The ascendancy of the capitalist market, he argues, made it natural "that the very concept of property should be reduced to that of private property—an exclusive, alienable, absolute individual or corporate right in things."[12]

But, as noted, a map of urban property, predicated on the ownership model, would also sustain a second claim: that there are many owners of land, "but, for practical purposes, . . . *only two classes of ownership*."[13] While private ownership is clearly the expected norm, forms of collective ownership are obviously acknowledged. However, these are carefully hedged: "either ownership is vested in private parties or it resides with organized governments. Thus, in the conventional lore, markets are based on private rights, or, when markets fail, property may be governmentally managed."[14] As Macpherson notes, state or governmental ownership is of a particular form. State property entails a right that the state creates and retains for itself (for example, public utilities or parkland). In effect, the state is acting as an artificial person or corporation.[15]

But the ownership model tells us not only what property is, but what it *ought* to be. State intervention is presumptively invalid, with the burden of justification resting with the state. As suggested above, the rights of the private owner are seen as legitimately trumping those of the collective, and are deemed both anterior and superior. This places a heavy burden on those seeking to regulate or limit the property right. Put in more popular terms, this conception is made explicit when a homeowner claims, "this is my land, and I can do what I like with it."[16] Although this may serve useful economic functions, the separation and privileging of property rights also sustains valued political functions—most importantly, that of the liberty of the owner. Maintaining the distinction between owner and state, in this sense, is critical. Property also promises a decentralization and dispersal of power: "Power allocated through property appears to have an independent, nonstatelike quality. It is "private power."[17]

The "ought" of property extends more generally. As I shall discuss below, private ownership is seen as good to the extent that it fosters valued behaviors, including responsible citizenship, political participation, and economic entrepreneurship. By extension, people who do not own property (insofar as the ownership model is concerned) are treated with a good deal of ambivalence, suspicion, and even hostility. This treatment extends to whole categories of people who do not enjoy the full exercise of private property rights, whether they be renters, occupants of social housing, or at an extreme, homeless. The ownership model has other important ethical associations. For example, many would argue that Mr. Luciak should be able to exercise his property rights to upgrade his property not only because of the importance of his essential liberties, but because we approve of his plan to "improve" the property. This would facilitate the "highest and best use" of the hotel, to use a widespread phrase. Property in this sense comes freighted with both economic and political meanings.

And of course, these definitional questions are more than a disinterested taxonomic exercise, but prove immensely consequential. Put bluntly, the adjudication of what is, and what is not property makes important things happen. And of course, what or who qualifies as an owner or object of ownership, and the precise nature of the relationship "against all others" has long been politically charged. Can people be owned, for example? Can individuals exercise private property rights over objects of shared cultural value?[18] Who is entitled to own? The ownership model is again important here, offering what seem to be persuasive and commonsensical answers. This is important: because of the institutional and ideological investments of capitalist society, naming someone as an owner or something as an object of ownership is important. As I discuss below, property relations acknowledged by the state are granted rights-status. So, put simply, because I am categorized as an owner, I have an enforceable right to my home. Others, such as indigenous people, may pursue a claim to "my" land. However, should a native person decide to camp out in my front garden, I could enlist the power of the state to expel him, using force, if necessary.

The tendency to view property as essentially private, and periodically public, reproduces the wider tendency to view legal orderings as binary, with a privileging of one pole. We should not be surprised by this, given the prevalence of a particular worldview, central to Western law, which offers a powerful view of law, society, and power. This liberal discourse assumes a view of rights, such as those relating to property, as belonging to atomized individuals located in a realm of private liberty, confronting a threatening collective (either the state or other institutions).[19] This clearly fits into the ownership model, with the centrality it accords the individual and the incoherence of collective claims to property.

The ownership model thus offers a consequential categorization of property that affects both the formal workings of the law and everyday understandings of property. Jennifer Nedelsky points to the "tenacity," "power and significance" of a particular view of property to conceptions of property, politics, and the world.[20] Like a more famous Hotel California, it feels like we may be able to check out, but never (conceptually) leave. The reified categories of the ownership model, moreover, remain persuasive in part because they are sustained by spatial categories. In both a practical and metaphoric sense, the ownership model is, in part, a spatial model. This is significant, given that legal and spatial representations, when combined, can have powerful effects. The ownership model presents property as fixed, natural, and objective, transforming "the contingency of social history into a fixed set of structural arrangements and ideological commitments."[21] This in part reflects the institutional power of law, reliant upon deeply engrained claims to formalist reasoning, reason, and closure.[22] Space, like law, has also been characterized as objective, appearing to have "an air of neutrality and indifference with regard to its contents, and thus seems to be purely formal, the epitome of rational abstraction."[23] The assumed objectivity of the spatial and the legal render them especially opaque to critical insight. Consider, therefore, what happens when legal categories are simultaneously and recursively spatial categories: when law and space are "spliced" together.[24]

Practically speaking, the ownership model relies upon spatial boundaries. As Singer notes, "we know the extent and the limits of the property by a physical description of the space that is to be controlled by the owner. The boundary separates the owner from nonowners. The owner's property rights are absolute within the boundaries of the property and nonexistent outside those boundaries."[25] Like the legal meanings of property, the boundary itself is imagined as determinative and transparent and as serving to separate and divide. These boundaries on the ground, as it were, shade off into metaphoric boundaries, notably that between the public and private spheres.[26] Metaphorical boundaries are important to legal liberalism, which Michael Walzer has described as turning on the "art of separation," predicated on the drawing of lines and the separation of different realms. "Liberalism is a world of walls. . . ."[27] But there's another spatial metaphor at work here. A number of commentators have alerted us to the centrality of the private home as a model for structuring our thinking on property rights. "For a man's house is his castle, *et domus sua cuique tutissimum refugium*," declaimed Coke.[28] Deliberation on property rights, Michael Robertson suggests, frequently turns to the model of the family home as a basis for evaluation.[29] Thus, even though the Hotel California was a home of sorts to many long-term residents, the model invites us as homeowners to identify with Mr. Luciak. In so doing, we attribute to corporations the qualities, rights, and protections of private individuals. The "walls that liberalism constructs do more than create liberties," it has been argued, "they also obscure and shelter the citadels of domination."[30]

The significance of space to the ownership model does not rest solely with the importance of geographic images, like the home, or of territorial markers, like the boundary. Real property, in particular, relies upon a notion of property itself as a finite space. Theorists of property frequently bemoan the widespread tendency to treat property as a thing, rather than a bundle of relations. Yet if asked to describe my property, for example, I would tend to delineate a space, rather than a bundle of jural relationships.[31] In selling property, we imagine transfers of land, rather than the alienation of exclusionary rights. It doesn't take long to realize that this is a rather strange view.[32] However, despite the protestations of legal theorists, we need to recognize the significance of such a spatialization. Treating property as a spatialized thing, rather than a bundle of relationships, locates its central relationship as that between the owner and the thing owned. The effect is to suppress our understanding of the undeniable and often differential relations between the owner and other people, such as Mr. Luciak and his tenants.[33] Edward Thompson notes the historic consequences: "since property was a thing, it became possible to define offences as crimes against things, rather than as injuries to men. This enabled the law to assume, with its robes, the postures of impartiality: it was neutral as between every degree of man, and defended only the inviolability of the ownership of things."[34]

As a result, the rules and spatial arrangements of private property appear prepolitical, obvious, and unproblematic. There is nothing particularly surprising about for example, Mr. Luciak's claiming and exercising powers which directly affect other people. Although we may object to the particular ways in which he exercises these powers, we take as given—even

	Private property	**State ownership**
Title	Clear—no prior or competing claims	Clear—no prior or competing claims
Owner	Single identifiable owner	Vested in the state as fictive individual
Priority	Anterior and superior	Secondary—guarantor of private rights
Property rights	Consolidated bundle (alienation, use, exclusion, etc.)	Rights presumptively inferior to those of private owner
Spatial organization	Clearly fixed by objective boundaries	Spatially delimited and finite
Spatial archetype	Private, detached house	City park or street

Figure 1.1 Property—the ownership model

as natural—the basis for this power; that is, the notion that Mr. Luciak can lay exclusive claim to a parcel of space.[35] Similarly, there is a naturalness to the spatial markers of property. As Patricia Seed notes, the boundary has long been used within English legal culture as a symbolic and practical marker of the bounds of property. We take as given the idea that a property claim can be spatially delimited, and that the boundary itself has a determinative meaning (marking mine and thine).[36] Both are of the order of things. The widespread tendency to treat both space and law as objective categories facilitates this.[37] Spaces "appear to have their own rules, not the rules constructed for them."[38] Through spatialization, property becomes self-evident and impersonal. However, as we shall see, if we recognize that space is socially produced, and socially productive, we need also to recognize that it can be remade for different social ends. The spaces of property in that sense can be powerfully disciplinary but also transgressive.[39]

Purification

Property law has, in effect, helped us to reimagine and reinvent what we understand to be the real world.
  —Theodore Steinberg, *Slide Mountain or the Folly of Owning Nature*

Representations, when allied with state power, not only depict the world, they can remake it. Thus a state cadastral map "does not merely describe a system of land tenure; it creates such a system through its ability to give its categories the force of law."[40] The ownership model similarly has had important effects. As noted above, it underpins a particular and consequential view of property, power, and social life. Definitionally, only certain relations are named "property," and certain social actors recognized as viable owners. Private, individual ownership is, of course, at the core of the ownership model, with provisional acceptance of state ownership in certain situations. "A way of seeing," however, "is also a way of not seeing."[41] Similarly, the ownership model has "a certain cultural myopia" toward other forms of property. Given the power of the ownership model, non-private forms of ownership "do not look like property at all to us, and we have tended to ignore them."[42] Partly, Carol Rose suggests, this is because they are complex and rather amorphous. Also, "communal claims are frequently made by what seem to be persons that are somehow deemed inappropriate to make claims of entitlement" (given notions of the "propriety" of property).[43]

The case of common property is instructive here: considerable scholarly investment has gone into marginalizing or ignoring its presence. This becomes interestingly evident when we turn to those authors who wish to celebrate property as a bulwark of liberty or prosperity. More accurately, they seek to laud *private* property: to do so, it is necessary to at least acknowledge other possibilities. While public (state ownership) is clearly recognized, and derided, common property must also be dealt with. For Pipes, this is easy: First, it is disappearing: "Except for a few isolated cases of self-perpetuating poverty, such as North Korea and Cuba . . . and except for the minds of a still sizeable but dwindling number of academics, the ideal of common ownership is everywhere in retreat," he confidently claims. Second, perhaps it never even existed. Thus, Pipes feels it necessary to track the antiquity of property (to prove its significance) but also then argues that "primitive" and hunter-gatherer societies do not regard land as common property but defend their territory with an animal like "ferocity."[44] Tom Bethell dismisses the very possibility of common property by drawing on the well-worn argument that its internal contradictions lead, inevitably, to systemic collapse. He goes on to challenge the high-minded moral justification for communal ownership by insisting that it is ethically dysfunctional, encouraging "greed, selfishness, idleness, suspicion and a brooding sense of injustice."[45] These claims have been powerfully countered by an array of scholars who point out, variously, that the dominant version is based on a misreading of the workings of common ownership and document the stubborn persistence of the commons, noting its remarkable resilience and flexibility.[46] Yet despite this, the commons appears marginal at best. The tragedy of the commons, perhaps, is less its supposed internal failures as its external invisibility.

J. K. Gibson-Graham's arguments about capitalism are appropriate here: they note the ways in which capitalism presents itself as a singularity, without peer or equivalent. All other economic forms—such as feudalism or socialism—appear as residual or marginal moments compared to a capitalism that appears fully realized and self-sufficient. This serves, they note, to discourage alternative economic projects, as they will "necessarily be marginal in the context of Capitalism's exclusivity."[47]

The centrality of the ownership model similarly renders other modalities of ownership invisible. Common property, declares one scholar, "means no property."[48] The case of indigenous institutions of property is an important one, to which I will return. These have long been both overlooked and misunderstood partly, perhaps, because they do not conform to the ownership model. Thus, in deciding whether indigenous claims to land constitute a proprietary relation, courts have tended to adopt a categorization that compares them with the assumed substance of English concepts of property.[49]

Native claims to land are also illegible if they fail to adopt the geographies of the ownership model. English colonists in the New World took as given that enclosing, fencing, house construction and agricultural activity were clear acts that signaled private ownership. The rightful appropriation of land in the New World for English settlers turned on certain culturally accepted practices, such as house building and agricultural "improvement" and the building of fences. This conferred definitive ownership. "And for the Natives in New England," observed John Winthrop, "they inclose noe land neither have any setled habitation nor any tame cattle to improve their land by."[50] The absence of these spatial markers was then taken as empirical proof that native people had no claim to land.

The centrality of a particular geographic model of ownership fosters one-sided colonial interactions. Stuart Banner discusses the cultural specificities of property's geographies in his exploration of the colonization of New Zealand. A powerful "geographic paradigm was embedded in settler consciousness," he argues, whereby ownership rights were understood to be allocated on a geographic basis.[51] "Land was divided into spaces, each piece was assigned to an owner, and the owner was ordinarily understood to command all the resources within that geographic area."[52] The Maori, however, allocated property rights on a functional, rather than a geographical basis: a person was not imagined to own "a zone of space," but would have the right to use a particular resource in a particular way. The right to trap birds in a certain tree, for example, did not necessarily entail other rights exercised within the same space. There were apparent cultural similarities however: the Maori cultivated and fenced land, for example. Yet these similarities, which encouraged settlers to imagine a common vocabulary of ownership, if operating at different levels of civilization, were crosscut by differences. The effect was often mistranslation and a cultural confusion that only dissipated when the colonial authorities were able to force the Maori to reconceptualize land as composed of geographic spaces rather than of use rights: "The colonization of land, the physical substance, could not have proceeded without the simultaneous colonization of property, the mental structure for organizing rights to land."[53]

This colonization continues, argues Ashinabe legal scholar John Borrows, describing land use planning in Ontario. Indigenous geographies have been mapped out by a "conceptual grid . . . which divides, parcels, registers, and bounds peoples and places in a way that is often inconsistent with Indigenous participation and environmental integrity." "The law," he argues, "has put a culturally exclusive vision of geography in its service."[54] The failure to acknowledge indigenous property claims not only constitutes a profound injustice, it also overlooks the value of alternative legal imaginaries and orderings.

The mapping out of aboriginal understandings of property, of course, has a very real association with the actual dispossession of native people, a point to which I return later. But it is not just private property that is differently conceived. "Public" lands, at issue in many treaty settlements, are frequently characterized as a common property resource, open to all (like a public park). In its brief to the Canadian Commission on Aboriginal Peoples in 1993, for example, the Ontario Federation of Anglers and Hunters argued that treaty and aboriginal rights did not give Aboriginal people an exclusive privilege. There are, in effect, only two classes of ownership—collective and private: "Crown [that is state] lands . . . are held in trust by the Crown for . . . the social and cultural well being of all the people of Ontario. Thus, together they are *public common property resources. . . . No one person or group owns them!* . . . Possessory rights to Crown lands are usually conveyed through tenure agreements and licences at fair market value, issued by the Crown for payment of fees/royalties."[55]

However, aboriginal property systems resemble neither private nor state ownership. Although the details of property arrangements vary amongst aboriginal societies, certain basic principles are said to be universal. Describing precontact native orderings within what became Canada, it has been noted that "[i]n no case were lands and resources considered a commodity that could be alienated to exclusive private possession. All Aboriginal peoples had systems of land tenure that involved allocation within the group, rules for conveyance of primary rights (and obligations) between individuals, and the prerogative to grant or deny access to nonmembers, but not outright alienation."[56] In this sense, property can be said to be a "sociocultural practice" that derives from specific ontologies: differences in conceptions of property reflect not only variations in modes of owning and possessing, but very different ways of "relating to the world at large."[57]

But the ownership model, when mapped onto the nonnative world, can also be disjunctive. Joseph Sax's discussion of U.S. parks policy offers a striking example of this translation problem. Parks, he notes, have increasingly been designated in areas that contain existing human settlements. The National Park Service, seeking to create natural preserves, seeks to "phase out" these settlements. The National Park Service takes a "disaggregative view," treating each individual and parcel within a settlement as separate entities. As long as each owner is treated equitably, justice is felt to have been done. However, "what is missing is the question whether there is some entity consisting of all the pieces taken together, a community, the interests of which are neglected in any such item by item approach. The current law does not agonize over this issue. . . . The interests of a community have no formal status; they are not, for example, property rights. In the law's eye, they are only sentiment." The "interests of a community," he and others suggest, may indeed be worth acknowledging, and may even constitute a property right. The problem, however, is that "the structure, or absence of structure" of the legal system itself renders these interests invisible.[58] The fate of the Golden Gate barrio in Phoenix, home to a Chicano community, attests to the consequences of this invisibility. City authorities removed six thousand of its residents in the 1970s and early 1980s to accommodate the expansion of the city's airport. Many residents wanted to be relocated together to maintain their community, but the city did not accommodate this desire. As one community representative noted: the city "has in short invoked a standard which says 'bricks and plumbing and home appraisals count, your social and cultural values do not.' "[59]

But there's a second consequence of the ownership model: it determines which property relations are assigned a value as rights. There's an obvious and important difference between property and property rights, insofar as the latter entails state enforcement. While property is a "social relation that defines the property holder with respect to something of value . . . against all others,"[60] a property right can be defined as: "[a]n enforceable claim to some use or benefit of something, whether it is a right to share in some common resource or an individual right to some particular things."[61] Assigning rights-status, of course, is immediately consequential. As a private property owner, I have an enforceable claim: I can call upon the state to expel the trespasser on my property, for example. However, even though I may regard the stretch of roadway outside my house as "mine," I do not have an enforceable claim, against all others, to park my car there.

Claiming a right, in this sense, can make things happen. More discursively, it can signal an acknowledgment by the state that certain issues are worthy of special protection. Rights are clearly important in constituting as well as resolving political struggles. As a claim upon the state, groups and individuals can use rights to mobilize the state and its disciplinary powers, and in so doing, receive an affirmation that the collective recognizes and acknowledges the justice of that claim. For Ernesto Laclau and Chantal Mouffe, rights are unique in offering a political yardstick that allow power relations previously understood as organic and natural to be reframed as political and conditional. *Subordination* can be recast as *oppression,* and thus politicized.[62] Put another way, rights offer a powerful vocabulary for "naming, blaming, and claiming."[63] Scholars have also argued for the historic significance of rights-based struggles for oppressed groups. In one justly famous essay, Patricia Williams argues that rights are important to the African-American experience precisely because they have so frequently been denied and negated. As such, they provide a site for political struggle that is at once politically necessary *and* expansionary:

> "Rights" feel new in the mouths of most black people. It is still deliciously empowering to say. It is the magic wand of visibility and invisibility, of inclusion and exclusion, of power and no power. The concept of rights, both positive and negative, is the marker of our citizenship, our relation to others.[64]

Although, as we shall see, the state is not the only arbiter in determining rights-status, it clearly plays a critical role. A determination that a property claim is not a property right, to the extent that it fails the ownership model's definitional test, can thus be immensely consequential. For a court to determine, for example, that an indigenous people do not have an enforceable claim to land can be politically, symbolically, and instrumentally devastating.

Unsettlement

> *[C]an't we give capitalism an identity crisis as well?*
> —J. K. Gibson-Graham, *The End of Capitalism (As We Knew It)*

But dominant maps of property, although institutionally and ideologically very powerful, offer only a partial reflection of the territory, I shall argue. As we have seen, property is a good deal more labile, multivalent, and complex than dominant mappings suggest.

A well-established body of legal scholarship has challenged the certainties of the ownership model. American legal realism, with its attack on legal closure and its distrust of legal formalism, sought to expose the political context to law. Property arrangements, for example, were predicated not on consent, but on the coercive power of law.[65] The fundamental legal distinctions between *dominium*—the rule over things by the individual—and *imperium*—the rule over all individuals by the state—was criticized as inaccurate, to the extent that it ignored the possibility that with property, dominion over things, "is also *imperium* over our fellow human beings."[66]

Many contemporary authors argue that the ownership model is similarly flawed and inconsistent. The presumptions of the model—consolidated, permanent rights vested in a single identifiable owner, who is identified by formal title, exercising absolute control, and distinguished from others by boundaries that protect him or her from others by granting the owner the power to exclude—are simply inaccurate. The model "misdescribes the normal functioning of private property rights by vastly over-simplifying both the kinds of property rights that exist and the rules governing the exercise of those rights."[67] Thus, for example, identifying "the owner" becomes challenging, when we recognize the presence of other parties, such as mortgage lenders, neighbors (who may have rights recognized by law), spouses, and those granted easements: "full consideration of property rights in the same person is the exception rather than the rule; most property rights are shared or divided among several persons."[68]

The division between the private owner and the state also turns out to be rather less determinate and clear cut. For example, the "private" space of the owner is regulated in all sorts of direct and indirect ways. Obviously, zoning law dictates (often in great detail) the kind of buildings I can erect on "my" land. For example, if I fail to maintain my yard, the authorities can enter on to my property without my permission, effect a clean up, and charge me with the costs. I am forbidden from removing certain trees from "my" land. Law requires me to help maintain the city's land by removing snow from the sidewalk outside my house. More abstractly, the very institution of private ownership depends upon the collective. At minimum, ownership require the assent or recognition of others. As Daniel Bromley notes, things are not protected because they are property. Rather, by virtue of being protected, they become property: "What I own depends on what you agree that I own, not what I assert that I own."[69] The state is thus not simply an external threat to an owner's solitary rights, but is the very guarantee of those rights. If property is "the boundary to governmental power," Nedelsky notes, "it is a boundary government itself draws."[70]

Others have argued that if ever there was a reasonable basis for the ownership model, it has long since disappeared. Thomas Grey, for example, has argued that the concept of property has disintegrated. The certainties of a land-owning society have given way before the complexities of modern capitalism, where increasing economies of scale and divisions of labor encourage owners to divide and recombine the bundles of rights that make up original ownership. The notion of property as "thing-ownership," so central to classical liberal thought, is no longer tenable. The "death of property," he argues, erodes the moral basis for a capitalism predicated on the existence and protection of private property rights.[71]

I am sympathetic to many of these critiques. However, as Singer notes, "[d]emonstrating that [property] can be deconstructed does not deprive it of cultural force as an organizing category."[72] And thus, it is to its "cultural force" that we must direct our attention. What is it, in other words, that makes the ownership model so persuasive, despite its flaws? Perhaps one reason is its promise of clarity and certainty. Property, like law more generally, offers determinacy and order in a disordered and ambiguous world. The ownership model, in other words, appears *settled*. By this, I mean several interrelated things. The ownership model presumes a clarity and determinacy in the definition of what property *is*, and tells us which relationships in the real world are to be valued as such, and which are not. In so doing, it encourages us to think of ownership as complete and secure. The visible geographies of property (the maps, fences, signs, and so on) give a reassuring legibility to property. I can see where mine becomes yours, for example. But the ownership model also reassures me of the apparent solidity of the all-important chain through which previous owners transferred title to me. The presumed clarity of the ownership model is deemed valuable, in part, because of its guarantee of secure and uncontested relations with others with respect to the use and disposition of things. Because we know who owns what, and where their title came from, and because ownership is complete and zero-sum, conflict should be minimized. "Clear" title brings "quietness of possession."

In their wonderful book, *The End of Capitalism (As We Knew It)*, Gibson-Graham ask a provocative question: "What if we were to depict social existence at loose ends with itself. . . . rather than producing social representations in which everything is part of the same complex and therefore ultimately 'means the same thing' (for example capitalist hegemony)?"[73] What if we were to similarly depict property "at loose ends," and refuse its circular and settled self-representation? If the city appears settled, perhaps this is more a "reality-effect" of the ownership model, than an accurate mapping of property in the world. If we accept property—as defined by the ownership model—as a hegemonized claim, rather than an assured reality, certain possibilities emerge:

> [O]ne might represent economic practice as comprising a rich diversity of capitalist and noncapitalist activities that had until now been relatively "invisible" because the concepts and discourses that could make them "visible" have themselves been marginalized and suppressed.[74]

In calling this book *Unsettling the City*, my goal is similarly to question the settlements of property and the ways in which property's ontological and political diversity has been rendered invisible.[75] I want to suggest that the spaces of urban property may be definitionally and politically more ambiguous and varied than the ownership model supposes. This "unsettled" nature of property provides a basis for conflict over who has what and how they acquired it. Conflict may also occur over the ethics of property. Such disputes may be partly external to dominant understandings of property. However, they may also draw on a similar vocabulary.

This takes us to the first of property's settlements—its definitional certainty. There is considerable potential in "remapping" property "as hegemonized while rendering the social world as economically differentiated and complex," seeking the "glimmerings and murmerings of noncapitalism" through a recuperation of various forms of economic alternatives both from within and without.[76]

Other Estates

> *Private property is a more subtle institution than scholars and judges have often realized.*
>
> —Michael A. Heller, "The Boundaries of Private Property"

Let me then focus on the ways in which the ownership model leaves no space for property that is neither private nor public. Looking more carefully at cities, I shall try and indicate the diversity of property on the ground, both in everyday practice, and in creative acts of resistant remapping. When we look carefully, it is clear that property is a much more capacious category than it first appears. The denial of these alternative possibilities begins to be seen, in this context, as almost willful. Property, as conceived by the ownership model, is as much aspiration as fact. The map not only records. It arbitrates. The arbitration of what is property is not an objective categorization, but an active form of boundary making and purification. The question is not so much "what is property?" as "what is to *count* as property?" Although these alternatives do not appear on official maps of property's spaces, they can and should be found. If property is theft, the larceny entails that of the diversity (and perhaps, the radical potential) of property. Property offers a rich, multivalent, and politically charged vocabulary. Cities are sites in which people live inside the ownership model, but they also depart from it. Collective claims to land and space are made. And private property itself turns out to be a good deal more multivalent, both ethically and analytically, than is supposed.

Even when we look more closely at relations that are acknowledged as property by the dominant model, we find "loose ends." I have already tried to suggest that the realities of private property confound the neat certainties of the ownership model. Private property, it has been noted, "is the most discussed and the least understood form of ownership."[77] Indeed, it is clear that, when viewed empirically, private ownership is a much more heterogeneous category than it first appears. Charles Geisler urges us to acknowledge the very real existence of recognized estates in land that are not captured by the traditional binary of public and private ownership:

These have public and private features, but their salience lies elsewhere. Though they rarely appear on maps, they occupy measurable space, have physical reference points, grow out of social relations, and represent formal value systems. They are part of our geography and culture, though often upstaged by the familiar public-private polarity.[78]

These include forms of ecosystem management, corporate estates, Indian lands, and common property estates (forms of collective private ownership), such as the regimes governing some inland fisheries or aquifers. While dominant mappings of property offer us very persuasive models of ownership as determinate, contained, and bounded, law recognizes a considerable diversity of possible tenurial arrangements of which individual ownership is only one. As Singer notes, housing law can also comfortably accommodate:

[J]oint ownership (tenancy in common, joint tenancy), leasing arrangements (perhaps subsidized by government welfare payments), cooperatives, condominiums, subdivisions, homeowners' associations, ground leases, charitable land trusts, limited equity cooperatives, tribal property (including original Indian title, recognized tribal title, and restricted trust allotments), public housing, and government property.[79]

These alternatives, he insists, are not variations on the ownership model: "Many of them depart so far from the basic model of a single owner with consolidated rights that use of that basic model is essentially misleading as a conceptual baseline."[80]

An interesting example is the community land trust model, or third sector housing, such as the limited equity condominium. This can be distinguished from either public or market housing "not so much how it is produced or how it is financed, but how it is owned, controlled, and conveyed."[81] A land trust disaggregates alienation from the bundle of rights associated with ownership, while retaining most of the traditional benefits. Although David M. Abromowitz suggests that this unbundling is not unprecedented, John Emmeus Davis argues that in so constraining the alienability of real property, the land trust model is an "affront" to central tenets of liberal property law.[82] The case of "privately owned public space" in New York is another intriguing example that complicates the categories of the ownership model. An "oxymoronic invention," a zoning law rewards developers who produce spaces of public access with increased density.[83] Ownership of such spaces, however, is vested with the developer, and conditional access is granted to the public.

But stepping outside state–sanctioned property arrangements, we can also find other claims to property that are neither clearly private nor public. Rose coins the phrase "un-real estate" to describe the way people "sometimes act as if they were asserting and acknowledging property claims, even though it is quite well known that these claims really have no legal status at all."[84] Jane Jacobs famously wrote of the "marvellous . . . complex order" that encourages "eyes upon the street, eyes belonging to those we might call the natural proprietors of the street."[85] Public spaces, such as streets and parks, are more or less successful and safe to the extent that private residents imagine and act upon a property claim to that space. Oscar Newman described certain spatial structure as conducive to this sense of "unreal" proprietorship over public space. Newman sees this as valuable in encouraging the policing of public space and the exclusion of the unwanted and criminal.[86] Some policing strategies attempt to encourage "un-real estate" in order to reduce public disorder. Spaces that appear to be unclaimed (that is, unowned) are to be avoided, as these are targets for petty crime. If a broken window is unrepaired, a building quickly becomes vandalized.[87] What is needed, therefore, is to encourage respectable residents to "take ownership" of public space and "reclaim" it from criminals.

But this can also occur without state sanction. In research I conducted with residents of an inner-city neighborhood in Vancouver, I explored people's reactions to, and involvement in, garden "encroachments;" that is, when "private" gardens extend outside the formal boundaries of the lot, onto municipal property. This seemed fairly widespread: in some cases, people had even erected low fences around "their" encroachments. One artists' collective placed old bathtubs and washing machines on the boulevard, and filled them with plants. A few respondents were adamant that this was inappropriate. This was "city" land. Bathtubs, one noted, belonged in bathrooms. Most, however, were tolerant of the bathtub planting, even delighted, regarding it not so much as a private "taking," but as a communal "sharing." One respondent described the bathtub garden as "art shared into space." Another noted that it was not "taking possession of public space in a selfish way" but "extending the care that you give your own space to the public space." Yet if this was not "private" space, neither was it "public" space. Most claimed that they would feel uncomfortable using the space as if it were, say, a park. Having visibly transformed and worked the spaces, the encroacher retained certain rights over the spaces: "I never thought about them encroaching on city land, which is actually our land, I suppose," noted one respondent. "It always seemed like theirs . . . Because they do all the work, plant the stuff, I never thought about it as mine."[88]

But collectives can also make property claims to both "private" and "public" space. These differ from purely private claims, given that membership in a more or less defined collective is a necessity. However, to that extent, these claims also depart from an open-access commons. Carol Rose considers the case of what she terms "limited common property" that is, "property held as a commons among the members of a group, but exclusively vis-à-vis the outside world."[89] This differs from public property, formally defined—indeed it may entail the appropriation of land claimed by the state as well as private owners. Such commons may not be protected by the state—indeed, the state may deploy property rights against these claims. However, group members may enforce their claims through other means, including appeal to rights, morality, and membership within a localized community as well as acts of exclusion.[90] Such arrangements, it has been suggested, are widespread, though often overlooked.[91] "The commons is ubiquitous. It is an underrated, much-ignored reservoir of valuable resources, system of social governance, and crucible for democratic aspirations . . ."[92]

These counterpublics may in this sense be "extra-legal."[93] Yet a prevailing legal centralism tends to gloss over "the plurality of 'legitimate' claims to, and interests in, land; and the plurality of ordering mechanisms that are capable of ordering rules and inducing compliance."[94] Omar M. Razzaz insists that "property relations which are endowed with the protection of legal rights and duties are only a subset of the universe of property relations"[95] and argues for the need to acknowledge both property claims and property rights.

Take, for example, surfing. Media coverage of the phenomenon inevitably christened "surf rage" has directed attention to the intricate, informal rules governing use and access to the surfing commons. Codes of etiquette, known sometimes as "Tribal law," govern appropriate behavior (condemning "snaking," or cutting in) and resource use (for example, the surfer farthest out or waiting longest has priority and right of way).[96] However, groups of locals have also long laid claim to certain beaches, dissuading outsiders with graffiti and occasional threats (fig. 1.2). Known as "localism," this apparently takes different forms from one beach to another. Veteran surfer Glenn Hening, founder of the Surfrider Foundation, distinguishes the "privileged sniffiness of Ranch mossbacks" from the localism of the "unemployed construction workers and cholos of Silverstrand."[97] With the explosive growth in surfing and the availability of Internet webcams, localism has become more intense. The "core issue," notes one surfer, is "wave possession."[98] Insiders, interestingly, condemn surf rage as an individualized violation of an imagined commons. "[I]n localism, it's about 'our waves,' " notes one surfer. "In surf rage, it's about 'my wave.' "[99] A 1999 referendum in California saw a proposal for an Open Waves Act which would make the Pacific coastline a place where no person "regardless of residence, lineage, social status or other reason, may lawfully claim the right to a wave."

Community gardens are a more terrestrial local commons. Often carved out of underutilized land, whether public or private, community gardens operate within the legal shadows. Many gardens are created extra legally, through occupations and horticultural "guerrilla" raids.[100] Most

Figure 1.2 The surfing commons. Graffiti: Trestles, Orange County, 1999. Reproduced by permission of Tim Rainger.

cities will only grant short-term leases to community gardens on city-owned land (if at all). Personal experience with community gardening in Vancouver suggests that city officials have a hard time granting "public" land to members of the "public," and often regard the garden as a semiprivatized space. Although some community gardens can be fenced (and are thus not an open-access commons) they are neither clearly public nor private. If anything, they "transcend the separation . . . [T]hey are part of the public domain and are the sites of many functions conventionally equated with the private sphere. Domestic activities, nurturing, and a sense of home are explicitly brought outside into the gardens."[101] This ambiguity has proven important: the continuing battle over the future of several hundred community gardens in New York, for example, turns on a "basic problem of classification and geography"; that is different appraisals of what constitutes public space. City officials regard community gardeners as temporary users of municipal land, whose interests can be superceded by the "public good." Gardeners, conversely, argue that community gardening produces truly public spaces, predicated on localized community, democratization and interaction.[102] For some observers, the community garden represents a blow against global enclosures, and a reclamation of a sacred premodern commons.[103] While they have often been used as a space for collective political organizing against privatization, their success in stabilizing and beautifying low-income neighborhoods may unintentionally contribute to processes of gentrification.

Another intriguing example of a set of property claims that escape or complicate the conventional categories can be found in the practice of squatting. A worldwide phenomenon, squatting is particularly prevalent in many third world cities, but is also found in developed countries. Driven by need, and occasionally political claim making, squats are created on vacant or under used land or buildings, usually privately held. Most immediately, squatter advocates see squats as providing for self-determination, independence, experimentation, and creativity,[104] encouraging personal empowerment and democratization. Squatting's relationship to private property is slightly more ambiguous. In one obvious sense, squatting is an affront to the ownership model. It impinges upon the rights of individual owners to dispose of their property as they see fit, even if that means leaving it vacant. Squatters may also advance a political argument that challenges prevailing inequitable distributions of, and access to property. Squatting can also rely upon a communal claim to land.[105]

Although squatters can, in some cases, acquire legally sanctioned property rights, the initial acquisition of land is, by definition, extra legal or even illegal. As such, squatting, according to the ownership model, makes sense only as a practice external to property, rather than as a claim for property rights itself. This, in a sense, is the basis for prescriptions from neo liberal pundits, such as Hernando de Soto, who insist that the solution to poverty is to turn property *claims* in the third world into enforceable *rights* through a process of formalization. Thus guaranteed, secure tenures can be translated into alienable commodities, credit and housing improvements. State–recognized private property rights appear as the master term, to which everything must conform. Informal property rights are defined, like the undeveloped world, by what they lack.[106]

de Soto's prescriptions are a telling example of the ownership model at work. As Ann Varley notes, he relies upon a spatial model in which property and extra legal claims to land (non property, in other words) occupy different and opposed territories.[107] Yet an interesting body of work not only has demonstrated the potentially negative effects of "titling" on the urban poor but, more interestingly for our purposes, has documented the poor empirical fit of the categories "legal" and "extralegal." The conceptual dualism, it has been said, "exaggerates the difference between the two opposing categories and underplays the diversity within them."[108] The experience of squatter settlements on private land, for example, differs from illegal settlements on *ejido* (common) land. Moreover, people do not seem to always need the state for property to be put to work.[109] In other words, many of the putative benefits of property—such as housing improvement, access to credit, and so on—occur absent state–sanction.

This is evident in other ways in the West. Squatters act as if they have viable and enforceable claims, even without obvious state sanction. In one fascinating inversion, the U.K. Advisory Service for Squatters provides a template "legal warning" to be posted at a squat, citing the Criminal Law Act (1977). This proclaims to the world "that we live in this property, it is our home, and we intend to stay here" and that "any entry or attempt to enter into this property without our permission is a *criminal offence.*"[110] At the same time, squatting can also draw upon ideologies of ownership through labor. In his discussion of the "philosophy to squat by," Anders Corr makes a number of arguments in support of squatting (as well as related struggles, such as land occupations and rent strikes). In considering concepts such as the importance of squatting to self-hood, an ethic of just deserts based on labor, adverse possession, and the relation between ownership and improvement, he draws creatively on the prevailing ideological underpinnings of property.[111]

A concrete example is given by the Ontario Coalition against Poverty (OCAP) that in a national housing protest called on the authorities to "give it or guard it." OCAP has proposed a "Use It or Lose It" bylaw which prohibits owners of residential property from leaving their buildings empty for a period exceeding six months.[112] There are intriguing echoes here of Locke's argument that enclosure was only justified if "as much and as good" was left to others, and that unworked property could be forfeited to others in need.[113]

The history of squatting in inner-city neighborhoods, such as New York's Lower East Side, reveal some of these complexities. Formed in the waves of arson and abandonment in the 1970s, squatting was born both from political activism and basic need. By the early 1990s, there were between five hundred and one thousand squatters spread through thirty-two buildings in the neighborhood. Although clearly countercultural in their orientation, some observers have noted the entrepreneurialism and real estate skills of some of the squatters. Sweat equity, political savvy, and a focus on improvement and habitability combine with friendly anarchism and social revolution. Indeed, several squats are becoming "legal" through the intermediary of the urban Homesteading Assistance Board, a New York nonprofit organization that helps establish low-income limited-equity co-ops. Yet, as one squatter noted: "I think this idea of having the building owned will be a big change. People will begin to have the concept of 'this is mine.' That wasn't what it was about originally, and I'm worried about that."[114]

As these and earlier examples reveal, there is nothing inherently inclusive about these alternatives. Whether by intent or effect, they can serve regressive or progressive ends. We cannot simply read from property to politics. Holders of common property need not have an adversarial relation to private property, for example—they may even be seeking admission to the realm of private ownership. Private property can also be politically complex.[115] Holders of common property may also act in exclusionary fashion—the gated community being an interesting case in point. Not only does the gated community exclude those outside the gates but also, as Kirby notes, the space of the "community" itself is far from communal, but divided, policed and hierarchical.[116]

So, to conclude, a closer examination of urban property reveals a greater diversity of possibilities than the map suggests. Private claims to property are routinely made in (often-accepted) ways that depart from the strictures of the ownership model. Further, a variety of claims are made to urban space that are more collective in orientation. Although often extralegal, claimants can act as if they had sanctioned property rights. The ownership model, however, invites us to overlook or ignore these other estates.

Uncertain Entitlements

As Singer argues, ownership rights are imagined as created at one moment in time and immutable thereafter. "Only two moments matter: the moment of initial creation or acquisition and the moment of transfer. Events that happen in between or after them have no effect on the rights of the owner."[117] However, it can be argued that property depends on a continued "doing." The enactment of property, I shall suggest, entails various forms of continuing persuasive practice designed to legislate what property actually is and what it ought to be. As we have begun to see, both these questions are far from analytically clear or effectively secure. Perhaps because of this, as well as the massive material and ideological investments associated with particular arrangements of property, notably private property, considerable social energy is given over to sustaining and reproducing a particular representation of property. Social categories, like property, are "never stabilized, normalized, sedimented or structured. Rather they are always in a process of dynamic unfolding and becoming." Such enactments constitute "the material acts and gestures that make texts recognizable features of social life."[118] These enactments do not just seek to ensure the reproduction of prevailing property arrangements and relationships more generally as I have suggested, they also serve to police the meanings of property itself and its association. Thus, the ownership model itself must be maintained, and alternative arrangements ignored or denied. Property, as particular relations on the ground and as an overarching set of institutions and understandings, must be settled. Yet, as we have seen, claims to property that escape the ownership model are also enacted. These claims are reliant upon varied and diverse enactments that are simultaneously practical and representational. Although often intentionally oppositional, these alternative enactments can engage in a creative bricolage. They not only draw upon suppressed meanings and practices, but also can rework dominant enactments, often by pulling out the very loose ends of those accounts. Thus it is, for example, that squatting activists and neoliberals alike can cite John Locke.

But there is a related claim here, that of *settlement:* the enactment of property not only presumes a definitional certainty (*this* is property, *that* isn't), it also invites us to imagine that property and settlement are synonymous. The unitary owner at the center of the model is secure in her entitlements, and the institution of property itself is rendered a means for preventing discord. The clear markers of ownership and the established expectations of property work to ensure the "quiet enjoyment" of the land. The ownership model is powerful, in part, because it promises a set of arrangements that minimize social discord. It is this claim that underpins several of the origin stories of private property. In the beginning was violence and conflict over resources—the war of all against all, in Hobbesian terms. Private property, so the story goes, was the solution to these conflicts. Property, for Bentham, is "an established expectation" that requires the security provided by law for it to exist; "Property and law are born together, and die together. Before laws were made there was no property; take away laws, and property ceases."[119] And thus it is that property's lands appear to be quiet lands. They are not only lands that are securely possessed, for which title is determinate. The land itself appears inert and quiescent.[120] The doing of property becomes invisible.

But what if property isn't clear and established, but open to overlapping and conflicting possibilities? As in Robert Frost's poem "Mending Wall," you could construe my fence, understood by me as a point of neighborly connection, as a crude divider. What if the moralities of property are open to various interpretations? What if property claims, meaningful to some people, are rendered invisible by prevailing assumptions? What happens when my possession depends upon your dispossession, whether now or in the past? Mr. Luciak's title to his hotel depends, ultimately, upon the dispossession of native peoples who claim the land upon which Vancouver now sits as part of their traditional territories. Further, the unfettered exercise of his property rights seems to threaten the property rights of his tenants. Moreover, the upgrading of his hotel may encourage other hotel owners to follow suit, thus facilitating a much wider displacement. What occurs when the enactments of property are reworked to different ends? Native people, for example, could appeal to a right of first appropriation, central to some threads within property discourse, to buttress their claim to land, while colonial settlers could argue for the primacy of their right given the "improvements" they had effected (thus appealing to labor as the basis for appropriation).

Conflicts can, of course, occur between private owners. They can also turn, as has been noted, on the contradiction between property's use-value and exchange-value.[121] But conflicts may also occur because of the multiplicity of claims to land. The ownership model invites us to focus on the solitary owner: in so doing, we overlook the fact that "almost every interesting dispute about control or access to property can be described as conflict between property holders or between conflicting property rights."[122] For my purposes, what is striking about these conflicts is the ways they challenge the certainties of both public and private property by drawing upon claims to land that are neither, both, or something in-between. Cuff argues, for example, that many disputes over urban development in U.S. cities can usefully be seen as a struggle over the rights and responsibilities associated with property. Community activists can contest the rights of the owner (for example, by insisting that he or she preserve "heritage") and thus argue that the developer's rights must be matched by a concomitant responsibility to a local neighborhood. Activists can also lay claim to a form of community ownership: "[C]ontemporary development contentions often pit the developer-owner's private property against the community's common property."[123] In Britain, urban activists under the banner "This Land Is Ours" have directly invoked a sixteenth-century language of revolt over land in a call for affordable homes in the city, appealing not only to social need, but collective entitlement: "The land bequeathed to all of us must be made to work for us once more. Today the dispossessed of Britain are starting to reclaim their inheritance."[124]

Property is a frequent basis for political claim-making in the city, and a site of contestation. Proponents of private property rights have mobilized across North America in opposition to urban zoning, insisting that it relies upon objectionable collectivist principles, and renders property rights nugatory: "Under zoning, a property owner may use his property, not by right, but by permission. Yet ownership without control is a fraud. Under zoning, land ownership is nothing more than nominal ownership."[125] The Alberta Real Estate Association, meanwhile, advocates the constitutional entrenchment of property rights in Canada, given a concern that property owners may see their rights overturned by governments at any time.[126] The problem with urban property, from this perspective, is that the promise of the ownership model has not been fully realized.

Yet property discourse is such that apparently similar claims can be made for very different purposes. For example, a protest occurred in San Francisco in 2001 in response to the mass confiscation of homeless people's property by the city. In return, activists symbolically confiscated city hall, occupying the mayor's office and hanging a banner that read "You took our home, we'll take the dome." John Viola, staff attorney of the Coalition on Homelessness argued that "a policy that allows the city to seize and destroy the property of homeless people not only violates their constitutional rights but punishes people simply for being poor." Another activist claimed that: "City hall's attitude towards homeless people and their property continues to be one of contempt in refusing to pass legislation which would respect homeless people's property rights." This ushered in a fascinating string of email commentary among Bay area activisits, who variously pointed out the perils of the defense of the right of property; noted the class specificity of property; considered the merits of giving the city back to Native Americans; reflected on the irony that many of the " 'Indians' are homeless on the streets of toxic urban America"; suggested that instead of treating property as sacrosanct, we value people or the land itself and claimed: "Property is theft. Property is liberty. Property is impossible. What does this mean? Hint: there are (sic) more than one kind of property."[127]

The ownership model, as noted, concerns itself only with initial acquisition and subsequent transfers. Contemporary entitlements are grounded on some originary act:

> How do things get owned? This is a fundamental puzzle for anyone who thinks about property. One buys things from other owners, to be sure, but how did those owners get those things? Back at the beginning, someone must have acquired the thing, whatever it is, without buying it from anyone else. That is, someone has to do something to anchor the very first link in the chain of ownership. The puzzle is, What was that action that anchored the chain and made an owned thing out of an unowned one?[128]

Now, of course, this is the dilemma that theorists such as Locke posed, locating the first link in the chain of ownership in an act of primary appropriation, realized through productive labor or divine gift, that vests ownership rights on the appropriator. But the issue of initial acquisition is decidedly "unsettled" in settler societies such as Canada, Australasia, and the United States. In cities like New York, Sydney, Honolulu, or Toronto, where do we locate that first link, given the prior presence of indigenous peoples? How settled are the links in the chain? Settler cities reassure themselves by supposing either that a legitimate transfer of title from native to nonnatives occurred (through treaty, deed, conquest, and so on) or, more bluntly, that the land was simply unowned and empty. Native lands were

WHO OWNS THE PARK?

Someday a petty official will appear with a piece of paper, called a land title, which states that the University of California owns the land of the People's Park. Where did that piece of paper come from? What is it worth?

A long time ago the Costanoan Indians lived in the area now called Berkeley. They had no concept of land ownership. They believed that the land was under the care and guardianship of the people who used it and lived on it.

Catholic missionaries took the land away from the Indians. No agreements were made. No papers were signed. They ripped it off in the name of God.

The Mexican Government took the land away from the Church. The Mexican Government had guns and an army. God's word was not as strong.

The Mexican Government wanted to pretend that it was not the army that guaranteed them the land. They drew up some papers which said they legally owned it. No Indians signed those papers.

The Americans were not fooled by the papers. They had a stronger army than the Mexicans. They beat them in a war and took the land. Then they wrote some papers of their own and forced the Mexicans to sign them.

The American Government sold the land to some white settlers. The Government gave the settlers a piece of paper called a land title in exchange for some money. All this time there were still some Indians around who claimed the land. The American army killed most of them.

The piece of paper saying who owned the land was passed around among rich white men. Sometimes the white men were interested in taking care of the land. Usually they were just interested in making money. Finally some very rich men, who run the University of California, bought the land.

Immediately these men destroyed the houses that had been built on the land. The land went the way of so much other land in America—it became a parking lot.

We are building a park on the land. We will take care of it and guard it, in the spirit of the Costanoan Indians. When the University comes with its land title we will tell them: "Your land title is covered with blood. We won't touch it. Your people ripped off the land from the Indians a long time ago. If you want it back now, you will have to fight for it again."

Figure 1.3 'Who owns the park?', 1969. Courtesy of the Bancroft Library, University of California, Berkeley.

the empty Eden from which private property was wrought: "in the beginning," argued Locke, "all the World was America." Thus, the chain begins with European settlement. As we shall see, the city itself becomes imagined as a settled site, conceptually uncoupled from a native world. This detachment is again evident in the academic literature: "[T]he construction of the city as the space of the settler," it has been noted, "has received little attention."[129] But when we look more closely at this colonial chain, settlement becomes less certain. An enduring indigenous presence and increasingly vocal land claim ensures that "a condition of unsettledness folds into this taken-for-granted mode of occupation."[130]

Interestingly, indigenous and nonindigenous settlements and their associated conflicts over land can fold back into each other. The case of People's Park in Berkeley is an interesting one. Created through direct action, when activists occupied an empty lot owned by the University of California, the Park was imagined as a liberated space that would allow for unmediated political exchange and a decentralized democracy.[131] This is clearly a struggle over publicity and the spaces of protest, but it also clearly implicates property. The concentration of the homeless in the park—denied any other space by the legal workings of real property and the economics of real estate—has also proved contentious, given dominant anxieties about appropriate forms of use and occupation of public space. But it also entails an attempt to carve out a people's commons from state space. *Public* space, in other words, is not *municipal* space. As one observer noted: "this is still a fight over territory . . . it's the whole issue of who has a rightful claim to the land."[132] But in raising the issue of who now has the rightful claim, the chain of colonial ownership also emerges as consequential. A 1969 poster, asking "Who Owns The Park?", challenged the colonial processes through which claims to land were made (fig. 1.3).[133] In so doing, the legitimacy of public (that is, state) ownership and associated exclusionary powers are challenged at the same time as a counterclaim on the part of the collective is made in the name of the historically dispossessed.

Conclusions

The Hotel California with which we began is now a Howard Johnson's, advertising itself as a "boutique hotel" that "makes you feel at home."[134] Those former tenants, for whom the hotel was "home," are long gone. The neighborhood has been upscaled, with a mix of entertainment and loft developments. Planning policy for the area embraced a policy of "densification," where the primary planning concern, as is normally the case, operates according to the calculus of "land use," focused on the utilitarian question: "Where do things belong?" As D. A. Krueckeberg has argued, this "sanitizes the essential query: 'To whom do things belong?' Where things belong cannot be answered justly until we know whose things we are talking about."[135]

The ownership model encourages us to think that this is an essentially settled question. Things belong to identifiable owners, who stand in a particular relation to others. As I have argued here, this model also relies upon a geography of property, predicated on finite boundaries and absolute spaces. The ownership model is easily challenged. Yet it remains powerful to the ways in which property is conceived, and not conceived. It renders certain other claims to land—especially those of a more collective nature—marginal, or even invisible, denying them legal standing and rights status. It misrepresents the actual workings of property law. It denies the ongoing enactments that sustain property. It obscures the inevitable conflict that occurs in and over property, including conflicts over the very "beginnings" of property. This is ethically important, of course, but it is also analytically consequential. It affects the ways in which we conceive of cities, the preeminent human "settlement." In the next chapter, drawing upon the case of Vancouver's Downtown Eastside, I try and demonstrate the existence and significance of claims to land that are not captured by the ownership model, unpacking the important geographic enactments of these claims.

CHAPTER 2

Property and the Landscapes
of Gentrification

There is a pressing need . . . for a better understanding of the various ways through which rights to land are established, contested, controlled, and renegotiated.
—Omar M. Razzaz, "Examining Property Rights and Investment in Informal Settlements"

The basic issue . . . is who owns the land. By "own" I mean in the very real sense, morally. And we believe that land belongs to the poor, literally, in every way, legally, morally. It belongs to the people. Because they were the people who struggled when nobody else wanted the Lower East Side.
—Community Activist, New York

The law of property shapes people's political rights, their actual and potential access to instruments of political leverage, and their objectives as political actors. . . . [P]roperty demarcations . . . constitute social relations on the Lower East Side.
—John Brigham and Diana R. Gordon, "Law in Politics"

Urban Contests

Most observers agree that the political economy of Western cities has undergone an important change in the past two decades. Cities are increasingly caught up in the dynamics of globalization and shifts in the structure of labor and property markets. Intersecting processes, such as deindustrialization, the globalization of the property market, the rise of the service economy, and the increase in transnational flows of commodities, people, and ideas, have all reshaped the urban economy. Urban politics have also shifted. Although place promotion has a long pedigree, the mobility of investment has encouraged many city governments to engage in more ag-

gressive programs of place marketing, positioning themselves as plat-
forms in an emergent economy of flows.[1] More entrepreneurial programs
of urban governance, in which cities compete aggressively to attract capital, tourists, and government funds, have been identified, with a conse-
quent shift from an emphasis on local livability and the life opportunities
of local residents to an externally oriented logic of the bottom line.[2]

But these strategies are entrepreneurial in another sense, given the increased importance of a market logic and vocabulary to state action. The
embrace of public-private partnerships, deregulation, fiscal austerity, cross-
subsidies, and market solutions have been characterized as a form of urban
neoliberalism:

> The doses do vary, but never mind what it says on the bottle, the basic treat-
> ment is pretty much the same: purge the system of obstacles to the functioning
> of "free markets"; restrain public expenditure and any form of collective initia-
> tive; celebrate the values of individualism, competitiveness, and economic self-
> sufficiency; abolish or weaken social transfer programs while actively fostering
> the "inclusion" of the poor and marginalized into the labor market, on the
> market's terms.[3]

Self-consciously radical, neoliberalism is, in part, a language of property—
a return to central axioms of eighteenth-century liberalism, which places
private property as the foundation for the individual self-interest, which
when exercised through the free market, is to lead to optimal social good.[4]
The city, moreover, provides a space in which neoliberalism is particularly
intense.[5]

Urban neoliberalism has been characterized as a "process," rather than a
"fully actualized policy regime." It is expressed through various forms
of "creative destruction" where the dismantling of Fordist relations and
forms goes hand in hand with the creation of new structures and modalities of rule.[6] This unfolding dynamic has an important geography. Not
only is neoliberalism contextually embedded and differentiated, and reliant upon particular spatial strategies, such as the tactical cleansing of
urban public space, it also has a particular intensity within downtown
areas. This is for several obvious reasons. First, the downtown has become
a site of massive reinvestment. It is here, for example that the service economy is localized in powerfully networked interactional districts.[7] Many
central areas have also seen significant public and private investments
in amenities such as libraries, waterfront redevelopment, sports com-
plexes, and convention centers. Some downtowns have also become sites
of middle–class residential investment and repopulation. Although in the
early 1970s, workers in advanced services were underrepresented in the
Canadian central city; by the 1990s, one was "more likely to meet a senior
white-collar white worker on an inner-city street than in a suburban

mall."[8] Second, many downtowns are experiencing increasing social polarization. The gap between the top and bottom deciles in income in inner-city Toronto, for example, increased from $31,000 in 1970 to $60,000 in 1990.[9] The result are "new dynamics of inequality," characterized by the valorization of certain spaces and people, and the simultaneous but interlocking devalorization of those deemed marginal, such as immigrants and the urban poor.[10]

Urban housing markets have become important sites for neoliberalization, as witnessed by the elimination of rent controls, state withdrawal from housing provision, and the facilitation of speculative investment in inner-city sites. As Smith argues, inner-city gentrification is one particularly important site for this reworking. Gentrification emerged as a "crucial urban strategy for city governments in consort with private capital in cities around the world" in the 1990s, he argues.[11] The result is more aggressive and generalized programs of gentrification (albeit often anesthetized under the banner of "urban regeneration"), motivated by the intensified logic of global interurban competition.[12]

But it is not just private space that has been reworked. Motivated by a class-based "revanchism," public space has also been subject to intensified surveillance and policing as the streets and parks of the city have become occupied by those evicted or squeezed from urban private space.[13] Expressed through a variety of legal interventions targeted at the poor and homeless—regulating not only panhandling but also behaviors that are unavoidable to those who have nowhere else to go, such as sleeping—and justified by an increasingly shrill language of "zero-tolerance," "compassion fatigue," and straightforward class hatred, this "public" policing has its roots, some argue, in anxieties over private property, especially relating to gentrification.[14]

But the rolling out of urban neoliberalization has been met by sustained and creative opposition, often in ways that depart from the traditional repertoire of political protest. Culture-jammers, union activists, ravers, and squatters rub shoulders, although sometimes uneasily, as the "Common Sense" of neoliberalism is fought, and alternative possibilities pursued. As neoliberalism works on reconfiguring the conditions of everyday life, so urban resistance has also increasingly focused on the "concrete life-worlds of people."[15] And often it is urban *spaces,* both private and public, that are consciously reworked and appropriated. Berlin's "Inner!City!Action!" movement, for example, targets the downtown given its large marginalized population and its symbolic and material significance as a center for investment. Its conscious reworkings of the spaces of property, such as picnics in a privatized park, or the entrance hall of a bank in a gentrified area of East Berlin,[16] compare to the campaigns of Britain's "Space Hijackers" who have arranged impromptu parties on London's Circle Underground line, and proposed nationwide booth hurdling competitions for McDonald's restaurants under the banner of "anarchitecture." Spatial form, the Space Hijackers argue, is like a language. Though powerful, its meanings are socially constructed and thus open to rescripting:

> [W]e oppose the hierarchy that is put upon us by architects, planners, and owners of space . . . [S]pace is designed in order to exert control over its users, for the means of the people who own it . . . It is through corrupting the language and signification of architecture that a real form of resistance can be found. . . . By setting up alternative realities for space, we confuse the meaning and language of that space, therefore reducing the authority of the people that own it.[17]

The Politics of Property in Inner-city Vancouver

Increasingly generalized, Neil Smith argues that gentrification has become more pervasive and organized. Jeff Derksen and Neil Smith argue that its increasing significance in Vancouver must be seen in this broader context.[18] That said neoliberalism, gentrification, and the politics of property take specific forms in different cities.[19] As we shall see, Vancouver's Downtown Eastside has it's own important historical geographies and local cultures of property. The meanings and politics of property in Canada, more generally, have their own specificities.[20] Drawing from my discussion in the previous chapter, I want to explore local resistance to gentrification and displacement and, in so doing, to demonstrate the importance of a set of representations and practices concerning property—viewed both as a force of exclusion *and* as a valued resource. In so doing, I will invoke landscape as a useful organizing category.[21]

The place that is now the Downtown Eastside, just to the east of the city's downtown core, has been produced in a complicated and fractured geologic layering of material and representational processes, caught up in local and increasingly globalized networks (fig. 2.1). From its very inception, competing narratives of the spaces of property have been evident in this richly layered landscape. This local property talk, caught up in a whole series of local entanglements with race, gender, and class, has been powerfully shaped by the evolving geographic context within which it is spoken. Powerful dynamics that center both on the commodification of land, and the structuring of dominant forms of ownership have been critical, shaping a landscape of real property and real estate.

The cadastral grid of blocks and lots that framed urban development in the 1870s and 1880s effaced the preexistent propertied landscape of the First Nations. Native peoples have occupied and used these lands since, they say, the beginning of time, establishing summer camps, villages, and fishing settlements; naming, using, and claiming the landscape in specific ways. The transformation of the landscape—"from the local worlds of

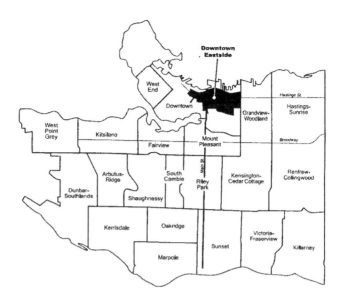

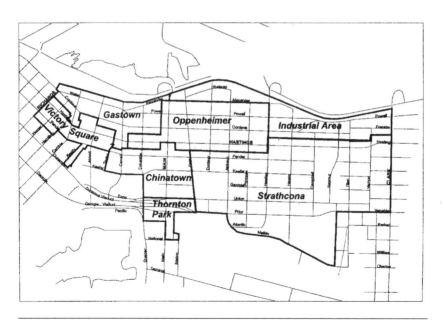

Figure 2.1 The Downtown Eastside, Vancouver. Reproduced by permission of the City of Vancouver.

fishing, hunting and gathering peoples to a modern corner of the world economy"—occurred with remarkable rapidity, as Cole Harris notes.[22] However, this erasure was not absolute. A significant First Nations population came to congregate in the area, and cultural memories of dispossession would crystallize into a province-wide political and legal movement for land claims as the twentieth century wore on. As we shall see, such struggles cast complicated shadows over contemporary contests over property and land.

As a material space, the Downtown Eastside was (and continues to be) produced in part through successive rounds of capital investment and disinvestment in urban "real estate." The area itself served as the original nucleus for European settlement in the 1870s. The fairly scrambled geographies of the frontier-city quickly crystallized into discrete residential and commercial spaces, cross cut by class, race, and gender. Shifts in investment capital facilitated the separation of a middle- and upper-class west side from a working-class east side that contained a large white immigrant population, as well as marginalized and racialized Chinese-Canadian and Japanese-Canadian districts.[23] A shift of capital to the emergent central business district to the west ensured that much of the built form laid down in the early years of the century—the frame houses of Strathcona, the residential hotels of Hastings Street, the clan houses of Chinatown, the brick warehouses of Water Street—was left largely untouched.

In the prewar era, the area was known as the "east side," and as such it remained the center of warehousing and transportation, as well as shopping for the city's working class. Loggers, miners, railroad laborers, and other seasonal workers between jobs could find inexpensive rental accommodation in the "dollar-a-day" hotels in the area. The era of migrant workers drew to a close after World War II. Area hotels increasingly became the permanent homes for many older single men, living on fixed incomes, who had worked in the resource industry. Deinstitutionalization brought many former psychiatric patients to the area. A significant number of native people also made the area their home. The Downtown Eastside presently contains a large, low-income population, which struggles to secure often substandard housing in the many residential hotels in the area. The average household income is one quarter of that of the city as a whole. This is overwhelmingly a population of renters.[24]

Yet this landscape is not just made of bricks and mortar, but of representations. Powerful interests have discursively produced the landscape since its very inception. Long coded as a place of dubious morality, racial otherness, and masculine failure, after World War II the area became labeled Vancouver's "skid road," a pathological space of interlocking moral and physical blight.[25] Unrelenting images of deviance, disease, and broken bodies, were increasingly framed by prevailing understandings of poverty, gender, and indigeneity. The Downtown Eastside has become a space of radical otherness, a zone that one senior city staffer describes as "no longer part of our city."[26] Local residents and activists counter by firmly linking its marginalization to identifiable economic and political processes, such as welfare policy, policing, and the housing market. While local residents acknowledge the undeniable presence of poverty, ill health, and crime, they juxtapose this by marking its strong sense of community. It is a place of death and love, art and anger; a "unique vulnerable troubled life-giving and death attacked community" as one community poet puts it.[27]

However, while "skid road" representations still prevail, they have begun to be overlain by other accounts of the area as the material production of the area shifts. Years of underinvestment and capital flight have depressed land values in the area. In the late 1980s, this cheap land, zoned for high densities, began to attract development capital because of its central location, an overheated property market,[28] a planning policy encouraging the "densification" of downtown space, and the changing function of the central city within the international division of labor.[29] In the past few years, a number of megaprojects on the periphery of the area—most notably, on the former Expo site to the south and west—combined with more recent incursions by loft developers into the neighborhood have occurred.[30] Social polarization has increased.[31] Combined with residential gentrification in Strathcona, in the east, the effect is to create a property frontier that encircles the area. Assessed land values have actually declined, in real terms, in the core of the neighborhood (fig. 2.2).[32] Real estate in the most depressed areas of the neighborhood is cheap: in 1997 land was worth around seventy dollars per square foot, compared to values around six hundred to nine hundred dollars per square foot for central downtown property.[33]

These changes in the land market have prompted a heated debate around the future of the area. Some development interests seem prepared to acquiesce at the "disappearance" of the low-income residents of the neighborhood, while others actively promote it. The threat to the residential hotels is also raising concern: for example, a city report revealed a significant increase in the proportion of downtown hotels and rooming houses that charged more than the basic welfare shelter allowance rate of $325 a month.[34] Planners and politicians vacillate between attempts at retaining affordable housing and policies that seem to facilitate gentrification. While realtors began to salivate over one of their "hotter markets,"[35] area activists called for a policy of "zero displacement."[36] Although these pressures abated somewhat in the late 1990s, low interest rates and pent-up market demand mean that the land market in much of the Downtown

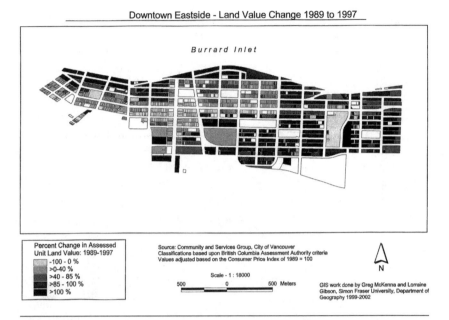

Downtown Eastside - Land Value Change 1989 to 1997

Figure 2.2 Downtown Eastside, land value change, 1989–1997. Map by author with the assistance of Greg McKenna and Lorraine Gibson.

Eastside is likely to heat up again. Although issues relating to drug use and health have come to dominate discourse around the neighborhood in the last few years, local activists are quick to note the ways in which gentrification continues to underwrite the debate.

Raising Shit

Bud Osborn is a street poet who lives and works in the Downtown Eastside. His poems, rich with anger, compassion, and an unrelenting political ethic, document and humanize the fierce realities of poverty and inner-city life. As an activist, he has also played a central role in struggles over housing and health care in the neighborhood. His "raise shit: a downtown eastside poem of resistance" interweaves references from scholars of gentrification with poetic commentary in a powerful mapping of the multiple displacements that threaten the Downtown Eastside. With "spaces and places for poor people shrinking," the poor are threatened by the "manipulations/exploitations confusions deliberate obfuscations/and seductions of the gentrification system." What is needed, Osborn argues is "to raise shit," "to actively resist/and we resist with our presence/with our words/with our love/with our courage." This shit raising, the poem tells us, cuts against the grain. Yet "our words and presence create/a strange and profound and strong unity" that rests on the memory of successful battles, "against the casino/for crab park . . . against hotel evictions/for poor people living in woodwards/against condominium monstrosities/and for our very name."[37]

In this chapter, I want to consider this shit raising, and provide more details of the struggles listed by Bud Osborn. I will draw upon the conflict over two development projects in the area (though there are many other flashpoints). In so doing, I want to point to the ways in which opposition relied upon some significant arguments about real property. I want to suggest that claims about property figure both negatively and positively; that is, that the oppressive characterization of dominant forms of property relies upon a positive claim to community entitlements in ways that are not easily captured by the ownership model, noted above. This conflict certainly centers on land. However, it is not "land use"—the allocation of uses to parcels of land—that is solely at issue. Rather, I want to suggest that we consider the conflicts as, in part, struggles over rights or property in land. Put simply, they entail people saying "it's mine" and, more interestingly, "it's ours."

In making sense of the ways in which such claims are advanced in the Downtown Eastside, I want to point to the significance of landscape, meant both as a physical environment and as a particular way of seeing a space. Thus, although Bud Osborn claims that "the word" is one of few weapons that Downtown Eastside activists have, I shall argue that these words are not free floating, but are worked out in a material and discursive landscape.

A word of caution. When I spoke to antigentrification activists, politicians, planners, and developers, property was not always explicitly discussed. Rather, people talked about "land," "rights," "obligations," "betrayal," and "displacement." Local activists, more particularly, seemed to find it easier to use a negative language of property to describe the actions of speculators and developers: less frequently did they explicitly invoke a claim to community ownership. This perhaps reflects a pragmatic realization that such a claim would not be very successful given prevailing legal opinion; alternatively, it may reflect the prevailing blindness to such claims. However, I hope to demonstrate the ways in which these conflicts, at least, are permeated by practices and languages of property. This is not to say that these struggles reduce to property. They are obviously entangled in many other axes of identification and power, including gender, class, poverty, and the state. However, property is also caught up in those dynamics.

Property, by virtue of the ownership model, embedded in turn in a prevailing legal paradigm, can easily appear to be an unhelpful analytical category. Ownership becomes disaggregated into a bundle of legal sticks, with which one can beat one's neighbor. Conflict turns on disembodied owners, detached from social context, who are forced to speak the arcane languages of Whiteacre, Blackacre, tenements, and appurtenants. Vested, supposedly, in individuals, it does not appear to have any social or cultural relevance.

But conflicts occur because property is important. Prevailing arrangements of property in land have important implications for social ordering. "The balance of power in a society," noted John Adams, "accompanies the balance of property and land."[38] Access to property, including land, is an important predictor of one's position within a social hierarchy, affecting class, race, and gender relations. Clear social differentials exist in access to real estate; 10 percent of U.S households, for example, held approximately 90 percent of equity in the 1990s.[39] This affects differences in wealth, health, and well being: property owners in many urban areas, for example, have seen their wealth increase significantly, while renters have not. The growing homeless population is also locked out of access to real property of any sort. Women and racial minorities are also often disadvantaged by the prevailing regime of property, whether as objects or legal subjects.[40]

Property is social in other important ways. Property discourse offers a dense and pungent set of social symbols, stories, and meanings. The formation of national identity is, in part, a meditation on the meanings and significance of land as property, evidenced in frontier stories in the United States,[41] or mythologies of the English garden.[42] Property also offers an important means by which we assign order to the world, categorizing and coding spaces and people according to their relationship to property. This has both material and symbolic effects. A homeless person, for example, can experience the exclusionary logic of property in a very direct sense.[43] At the same time, one's standing in relation to property has long been used in evaluations of one's political and moral worth. Despite its apparent individualism and rarefied legal appearance, property must be acknowledged as social and political, whether in its effects, origins, or ethical implications:[44]

> If the core of property as a social institution lies in a complex system of recognized rights and duties with reference to the control of valuable objects, and if the roles of the participating individuals are linked by these means with basic economic processes, and if, besides, all these processes of social interaction are validated by traditional beliefs, attitudes, and values, and sanctioned in custom and law, it is apparent that we are dealing with an institution extremely fundamental to the structure of human societies as going concerns.[45]

In large part, my goal here is to "surface" property as it works itself out in the spaces of the city. And when we reframe the struggle in this way, property emerges as crucial. It effects the moral and political claims that are made, the ways in which they are articulated and the issues that are excluded from discussion.

The Department Store

Will the Woodward's building become the Tompkins Square park of Vancouver?
Symbolically and materially it could well be.
—Neil Smith and Jeff Derksen, "Urban Regeneration"

A large red brick building fronts the north side of the one hundred block of West Hastings Street. It used to be occupied by the flagship store of a regional department store chain, named Woodward's after its founder. It grew through the century in a rather haphazard way, linking together several separate buildings. The building now covers most of a city block. Over top of the building stands a pylon with a large "W." Although its six stories are imposing, it is, frankly, an ugly building. In 1993, Woodward's closed its doors for the last time. The westward shift in services and investment had made it something of an historical relic. Although it remained a vital retail and—as we shall see—social resource for the poor of the eastside, spatial shifts in retail capital had made it increasingly noncompetitive.

In 1995, a group of area residents and antipoverty activists gathered on the street outside the Woodward's building, and started to sweep the streets and clear up litter. In a neighborhood that has seen it's share of creative and vocal protest, this action seemed unusual. At a subsequent demonstration, people painted pictures and slogans on the window glass, using water-soluble paint. Some of these messages were overtly political, with calls for affordable housing, yet many others painted mountains, rainbows, and flowers (fig. 2.3).

What motivated these actions? In part, the goal was to demonstrate that the poor residents of the area cared for this building. Vacant for two years, civic observers had been bemoaning the decline of Woodward's site and its surrounding streetscape of now apparently abandoned and boarded-up properties. In so doing, they challenged the deeply engrained assumption that the decline of the built environment was a function of the presence of human derelicts—the poor of the neighborhood. By taking care of Woodward's, activists wished to demonstrate that if the building had been abandoned, it was by capital, not the poor: "We will . . . take some pride in a block that developers and speculators have neglected in the hopes of maximizing their profits at the expense of the community and the city."[46] In that sense, the demonstration was aimed at countering the perceived negative influences of the property market. But at the same time, another claim was also being made. The acts of cleaning and painting are domestic acts. I clean my house. I decorate its walls. They are, of course, dependent upon an entitlement and an obligation. If it's my house, I *can* and *should* maintain and improve it. Similarly, in cleaning and painting Woodward's, activists were enacting a claim of ownership. For one of the organizers: "Woodward's belongs to the neighborhood."[47]

Figure 2.3 Window painting and graffiti, Woodward's. Photograph by author.

But Woodward's did not belong to the neighborhood, at least insofar as the ownership model is concerned. It had been optioned by a local developer, Fama Holdings, whose CEO, Kassam Aghtai had a proposal before the city to build 350 condo units.[48] Although this proposal was celebrated by many local merchants and loft dwellers as a needed entrepreneurial kick-start in a depressed locality, local activists were horrified, and expanded their lively, engaged, and still unresolved campaign concerning the development of the site. The opposition to Aghtai's proposal seemed to stem from two claims. The first was a pragmatic one: surrounded as it was by residential hotels, the private redevelopment of Woodward's would signal a massive influx of middle-class property owners, many of whom were elsewhere seen as hostile to the poor. It would also prompt other neighboring property owners to upgrade or convert their properties, displacing local residents. Although there had long been megaprojects on the edge of the Downtown Eastside, this was really the first within the core of the neighborhood.

But, as noted, the opposition was related not only to the perceived dynamics of *real estate*, but also, if you will, to *real property*. Activists claimed an enduring symbolic relationship between the building and the "community." Used for years for shopping and entertainment in a neighborhood that lacked both, the building had become invested with meaning and value. The private rights of Fama, it was argued, had to recognize the collective claim of the community.[49] Amazingly, such was the pressure that in early 1996 the provincial government forged a partnership with the City, Fama, and community representatives, from which emerged a revised proposal for a mixed-use development.[50] While this was hailed as a great victory for the poor, there were others who continued to complain, insisting that it should be entirely nonmarket housing, such was the need. Over a year of complicated negotiations among the various stakeholders ensued. I sat, briefly on a committee made up of community representatives, and saw first hand some of the tradeoffs that were made.

But then, in 1997, Kassam Aghtai walked away from the table, insisting that the process had become too bureaucratic. He then returned to his original market-only proposal, successfully submitting a formal proposal to the City of Vancouver. Protests began anew. However, claims to community ownership were now even more in evidence. A poster for a demonstration in April 1997 claimed: "Woodward's belongs to us. . . . Not to Kassam Aghtai" (fig. 2.4). Aghtai, it was said, had "betrayed" the community: "It is true that Kassam Aghtai has money. But no one developer has the right to determine Woodward's future. We have given Woodward's its history. Now we are coming together to *reclaim* that history." Echoing the sense of betrayal, one activist claimed: "We're not going to let go of the Woodward's site, even if someone else does own it."[51]

Vowing increasingly radical action, activists painted the now boarded-up windows—not with flowers, this time, but with stenciled graffiti that read "give it back," "100% ours," and "community property." The official signs, trumpeting property's power to exclude, that read "Another premises protected by Vancouver Security K9 Patrol," were subverted by an activist whose stencil countered: "These premises are protected by the community of the DES" (see fig. 2.5). This "protection" was also physically expressed: protestors attempted to encircle the building with a human chain and surveyor's tape (fig. 2.6). This pressure proved successful. In 2001, the outgoing provincial government acquired the site, and promised

Figure 2.4 'Woodward's belongs to us', 1997.

to create three hundred co-op housing units, with the balance to be used for commercial and retail purposes.

In the spring of 2001, the election of an avowedly neoliberal provincial government ushered in a new chapter in the Woodward's conflict. Although the previous provincial government had sympathies for the arguments of area activists, the new government soon looked to unload the building—to a private developer, if need be (Wal-Mart was identified as one potential bidder). In September 2002, driven by increasing frustration, a number of activists and homeless people pulled the plywood from the windows and entered the empty shell, establishing what soon became dubbed as "Woodsquat." Claiming a concern for public safety, the province sent in the police and evicted the squatters. Somewhat surprisingly, they allowed the establishment of a protest encampment on the streets around

Figure 2.5 Exclusion and community ownership. Photograph by author.

Figure 2.6 Encircling Woodward's with surveyors tape. Photograph by author.

Figure 2.7 'Woodsquat', December 2002. Photograph by author.

the building that grew in size until it was finally disbanded in December 2002 (fig. 2.7).

Given local exigencies, the language of protest shifted slightly. Vancouver and the nearby ski resort of Whistler had made the shortlist for the 2010 Winter Olympics. Realizing that the squat could be used to embarrass the authorities (and recognizing that public homelessness can be bad for business) protestors now yoked the Olympics bid to social housing and urban poverty, with slogans that read "No social housing; no Olympics." However, the language of property remained firmly in evidence. Activists pushed for changes to property rights more generally (for example, by calling for a civic antivacancy by-law to seize empty, abandoned buildings and convert them to social housing), and their claim to Woodward's itself remained powerfully in evidence. As one community activist noted at the earlier demonstrations, the building itself was symbolic: "Like, if it were 400 condos in a parking lot I don't think you'd be able to get the same feeling."[52] Slogans reading: "Our community, *our* building!" were posted next to "Home, sweet home." The physical presence of the tent city, complete with mattresses, chairs, and tents made this sense of ownership manifest. Walking down Hastings Street, one entered people's bedrooms. Rumored buyers for the building were publicly shamed in posters that claimed: "This building is not for sale. It belongs to the community." Although life in a tent on Hastings Street was far from ideal, some occupants insisted that "We can't leave the big Dubbya, it's our symbol. The building is ours, we're staying right here until they let us in!"[53] The fact that the building was now "public" property was also invoked. As one squat organizer noted: "Campbell [the provincial premier] says the government owns the building. Therefore, the people own the building, so we're taking what's already ours."[54] Media interest became intense, especially in the run-up to a municipal election in which the Downtown Eastside received particular attention. A left of center party—with strong associations with the Downtown Eastside—swept to power in Vancouver late in the year. In December 2002, the squatters finally agreed to leave the site when offered alternative accommodation.[55] In late January 2003, the province sold the building to the city, with a promise of funding for one hundred units of nonmarket housing. As I write, discussions continue over its redevelopment.

The ownership model, as noted earlier, categorizes as property only that which meet clear definitional tests. It prescribes certain relationships as appropriately "property" and, as I suggested earlier, rules out of court a variety of other estates in land, especially those of a collective nature. It should not surprise us, therefore, that on the rare occasions when a community claim is heard by outside observers, it is quickly dismissed. For one commentator, discussing Woodward's, it was absurd that nonowners could claim property: "The downtown eastside is home to militant community activists who view the district as their own, despite the fact that few of them own property."[56] The only property rights that are recognized, on this account, are those of the developers. Thus a city councilor lambasted the actions of the area's provincial representative, who had joined in a community protest to Fama's proposal by painting a flower on the Woodward's hoardings, as an affront to the rightful owners: "How can a minister of the Crown, of the province, paint private property? . . . It's ridiculous." He used the same terms to complain at the attempt of activists to force the owner to build affordable housing: "if it were a city building or a public building I could see them holding up the development for social housing. But it's private property!"[57] The possibility that this population would have any ethical claim to this space is consequently hard to sustain. That they may enjoy certain rights to the space, even extending to property, is almost incomprehensible.[58]

Yet Woodward's activists make at least two powerful claims about property. First, private property relations are seen as a threat. They are monetarized and individualized, yet simultaneously relational. Private owners, like Aghtai, have money and legal title—the where withal and legal authority to develop. However, the exercise of that power entails betrayal and exclusion. Second, private ownership threatens a more positive property relation, a claim to collective ownership of the building, vested in the low-income residents of the Downtown Eastside. Woodward's, they argue "belongs to us." Its history was something "we" created. Aghtai's actions, then, were a betrayal, *and* a taking. The tension between "bad" and "good" property is a recurrent theme, as we shall see. I will return to this point below.

The Park

> *To exist today means to tread on the property of others.*
> —Department of Space and Land Reclamation

The lesson of Woodward's is that a building is never just a building. Woodward's is a contested site, where the dynamics of real estate and real property intersect. There are other spaces in the Downtown Eastside that speak to similar struggles over property, although for somewhat different reasons. A few blocks northeast of Woodward's is a small waterfront park, hemmed in by rail yards and industrial buildings with a large parcel of undeveloped land to the west. Although it may seem strange to see parkland in what appears to be a largely nonresidential area, taken superficially the landscape is not particularly striking. Officially, the site is known as "Portside Park," one of a number developed on land leased by the owner, the Vancouver Port Corporation (VPC), a federal agency responsible for greater Vancouver's dock lands.[59] VPC claimed the park's development was largely the result of a trade-off between the Port and the city.[60]

The ninety-four acres of undeveloped VPC land to the west of the park (designated as the "central waterfront lands") were the subject of another surprise announcement in 1994. In February, VPC announced its "Seaport Centre" proposal, which entailed a cruise ship facility, a hotel, and—most contentiously—a for-profit casino. A consortium made of Mirage Resorts Inc., a Las Vegas–based casino developer, and local developer VLC Properties Ltd.[61] was established, and a million-dollar campaign was launched to sell the proposal.

As with Woodward's, the Seaport proposal caused grave concern amongst Downtown Eastside activists, particularly in relation to the possible effect on the adjacent housing stock. Of the 7,400 single room occupancy (SRO) units in the city, 3,700 were within six blocks of the Seaport site. 85 percent of hotel rooms in the Downtown Eastside were rented monthly, most at welfare rates.[62] Activists feared that neighboring hotels would evict their long-term residents, and re-rent their units to service workers, employed by Seaport. More generally, there was a fear that the Seaport development—like Wood-

Figure 2.8 Portside/CRAB Park. Photograph by author.

ward's—would be a catalyst for speculative development, leading to the loss of affordable housing in the neighborhood.

But, as with Woodward's, the concern was not only that the Seaport development would affect private space. There was also a sense that the development would threaten "public" space. Of particular saliency to the casino debate in the Downtown Eastside was the park, just to the east of the proposed site (fig. 2.8). This green space, it was felt, was threatened by the proposal in a number of ways. Yet to many outsiders, there was little redeeming in the Central Waterfront. The land was seen as derelict and abandoned: "there is almost no land there at all, [it is] currently occupied by weeds, rocks and junk, and desperately polluted with toxic silt."[63] A representative of VPC complained that the park was largely wasted: "this is not a heavily used park. It could use some traffic. It could use some tourists, it's a very nice site. We spent a lot of money. It's a beautiful park. . . . I mean the hookers take their johns down there at night."[64]

However, the park wasn't just "weeds, rocks, and junk" as far as neigh-borhood activists were concerned. They saw "Portside Park" very differ-ently. For a start, they knew it as "CRAB Park." Seeking waterfront access on what had been semiderelict industrial land, a number of activists had rallied behind the slogan "Create a Real Available Beach" in 1982. From the beginning, this was to be no ordinary park: the CRAB committee called for a large, natural green space, with planning input from the community. The park was envisioned as "noncommercial," that is as consciously different from other proposals for the land, some of which included private "improvements." The park was designed to "provide community stability in the face of . . . numerous, big buck Megaprojects."[65] Of particular significance was a proposal from the "Vancouver Renaissance Townsite Group" who sought to upgrade the area. Pressure on the authorities failed, prompting direct action, including an extended occupation (or "campout") on the site over the summer of 1985 (fig. 2.9).[66] CRAB Park, say local activists, was won for the community, by the community. It was "the People's Park."[67]

The particular historical geography of the site made a privatized, non-neighborhood development like Seaport all the more controversial. The interests of affluent gamblers and tourists, it was claimed, would clash with local practices and use. An "open-minded" space would become "single-minded."[68] Where locals saw difference, outsiders would see aberrance. Security officers would drive away low-income park users, it was argued, to ensure that cruise ship passengers and high-rolling gamblers would not have to encounter them. As with Woodward's, this was presented as an illegitimate taking: one resident worried that the rich would decide "that we are fair game, that they will throw us out and take the place."[69] "I think that *our* people would feel uncomfortable and there would be people uncom-

Figure 2.9 'CRAB people invade waterfront', *Vancouver Sun,* August 20, 1984. Reproduced by permission of the *Vancouver Sun.*

fortable with *us*. If development takes the shape that creates that kind of class difference, it could dilute the *community's hold* on the park."[70]

Public spaces have become flashpoints in the neoliberal city more generally. For example, April 2001 saw a weekend of creative action in the spaces of Chicago:

> At the Chicago Board of Trade, a group . . . called the Society for the Representation of Society break-danced and performed stunts around a rolling piece of random objects and debris, entitled the "Nomadic Apocalypse." Heavy breathing, moaning, and other "Zombie sounds" emanated from trash cans and subway tunnels. Cars did a loud automotive ballet in a lot off Lake Street. . . . [B]ands of . . . women roamed the streets harassing men, subjecting them to the kind of catcalls and obscene comments that women are all to familiar with. . . . Ladders mysteriously appeared on fences and walls across the city, offering a symbolic route over these metaphorical and physical barriers.[71]

Organized by the "Department of Space and Land Reclamation," echoes of state ownership are here used to enact a claim of popular ownership: "Our mission is to reclaim all the space, land, and visual culture of Chicago back to the people who work for it, live in it, and create it." The stated aim is to resist the manipulative city under the banner: "Take to the streets. Take back what is ours." Global capital has reached such a point, it was argued, that the physical and intellectual landscape have been completely purchased. Activists noted the intensified enclosure of space through advertising, public order legislation, gentrification, and the commodification of popular culture. Hence, "to exist today means to tread on the property of others."[72]

Parks, such as CRAB Park have also been sites of struggle. As noted, the struggle over People's Park in Berkeley implicated, in part, questions of title, right, and appropriation. Similarly, Tompkins Square Park on New York's Lower East Side has been identified as the geographical focus for that city's "homeless wars." When a growing population of "evictees from the private and public spaces of the official housing market" began sleeping in the park, periodic police sweeps, counter protests, and state violence began to unfold. Under the slogan: "Whose fucking park? It's our fucking park" more organized opposition was met with force. The homeless, the *New York Times* argued, had "stolen it from the public" and the park would thus have to be "reclaimed."[73] The authorities evicted between two hundred and three hundred park dwellers, and fenced off public space from the public, in the name of the public.

Although also seeking to "reclaim" space, the politics of CRAB Park were slightly different. The concern was not just to resist private enclosures in general, but also to contest the taking of a particular local commons. For many local activists, CRAB Park is space over which the community had a special claim, given its location and the process by which it was created. It is seen not only as a general amenity for the city, but also as a space over which the poor of the Downtown Eastside have a particular entitlement. As with Woodward's, this does not mesh with the prevailing model of property. If Woodward's is imagined as privately held, then CRAB Park is seen as state property, held by the municipality, acting as a fictive individual.[74] As a park, it is imagined as an open-access commons, accessible to all residents of the city. CRAB activists, conversely saw themselves as "sharing" a community resource with like-minded outsiders, rather than being one "user-group" among many, granted provisional access to state-owned land. As with Woodward's, this claim proved rather puzzling to observers, if they acknowledged it at all. One parks commissioner, responded to the claims from a rival representative that "the community fought for years to get CRAB park" and that "they will lose it" if the casino goes ahead, by arguing that "[t]he park is not the private domain of a few people."[75] A representative of VPC also criticized the assumption that the park was a "neighborhood park" as opposed to a "Vancouver park."[76]

Enacting Property

Let me, for the moment, explore the ways in which these property claims are articulated and enacted by local activists. How, for example, is it possible for Woodward's or CRAB Park to be "ours"? As noted, many would regard such a claim to be by definition absurd. However, property emerges as a site for conflict, not concord, and people seem to be making propertylike claims in ways that depart from the conventional definition. These local claims complicate the settlements of property. Fama Holdings may indeed hold title and "have the money," activists argue, but that does not necessarily mean that Fama can claim exclusive ownership of Woodward's. The park may formally be "state property," but it is also claimed as a local commons.

Property, I have suggested, relies upon enactments that are both practical and discursive. In part, such enactments seek to persuade the world of the validity and continuation of a property claim. Such persuasive claims, moreover, need to be reiterated.[77] Thus, the claim to "my" land is sustained not only by the original act of acquisition, but by continuing acts, such as fence building, maintenance of the property, and relations with my neighbors.[78] Fama's claim to Woodward's is similarly enacted (by putting up plywood in the windows, hiring security patrols, attending planning hearings, getting media coverage, and so on).

One critical way in which property is enacted is through narratives. To make sense of our world, we tell stories.[79] With the claim that stories are pervasive and powerful ways of "world-making" many legal theorists have argued for narrative analysis.[80] For narrative is far from innocent. Narratives are held to be powerful not because they serve as a framework imposed upon social processes, but because they constitute that which they narrate. The very coherence of narrative, the emplotting of people and processes, can render dominant stories persuasive and preordained, making alternative stories hard to tell. "The events seem to speak for themselves," note Patricia Ewick and Susan Silbey, "the tale appears to tell itself."[81] In these senses, narrative can suture hegemonic understandings of the world; in so doing, the contingent politics of social relations disappear. This is not to say, however, that narratives are simply used in the service of domination. What Richard Delgado terms "counterstories" are also told, constructing new communities of meaning at the same time as they reveal the cruelties and exclusions of dominant stories.[82]

As we shall see, story telling more generally plays a critical role in the enactment of property. Such stories can be metanarratives, such as Locke's account of property's beginnings and ends. However, they can also provide an enactment of property on the ground. Thus, for example, Neal Milner reveals how popular struggles over ownership in Hawaii involve the recounting of stories of identity, settlement, and struggle, offering accounts of "the way people describe a proper life and the role that they think rights should play in helping them maintain that life."[83] Lynne Heasley recounts the "stories" of property as told by different groups in southwestern Wisconsin, engaged in conflicts over the definition of public and private ownership.[84]

In the community land-claim in the Downtown Eastside, the most immediate argument is that the property rights of low-income residents need to be acknowledged. The rights of residents of SRO hotels to their rooms in upgrading areas around a new development, although often degraded and substandard, need protection.[85] The attempt by area activists to ensure protection for hotel residents has a long and important history. In mobilizing area residents, the story of Vancouver's Expo '86 World's Fair, which saw the mass displacement of between 500 and 850 hotel tenants as hotel owners prepared to receive the expected influx of tourists, was drawn upon time and again as an example of the likely effect on the neighborhood of the Seaport and Woodward's proposal.[86]

The narrative of the "Expo evictions" has become a political touchstone within the Downtown Eastside.[87] It seems to serve several functions. First, it configures dominant property relations in a particular moral light, evoking the language of "slum landlords," interested only in a quick economic return. This can feed into a more general critique of capitalist property relations, as individualized and fungible.[88] Second, for many local commentators the Expo World's Fair marked a geographic watershed, as Vancouver became increasingly integrated into global capitalist networks, many of them centering upon downtown property development. For Downtown Eastside activists, not surprisingly, these globalized processes are also cast in a largely negative light. Associating a proposed development with Expo, therefore, is to position its developers as "bad outsiders."

The case of one long-term resident—Olaf Solheim—has entered the collective history of the community. A retired logger, he had lived in the same hotel room for thirty years, only to be displaced in preparation for Expo. Although he found another place to live, he died soon after. Solheim's story—combining the retired resource worker, the heartless landlord, and the attachment to place is a powerful and oft-repeated one. This narrative was told again and again, in relation to Seaport, reminding listeners that one uncouples people from their "home landscape"—albeit a degraded hotel room—at a cost:[89]

> Do you remember Olaf Solheim? Olaf was an eighty-seven-year-old former logger who had lived in the Patricia Hotel for more than forty years. It was his home, but his long tenure didn't save him. Like a thousand other low-income residents, he was evicted from his home to make way for the rich tourists during Expo 86. . . . We must never let that kind of tragedy happen again. But there is a new, even more ominous threat—the proposed casino/destination resort on our waterfront. This development would destroy our community.[90]

This argument has, in some ways, been successful. Planning policy and general public discourse acknowledge the retention of affordable housing, including hotels, as a valid goal (although less, I think, because of an explicit acknowledgement of the property rights of area residents, than a concern for charity or the social costs of widespread homelessness). If the rights of Downtown Eastside residents are recognized at all, the common tendency is to focus on the need to preserve individual units of property. At an extreme, it is the number of units that is critical, rather than their location. Thus some business interests, intent on the areas "revitalization," have suggested that, given the value of inner-city land, policy would be better served if poor residents were simply relocated to peripheral areas, where land was cheap.[91]

The argument made by many activists is that such claims ignore the collective constitution of the "community," and its moral right not only to continue as an entity, but to remain *in situ*. For activists, the injustices wrought by gentrification and displacement extend beyond the denial of the property rights of individual residents to the use of their hotel rooms. Development pressures challenge the collective entitlement of poor community members to the use and occupation of the *neighborhood as a whole*. This is a central point, and one that is easily misunderstood by those who might otherwise tolerate the "movement" of residents. For it is also argued that the neighborhood itself is imbued with local meanings that speak to a collective entitlement. "History," as Shlomo Hassan and David Ley astutely note, "hangs heavily over the Downtown Eastside. . . . It is a place of shared sentiment and symbols, of collective memories."[92] Those shared memories—such as those of Woodward's—are constantly evoked by area leaders and local commentators, in the creation of an "imagined community" that speaks to past struggles, such as Expo, or the creation of CRAB Park. The streets of the Downtown Eastside may be mean and degraded to many, but they are also "home." It is the people of the area and the shared histories and material experiences that constitute the neighborhood: "It was your life's history, your community's history, and it's an organic thing."[93]

Landscapes of Property

However, these stories are entangled in, and actualized through, a local landscape that is at once material and representational. Put another way, this unofficial, yet powerful property claim is enacted not just temporally, through narrative, but spatially. Landscape, a concept "in between,"[94] is a term that can denote both "a material, physical form,"[95] and a visualized representation of the world. A landscape, then, can be morphology and scenery, site and sight. Although the two meanings of landscape are often treated as distinct (indeed, as a "visual ideology," representational landscapes presuppose a divide between the sovereign eye of the viewer and the space of the material world), Don Mitchell argues that such a separation is as analytically untenable as it is politically perilous.[96] Espousing a dialectical analysis of their interrelation, he argues that morphological landscapes can be generalized in landscape views, even as these ways of seeing, structure the social relationships that produce these material landscapes. In both senses, landscape is continually in a state of contestatory becoming.[97] Mitchell draws on Bruno Latour to argue that landscape is "*enacted* in the process of struggle." Landscape is a social embodiment of the relations and struggles that went into building it. Such struggles are relational; that is, they are not situated between two autonomous political positions, so much as they are constituted by articulations, flows, and heterogeneity. However, Mitchell notes, although the landscape is "always in a state of becoming," powerful social actors continually seek to represent the landscape as "a fixed, total, and naturalized entity—as a unitary thing."[98] Contemporary representations of the English rural landscape with their static evocations of "heritage" and subsequent denial of the generations of struggle and dispossession are an obvious example. But such essentializations can be challenged; contestatory landscapes can be produced, that often rely upon other temporary "fixings." Clearly, the definition and policing of boundaries between "us" and "them"—between demonized yuppies from "outside" and heroic hotel tenants who live "here," to foreshadow my later discussion—are constantly invoked. The landscape, in other words, is not a backdrop to such struggles, but is itself created through that contest, serving in turn to become a vital symbolic and practical component in future contestations.

But the significance of landscape, in both senses, to property runs deeper. As Barbara Bender notes, "landscape" can be derived from the Germanic form, "landschaft." The original meaning of the term was a material one: "a patch of cultivated ground, something small scale that corresponded to a peasant's perception, a mere fragment of a feudal estate, an inset in a Breughel landscape." It also denoted a localized realm of customary law and common property. Only in the seventeenth and eighteenth centuries did the term emerge as a "way of seeing," "a particular experience either in pictures or practice."[99]

The creation or reworking of a material landscape continues to be one critical means through which property is enacted. Forest landscapes in Indonesia, predicated on traditional property rights, are shaped by both government interventions and local mobilizations. For one observer, the emergent forested landscapes "can be seen as physical evidence of local resistance to, and counterappropriation of management and property rights."[100] As noted earlier, landscape claims can also be materialized within the West. Thus, "Englishmen occupying the New World initially inscribed their possession . . . by affixing their own powerful cultural symbols of ownership—houses and fences—upon the landscape."[101]

However, to say that landscapes are produced is not to deny that they are read. The ways in which landscapes are visualized and represented are also caught up in the politics of property. In a careful reading of the emergence of the meaning of visualized "landscape" in early modern Europe, Denis Cosgrove insists on the importance of a particular "way of seeing" in emergent capitalist property relations.[102] The landscape view of the artist and designer, on this account, was implicated in the process by which landed property was detached from the localized worlds of feudalism and inserted into increasingly mobile and commodified circuits of exchange. This helped inaugurate a view of property relations as concerning the owner and the space owned, rendering invisible those others who produced the land yet were now excluded from it by enclosure.

The landscapes of property are then particular ways of seeing. Remembering the fact that "*sight,* both real and metaphorical, dominates the persuasive and rhetorical aspects of property," and that "visibility runs through property law as perhaps no other legal area," we need also think of the map as a particular form of landscape representation.[103] The functional association between maps and property is a deep-rooted one, whereby the apparent objectivity and certainty of the formalized cartographic projection lends certainty to the definition of property claims. The ability to "map" one's property—whether as a householder or a First Nation—is a prerequisite for quiet possession. But the role of maps is a complex and symbolic one. Mapmaking and maplike visualizations play a central role in power relations and the construction of space, property, and social identity.[104]

But the ways in which property maps "work," then and now, demands more careful thought. For the moment, perhaps we can point to the very abstraction of the map as encouraging a view of detached things, set before an autonomous viewer. One important implication of this division is to help make possible the very idea of "space" as an abstract category, separate from the processes by which it is portrayed.[105] If space can be imagined as abstract, perhaps, it begins to be possible to treat it as the reified and alienable "object" of property. Dominant forms of mapping, arguably, "create a geometrical, divisible, and hence salable space by making parcels of property out of lands that had previously been defined according to rights of custom and demarcated by landmarks and topographical features."[106] Such maps, as Timothy Mitchell suggests, are immensely persuasive, relying as they do upon deeply engrained cultural assumptions of rationality, detachment, and Kantian space.[107]

But the temptation is to suppose that such landscape and their embedded property relations speak only the language of the powerful. Certainly, to the extent that individualized, commodified conceptions of property dominate under the sign of the capitalist economy, such a claim is plausible. Maps reify. Names are erased. Perspectivalism presents space as the visual property of the detached observer. Material landscapes speak to the domination of powerful landed interests. However, I have also been suggesting that landscape, like property, is a site for a struggle that is simultaneously material and representational.

To document the hegemony of dominant spatializations of property, in other words, is not to presuppose its ubiquity. There is also striking evidence of other understandings of property. Interestingly, such divergent, and sometimes oppositional understandings of property can entail very different spatial representations and practices. Land may not be mapped as an alienable abstraction, but represented as dialectically inseparable from local identities and hierarchies. Such alternative landscapes of property are consciously grounded in locally lived experience: the divide between abstract representations and grounded materiality collapses.

Material Landscapes

We can see the implication of landscape to property, and its reworking, when we return to the inner city. In their study of New York's Lower East

Side, Brigham and Gordon note the ways in which property can be made both *discursively* and *materially* present:

> The legal distinction between ownership and opportunity for use is constantly at issue on the Lower East Side. Walking (down the sidewalk usually), one is made aware of what is public and what is not. For a homeless person sleeping, tentatively, on the steps of the 10th Street public library, the possibilities contained in the laws of property become behaviors. *Ownership is presented in material ways (locks, fences, razor wire) and more discursively (in language that says "Get out," "Where is the rent?" "Come in).*"[108]

But those articulating an oppositional collective property claim, as in the Downtown Eastside, can enact that claim through a local landscape (I shall consider privatized claims to ownership and their relation to landscape later). For local activists, the Downtown Eastside is locally owned, we can argue, in at least two practical ways. First, collective "investment" in the physical landscape has occurred through histories of co-present *use* and *habitation*. For example, to say that the Grand Union, a local residential hotel (SRO), is owned by M & C Reserve Investments, Ltd., is from this perspective to deny the generations of people who have lived, died, suffered, loved, and survived there.[109] Second, the landscape has been locally *produced* through collective action and political struggle. The resources that were won for the neighborhood—such as the social services, the housing, or the Carnegie Community Centre, which not coincidentally served as a focus for opposition to Seaport—were achieved through grassroots organizing by local people and the overcoming of external hostility.

Woodward's is an example of the former. As activists have claimed: "[W]e have given Woodward's its history. Now we are coming together to *reclaim* that history." Such a collective claim implies a specific conception of the relation between individuals and the "objects" of property. As one community leader noted:

> [T]he Woodward's coffee bar, you knew that's where you found an awful lot of older people. . . . you'd see the same old guys mostly, going back and forth, you know, in their routine. . . . And the women . . . they'd go to the classier coffee shop upstairs and have strawberry shortcake every June. You know, dress nicely, and it's interesting that it soon became very apparent that Woodward's was a big part of the community and one of the places people could go and feel like an ordinary person rather than a poor person. . . . And so when it closed, people felt a real loss and, you know, the main issue was the loss of one-stop grocery shopping. But the other loss was just a meeting place, stability, something that had been there for a long time.[110]

While Woodward's has always been "private property," insofar as the ownership model is concerned, it has also been informally appropriated by local residents in ways that seem to complicate the model. Perhaps it has become what one author describes as an "everyday public space" "claimed for new uses and meanings by the poor, the recently immigrated, the homeless, and even the middle class. These spaces exist physically somewhere in the junctures between private, commercial, and domestic. Ambiguous and unstable, they blur our established understandings of these categories in often-paradoxical ways."[111]

The claim that histories of past use can socialize private property may seem surprising. However, such an appropriation is far from unprecedented. Public access is often legally predicated on continued, active use.[112] Another possibility, noting the claim of activists that "we have given Woodward's its history," is to recognize that the "private" successes of the firm were a reflection of local patronage. As such, local residents should be recognized as having some rights in decisions over the store's future. Roy Vogt provides a related example in his analysis of local opposition to the closing of a supermarket in a neighborhood in Winnipeg, where residents argued, in effect, that the store was both a private and a social institution.[113] Some legal scholars have claimed to identify a "reliance interest" within law that acknowledges and protects relations of mutual dependence between "private" enterprises and the communities in which they are located. Decisions on the part of private actors that destroy this relation— for example, a factory's decision to relocate—are thus seen as problematic. In response to the devastating closures in the steel industry in Youngstown, Ohio and Pittsburgh, Pennsylvania, residents began to articulate the idea that "some kind of community property right arises from the long-standing relation between a company and a community."[114] Others have argued that similar relationships constitute "a central aspect of our social and economic life—so central that numerous rules in force protect reliance on those relationships." However, the power of the ownership model invites judges to search for a solitary "owner." Such an approach has been deemed misleading: "Property rights are more often shared than unitary, and rights to use and dispose of property are never absolute."[115]

We might also find support for the collective claim of the Downtown Eastside by drawing from a strain of argument that justifies property by its relation to subject formation. Hegel, in particular, held that private property is necessary to actualize individual will, which is a basis for freedom and personhood. Margaret Radin has drawn from this argument to argue for the elevation of "personal" over "fungible" property relations, where the former concerns specific categories in the external world in which "holders can become justifiably self-invested, so that their individuality and selfhood become intertwined with a particular object."[116] Unlike fungible property, these objects are not easily alienable but take on a unique value to an individual: consider the distinction, for example, between the ownership of a family heirloom and the ownership of corporate stock. She applies this distinction in relation to rent control, arguing that residential tenants, such as occupants of SRO housing in the Downtown Eastside, may have a moral claim that takes priority over landlords, whose interest is fungible.

This can also provide a basis for collective property claims, she argues, given Hegel's argument that freedom was only possible in the context of a group. While for him this was the state, "one may still conclude that in a given social context certain groups are likely to be constitutive of their members in the sense that members find self-determination only within the groups."[117] And perhaps we can also extend her argument to include Woodward's: certainly, that is what the activists do when they note that the owner "has money" but "we have given Woodward's its history." While Fama or the state has made a fungible investment, the activists invoke a language of "personal" investment.

Although CRAB Park also has undeniable importance as a site of use, the fact that area activists can also claim to have coproduced it gives it even greater significance. As noted in chapter 1, property claims are powerfully buttressed by claims of acquisition, whereby people are deemed to own those things that are the product of their own labor. Interestingly, the occupation of the waterfront in 1985, and earlier community events, made reference to the language of possession, both negatively and positively. For example, photos of protestors referred to them as "crabbers" staking out their "beach claim."[118] Fake development permits (claiming the area as CRAB Beach) were posted in an ironic reference to the proliferation of threatening developments in the area that also enacted a community claim.[119] Parties and gatherings were held on the site. As a CRAB organizer put it: "We were just there claiming the beach. We were there. We were the people. We were real. And we had a good time."[120] During the "camp-out," direct reference to the moralities of possession was made by activists, particularly given surrounding developments: "Maybe some people think of us as squatters, but compared to the land grab that Expo and BC Place are putting on, the CRAB people are small fry."[121] But at the same time, there was a clear claim that the park was collective property: "everything finally depends on how badly, how many in this community want what is rightfully theirs."[122] At the same time, the productive labor expended by the poor residents of the neighborhood elsewhere was also yoked to the claim to CRAB Park. As one DERA leader noted: "The people in this neighborhood are the people who built this province—the loggers, the fishermen—they deserve that park" (fig. 2.10).[123]

CRAB activists also justified their claim by linking it to First Nations' title (a number of native organizers were involved with the campaign). This association, which was also made during the casino fight, is particularly consequential. The issue of First Nations land claims is an explosive

Figure 2.10 Jim Green, DERA, addressing CRAB rally. Photograph by Kris Olds. Reproduced with permission.

one in British Columbia, given its colonial history. The waterfront itself served as a native encampment in precolonial and early colonial times, and is presently claimed by at least two First Nations. It is not surprising, then, that the connections between historic native title and contemporary local entitlements were clearly defined. One pro-CRAB article was headed with a sketch of "Native people encamped at proposed CRAB beach park site in 1896" juxtaposed with a photo of the Second Annual CRAB Beach party.[124] When protestors first occupied the site during the "camp-out," one of their first acts was to erect what one activist described as a "white man's totem," inscribed with the names of institutional supporters.[125] Clearly, the implication is that historic claims to the land were being realized by contemporary acts of physical occupation and material use. As with the occupation of People's Park in Berkeley, the effect is also to unsettle the legitimacy of state ownership.

The landscape of the Downtown Eastside is studded with other sites that serve to map out a politicized claim to place.[126] For example, the Downtown Eastside Residents Association (DERA), as well as other groups, has managed to build a significant amount of social and co-op housing in the neighborhood over the years. The naming of these buildings, as well as their mere

Figure 2.11 CRAB demonstration. Photograph by Kris Olds. Reproduced with permission.

existence, is locally significant. DERA's Solheim Place, for example, commemorates Olaf Solheim, both as a martyr to displacement, and as an expression of resistance and local ownership (fig. 2.12). Solheim's private claim thus is socialized. The physical landscape itself is made to speak to property relations, both negatively, as a reminder of oppressive property relations, and positively, by inscribing a collective claim to ownership in the landscape. Past histories of dispossession and unjust property relations are not only commemorated, but are repositioned as defiant statements of con-

Figure 2.12 Solheim Place. Photograph by author.

tinuity and collective entitlement.[127] The name of the Four Sisters housing co-op, also built by DERA at the time of Expo, alludes to the sister cities of Vancouver in a conscious attempt to counter the discourses of globalization and economic linkage. Again, it is not simply the buildings that are important, but their political meanings. The claim that the space of the neighborhood is "owned" by the community because it was produced by the community is implicitly ever present.[128]

Bruce Eriksen Place, another housing development, commemorates one of the original DERA organizers. His face, surrounded by images that evoke resistance, struggle, and polarization, is prominently displayed on a mural on the building, as well as keywords, such as "dignity," "share," "work," and "dream." (fig. 2.13)

But the material landscape, produced, used, and hence "owned" by local residents is differentiated. Given the dialectic of "good" and "bad" property, many sites are bittersweet, with commingled memories of private oppression and community appropriation. The hotels are a case in point, as one community activist noted, in an interview: "I'd been going to the Patricia Hotel for beer every day from 1971 to 1986. I knew every person in the pub. I knew every person that lived upstairs. I lived [there]. . . . It was like being in a union hall, you know. And then Expo evicted everybody from it. . . . I have not been in the door of that place in ten years. . . . If I knew anyone that would've had, I wouldn't speak to them again as long as I live."[129]

Such community "landscapes" are also drawn upon as concrete examples of local agency, countering the political fatalism and discourses of inevitability that characterize dominant narratives of gentrification and redevelopment. Writing a few months after the defeat of Seaport, when the initial Woodward's development proposal had just been mooted, one activist made the connection explicit:

> It's not time to give up, but to fight for what is right. Not too many years ago, residents of the DES [Downtown Eastside] were told that they would get no part of the old Carnegie Library. . . . People in the neighborhood did not want a handout, some crumbs, and fought for what they thought was right. The Carnegie Community Centre stands as a monument to that spirit. . . . Sometimes the Downtown Eastside seems like a *place of impossibilities. But all we have to do is look around and see what is possible when determined people work together.* . . . We are being invited to give up and buy in. Let's stand up and speak out.[130]

Again, these claims seem alien to the legal universe. The idea that the "community" has a legitimate property interest in CRAB Park because it played a critical role in producing CRAB Park seems, at first cut, rather odd. However, closer reflection reveals the centrality of a model of property which vests title in those who labor upon the land. John Locke, most famously, argued that if a man owns his own person, he has a logical right to the fruits of his labor: "Whatsoever, then, he removes out of the state that Nature hath provided and left it in, he hath mixed his labor with it, and joined to it something that

Figure 2.13 Bruce Eriksen Place. Photograph by author.

is his own, and thereby makes it his property." For Locke, this is the basis for a privatized appropriation which, as we shall see, has been subsequently put to work to exclusionary ends, despite his insistence that such appropriations leave "enough, and as good left in common for others."[131] Scholars note that the labor theory of property is culturally very pervasive. As Nancy Peluso notes, a doctrine of property as a reward to useful labor seems to have purchase "in both Western and Eastern societies, and has correlates in both ancient and contemporary property systems."[132] Such a claim can be used for many ends, however. In his "philosophy to squat by," Anders Corr argues that it provides a "perfect justification for squatters."[133] For if property is acquired from the commons by taking and using it, "can we not sympathize with someone who does likewise with owned but unused property . . . ?"[134]

But there is another definitional problem, insofar as the ownership model is concerned. The ownership model seeks one, determinate owner—in this case, Fama, or the city. The idea that ownership could be located in the collective is, as I have argued, challenging. It seems to threaten basic liberal tenets of individualized, private action. However, one can find intriguing strains within legal doctrine that begin to acknowledge collective claimants. Property, formally speaking, again turns out to be a little more commodious than the ownership model supposes. Joseph Sax has noted the significance and value of the public trust doctrine to Anglo-American property law, which vests ownership in the public, not the state.[135] While the state may act as trustee, there is still a recognition of "the public at large, which despite its unorganized state seems to have some propertylike rights in the land held in trust for it—rights that may be asserted against the state's own representatives."[136] Ownership need not be only vested in private parties or organized governments: "[T]hese two options do not logically exhaust all the possible solutions. . . . the common law of both Britain and America, with surprising consistency, recognizes two distinguishable types of *public* property." State owned property is legally distinct from "property collectively 'owned' by society at large, with claims independent of and indeed superior to the claims of any purported governmental manager."[137] An exchange with a CRAB activist, describing the success of early occupations of the site, is instructive here:

> So the cops went away, anyway. 'Cos they realized we weren't going away. We're here. And that was probably the best thing. That attitude. It's not like we were superman or this or that, but the attitude of a certain bravery, if you like. But just that we had the right to be here and that's a very important attitude because society is always saying you don't have the right to be here, especially if you're poor people. They don't have the right to be anywhere, or really do anything, except for some subservient type person.

Q. Where does that right come from?
A. The right to be there? It's like your belly button. As a human being, you do have a right, as well as anybody else, to be there or be anywhere . . .
Q. That was private land?
A. Yeah.
Q. So you don't have a right to be there, according to the court?
A. Well, it's *kind of in the middle.*[138]

These, and similar justifications for a property right "in the middle" may be more or less judicially convincing. What I find interesting, however, is the ways in which these justifications can be found *within* the formal realm of property discourse. Rights in general have been shown to have an expansionary potential, bursting the bounds established by a dominant order.[139] The same would seem to apply to property. While the ownership model defines and justifies property rights in limited terms, it is also possible to find property being claimed in very different ways, yet sustained using similarly legitimatory logics. This is important, if we think of rights as a political yardstick that allows power relations previously understood as organic and natural to be reframed as political and conditional.[140] *Subordination* can be recast as *oppression,* and thus politicized. Rather than reflecting false consciousness, rights struggles, from this perspective, are "intensely powerful and calculated political acts."[141]

Visual Landscapes

Although the argument above concerns landscapes of property in both their representational and material form, I want to focus a little more carefully on the role of landscape as a "way of seeing." For the moment, I want to consider the Seaport struggle and the various ways visualized landscapes were deployed by competing interests. (I will return to Woodward's in the next chapter.) These different visualizations are particularly evident in the maps and "countermaps" used by the different groups. In part, the different visualizations of space rely and help constitute very different visions of the spaces of property.

The Seaport consortium deployed the standard repertoire of glossy maps, photos, and diagrams of the proposed development and the site. Prior to the Seaport proposal, the planning authorities had been concerned with the Central Waterfront. The proposal ushered in another round of documents, which, as is commonplace, presented material in cartographic form. The urge to map and to visually fix by the planning authorities seemed almost unstoppable. A brief policy document on the Central Waterfront contained no fewer than fifteen prominent maps, and displayed an annotated aerial photo on its cover. Maps serve not only to display information, but to mark out specific spaces into which activities are to be located. In its central mandate of seeking to "reinforce key port, regional, civic, and community functions and requirements, while sensitively integrating all new development with its diverse neighbors," planners mapped out three zones where separate activities could be regionalized and supposedly "integrated." A "downtown-oriented" area to the west would become "a preeminent civic destination . . . characterized by intensity, diversity, [and] vibrancy," while a "community-oriented area" to the east would be "an attractive and comfortable place to go for neighborhood people," with a "transition area" between the two that will enable the former two zones to "develop their own identity and synergy, while allowing them to co-exist side-by-side" (fig. 2.14a).[142] Having thus spatialized the issue, the task then appeared to be that of the correct positioning of material objects by, for example, locating any higher buildings on the "west part of the site, stepping down in significant transitions toward the east."[143] Interestingly, the map fixed many of the potential conflicts and planning tensions in visual terms. The effect of any development on "sight corridors," for example, was traced via an intricate network of mapped flows, arrows, and trajectories (fig. 2.14b).[144]

In asking what functions such mappings serve as "landscapes" of the area, we need to be cautious of idealism: that is, of supposing that such maps "work" independently of their social and political contexts. Area maps were clearly put to work within particular networks, whether it was

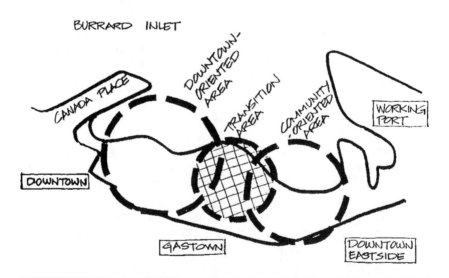

Figure 2.14a 'Development areas'. City of Vancouver, 1994, *Central Waterfront Lands Policy.* Reproduced by permission of the City of Vancouver.

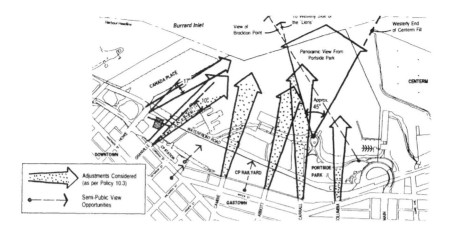

Figure 2.14b Public view corridors. City of Vancouver, 1994, *Central Waterfront Lands Policy.*
Reproduced by permission of the City of Vancouver.

the glossy brochures mailed to every Vancouver household by the developers, the maps produced by planners, or as we shall explore later, the intentionally oppositional maps and other landscape views produced by area activists. More generally, such representations of space did not work alone, but must be seen as part of a much more systematic dominance of what Henri Lefebvre has termed abstract space.[145]

This caution in mind, I think a few points can usefully be made concerning property and dominant landscape views. First, dominant maps speak the language of authority and expertise, precisely by virtue of their detachment. The authority of Cartesian projections, of course, is largely taken as a given. However, as rhetorical devices, they can serve to legitimate varying claims. Lefebvre speaks of the currency of such "representations of space" as the "conceptualized space, the space of scientists, planners, urbanists, technocratic subdividers and social engineers . . . all of whom identify what is lived and what is perceived with what is conceived." Such representations, he argues, are "tied to the relations of production and to the 'order' that those relations impose."[146]

Second, they offer an enframing of space, as discussed earlier, that helps make possible the very idea of "space" as an external category. This, I think, is of critical importance in relation to property, which is thus concerned with spaces—as "things"—rather than political relations. The issue is first and foremost that of the correct placement of buildings—of land use—rather than the just organization of spatialized property relations. Indeed, to the extent that the map directs us to the former, the latter become more opaque. Timothy Mitchell notes that:

[T]he act of distributing and fixing in place, repeated again and again in a sequence of exact and equal intervals, creates the impression that the intervals
themselves are what exist, rather than the practices of distribution.... The
appearance of order means the disappearance of power. Power is to operate
more and more in a manner that is slow, uninterrupted and without external
manifestation.[147]

This is not to say, however, that the maps move in some pure realm of representation, despite appearances. They were produced through some intensely practical and embodied processes, both "on the ground" and on the
drafting table, and they create an "actionable" space that can be intervened
in. However, they speak the implicit language of detachment, relying upon
several hundred years of perspectivalism.

Third, such a space seems empty and transparent. There are no "hidden
spaces" but all appears open to visual inspection. Cartographic space is
emptied of the complexities and particularities that give it meaning on
the ground, and presented as an isotropic surface. "Through a variety of
abstract codes and conventions . . . [maps] shut out the city's noise and
confusion, its energy and incessant movement, and transform its messy in-
coherences into a fixed graphic representation."[148] Emptied from the map,
of course, are the complex historical layerings, such as the First Nations
presence, and the human labor with which material landscapes, such as
CRAB Park, were produced. Indeed, "nature" itself is erased. The "Port
Lands" delineated on city maps are actually mostly water.

Fourth, while abstract space is emptied, it is of necessity authoritatively
bounded and named. Official documents produced both by the developer
and by the city frequently named CRAB Park "Portside Park"—the official
designation approved by the Port Authority—effacing any local "beach
claim."[149] On a number of maps, the Downtown Eastside is chopped up into
balkanized sections. On some projections, the name disappears completely.[150]

Spatial naming as a means of ordering is of immense political significance. The naming of our immediate environment provides a way of
"entering into relationships with those places, of making them our own,
of creating a home." Under these conditions, the denial or effacement of
names can be seen as an erasure of alternative forms of property, as many
colonial subjects can attest. As Forbes notes, "when we are forced to live in
places according to boundaries, maps and names that are created elsewhere, we in turn become alienated from those places."[151]

The politics of spatial naming has become an issue of particular concern to local activists (fig. 2.15). The authoritative production of space
through dominant maps, they note, has long been used to dispossess: the
line between cartographic dispossession and material displacement is a
thin one.[152]

ᴶ✓ewsletter of the 𝒞arnegie 𝒞ommunity ℰ𝒜ction 𝒫roject

──────────────────── November 1995 ────────────────────
Want to get involved? Call 689-0397 or   Come see us at the Carnegie (2nd floor)

Can You Find the Downtown Eastside on these Maps???

The City has a bag full of plans for this part of town --but seems like they don't include the Downtown Eastside community. Take a look at these two maps. There are 10,000 people with low incomes in the downtown and our community -- the Downtown Eastside -- doesn't even appear on either map.

In one map, it is absorbed into what City planners like to call "the East Downtown neighbourhoods." In the other map, they have all kinds of neighbourhoods, like the Central Waterfront, where nobody lives. But they don't have the Downtown Eastside.

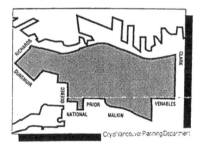

There's an old saying that the best way to make people powerless is to make them invisible. Maps are a good way of doing this. When Europeans first came to North American, they made Indians invisible by leaving large blank spaces on maps, even though lots of native people lived in those areas. That way they were able to rationalize stealing other people's land. They reasoned that if it was blank on the map, it should be free for the taking.

Figure 2.15 Cartographic erasure. CAP *Newsletter,* November 1995. Reproduced with the permission of the Carnegie Community Action Project.

There's an old saying that the best way to make people powerless is to make them invisible. Maps are a good way of doing this. When Europeans first came to North America, they made Indians invisible by leaving large blank spaces on maps.... That way they were able to rationalize stealing other people's land.... if it was blank on the map, it should be free for the taking ... the City insists that the Downtown Eastside must be gentrified.... One way they can do it is by eliminating the Downtown Eastside from city maps. By leaving a community off a map, they erase the people who live there and make them invisible. That way, the neighborhood is left open for whatever changes they have ... in store.[153]

The response to the Seaport proposal from within the Downtown Eastside also drew, in part, upon a visual and cartographic imaginary. However, the nature of that representation was different. While the coded claims and assertions of the "dominant" maps were implicit, the countermapping that occurred within the neighborhood was avowedly politicized. Not only does the language of these maps—the geographic names, texts and so on—advance claims to local entitlements, but the representations of space attempts to both destabilize the enframings of dominant maps—with their perspectival distance between space and the detached, expert viewer—and reframe space in ways that speak to local histories of use and entitlement. All four of the above issues: expertise, detachment, spatial emptying, and naming/bounding are at issue in these alternative maps. Two particularly powerful cases are worthy of note.

At a community gathering in August 1994, mock-ups of the proposed Seaport Centre were superimposed over the sight line from CRAB Park. The intent was to reveal the massive bulk of the proposed development, with the suggestion that it would "rob CRAB Park of its sunset."[154] The Seaport proposal is here clearly situated in the localized grounded realities of area residents, with a conscious dismissal of the abstractions of the dominant cartographic image (fig. 2.16). An undated announcement produced by the Carnegie Centre (headed "seeing is believing") notes that:

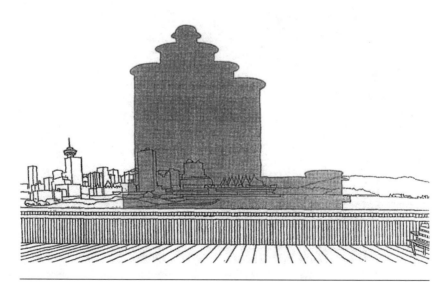

Figure 2.16 Orthnographic view of Seaport Centre, as seen from CRAB Park. CAP *Newsletter,* August 1994. Original artwork by Michael Banwell and Lawrence Lowe. Reproduced with the permission of the Carnegie Community Action Project.

> [I]t is hard to picture the unprecedented scale of this project because the Mirage/VLC media machine has only released glossy birds-eye-view drawings showing it nestling comfortably among the other downtown towers. To really grasp what a massive intrusion Seaport Centre would be on the fragile environment around it. . . . *you have to see it from ground-level, the level where it would be experienced every day by people, not just by birds or developers artists.*[155]

In a media interview, the artist responsible noted that "we always look at things from either a plan or a bird's-eye view. . . . We never get to look at things from the community view."[156] This mapping is all the more significant given the context within which it was produced. The mock-ups were unveiled at a community demonstration and celebration that was held at CRAB Park. Participants were physically obliged to "look at things from the community view." Rather than the apparently disembodied maps of dominant interests, mapping was now occurring with direct reference to the grounded bodies and localized spaces of the "community." In so doing, perhaps, the physical occupation of the site also echoed the earlier "camp out."

But rather than being purely reactive, community activists also sought alternative visions for the Central Waterfront through an extensive series of locally based "community planning" exercises. Area residents were encouraged to imaginatively regain control of the site from the developer and construct their own landscapes, based on their own lived experiences and felt needs. With the help of an artist, these individual images were combined into a series of sketches (fig. 2.17). The results are striking on a number of grounds, as noted by the accompanying text:

> The four large colorful community creations are neighborhood works in progress. These drawings are the ideas, inspirations and vision of some residents of what the Central Waterfront might look like as a public space (not a corporate space). But these visions are not only about the waterfront. They are about our neighborhood—the Downtown Eastside. They are about history, people, belonging, sharing, and the spirit that has built a community and keeps it going. . . . IMAGINE: *a place that celebrates our past, present, and doesn't block our view of the future. Imagine a public space that is safe and welcoming for residents and visitors alike. . . .* We are the experts! We know what the neighborhood needs and what works well. After all, the residents have a long history of deciding what is best for the community. We just have to look at the Carnegie Centre, CRAB Park, the social housing, the Four Corners Community Savings, the neighborhood-based programs, and much more to see what we can do when we work together.[157]

Although clearly an optimistic, even insolent countervailing proposal to the planned use of the site, residents are encouraged to "imagine the impossible" based on a past experience of successful intervention into the built landscape. In so doing, a collective property claim is figuratively staked out. The Central Waterfront is presented not as a separate space, but

PICTURE: a pedestrian overpass at Columbia Street: a community inspired, creatively designed gateway linking the neighbourhood to a larger CRAB Park, with a protected marsh, tidal pools, a longer pier, and even more access to the water's edge....

IMAGINE: more green space, more trees, community gardens, maybe a small botanical garden....

Now moving west from CRAB we enter the Community Area. Picture a group of low-rise buildings that don't block the view to the water. They are surrounded by greenspace and contain:

- a multi-purpose recreation centre with an indoor pool, ice rink, meeting places, a gymnasium, and ....(You fill it in).
- a childcare and family centre which includes daycare, afterschool care, children's programs, a family recreation centre — and just outside, a small recreation and picnic area....
- a community health centre....
- a full recycling depot....

JOBS: envision Downtown Eastside residents hired and trained to work in these centres.

As we leave the Community Area, we travel west again to an active Transition Area. This area is also accessible by pedestrian overpass, and has at its centre:

- A Public Market. This market of many shops has a creative design that brings it right down to the water.

This area is a sea of colour and activity, and includes:

- a public square, perhaps with an elders circle and speakers corner....
- a centre for theatres and cultural activities that keeps the area open and active at night....
- artist studios and areas for the display of public art....
- an educational centre with a focus on skills upgrading and training....

A PUBLIC PLACE: a place for work opportunities. A place to see and meet people, to relax, and to be close to the water.

After a short rest, we continue west, leaving this open area, and entering the most western part of the site. Here the buildings are higher, but still kept to the human scale of Gastown and the Downtown Eastside. And it is here that we find:

- First Nations Historical and Cultural Centre, uniquely designed and built with traditional materials and form....
- Vancouver Historical Centre with a library and gallery with materials of the City's history....
- A Maritime Museum....
- Maybe even a Town Hall with community planning facilities and meeting spaces.

Once again, open and well lite walkways run between the buildings and facilities. It is very close to a new Integrated Transportation Facility (ITF) which brings together the Sky Train, Sea Bus, and the new Commuter Rail system.

EASY TO GET TO: The whole waterfront is accessible by foot, bike, wheelchair, and public transportation. Car access is limited.

IMAGINE: a place that celebrates our past, present, and doesn't block our view of the future. Imagine a public space that is safe and welcoming for residents and visitors alike. Now put yourself in the picture of this model of unique and creative community planning. Only with you will this and other visions for the Downtown Eastside come true.

Figure 2.17 "Picture This: Drawings created by Downtown Eastside residents." Carnegie Community Action Project, 1994. Reproduced with the permission of the Carnegie Community Action Project.

as a functional, historical, and political part of the neighborhood. Rather than the abstract maps of the developers and the planning department, these "ground-level" sketches clearly situate the Central Waterfront as the neighborhood's "front yard." The Central Waterfront is visually positioned and functionally integrated with the Downtown Eastside. At the same time, the claims to expertise embedded in dominant maps are directly challenged ("we are the experts!").

The allusion to the history of the site in the context of the broader neighborhood is also instructive. The empty cadastral space of the Cartesian map is filled with a thick history of occupation and use, both by Native peoples, and then by working-class activity. Many of the proposed developments of the community map, such as a Maritime Museum, speak to the rich layering of human activity and human struggle that has gone on, in, and around this site, formerly part of Vancouver's working waterfront. In historicizing this space, it not only becomes positioned as inextricably linked to the Downtown Eastside, but also appears as a "place," rather than an empty speculative platform.[158]

Interestingly, the community proposals again included references to First Nations' history and contemporary needs: elders circles, sweat lodges, and other curative spaces are proposed not only to reflect the needs of many of the community but also to reference the original owners of the land itself. One proposal, for example, entailed a cruise ship facility designed to resemble a native longboat—an ironic colonial counterpoint to Canada Place, the Port–owned convention center to the west, built during the 1986 Expo, to echo the sails of a European tall ship.

Interestingly, the "community vision," as it is termed, does allow for three areas, echoing the planning zones noted above. However, even the (unnamed) western area allows for higher buildings, yet they are "still kept to the human scale of Gastown and the Downtown Eastside."[159] Moreover, inclusive uses—including those that would appeal to outsiders—are proposed. However, they speak to local aspirations rather than the supposed emptiness of a "destination resort casino," with its simulacra of other places and other times. Proposals include, for example, a "First Nations Historical and Cultural Centre, uniquely designed and built with traditional materials and form" and a proposed "Vancouver Historical Centre with a library and materials of the City's history."[160]

We must be cautious in supposing that such remappings were somehow intrinsically more contextual and practical, whilst "dominant" maps were somehow necessarily abstracted. As noted, the latter are also material, both in their production and use. However, they implicitly made claims to abstraction and as such, oppositional maps were able to turn these claims of expertise and detachment against them. For the community-based representations, expertise, and the associated entitlements to space, were predicated upon local histories of landscape production and occupation.[161]

Conclusions

Formally speaking it appears absurd to imagine that a building such as Woodward's, or a public space such as CRAB Park, can be owned by anyone other than a single private owner or the state, acting for an abstract "public." However, I have tried to suggest that the issue is far from settled. Thus, low-income residents act as if they have some degree of entitlement to these spaces—indeed, to the entire neighborhood. Although this is not necessarily at the exclusion of others, it seems to grant local residents some particular role in the disposition of a site. They do not claim rights of alienation, but rights of use and access. They also insist that these sites must not be developed in exclusionary ways. Property may be configured in individualized ways, they note. While this can provide a basis for oppressive forms of exclusion, it can also be defensible, as in the case of the long-term hotel resident. However, a localized property claim is also undeniably collective. It is not claimed in the name of an abstract "public," but predicated on membership in a local community, and sustained through acts of occupation, use, and representation. A material and visual landscape is one critical site in which this enactment is realized. This claim, while clearly distant from the definition of the ownership model, is not entirely foreign to core conceptions of property, I have suggested. Justifications for property based on labor, for example, or on subject formation, can also be used to sustain the community claim. Property rights, in this sense, have a powerfully expansionary potential.

The existence of the community claim, I have suggested, is important. It helps explain what is seen as at issue in contests over development and gentrification. It provides a powerful political vocabulary that can be used for "naming, claiming, and blaming." It can be used for mobilization, and to demonstrate community agency and efficacy. The defeat of the Seaport Centre and the proposed development of lofts in Woodward's is testament, in part, to its power. However, the prevalence of the ownership model makes it difficult for those outside (and, perhaps, even for some inside) the Downtown Eastside to acknowledge the purchase and significance of this alternative claim to land. Mistranslations remain; such as the controversies over the remapping of the neighborhood, or the presumption that redevelopment can occur, as long as replacement housing units are provided, even if they are outside the neighborhood.

Yet when activists encircle Woodward's and say "it's ours" they do more than complicate the question of what property *is*. As touched upon here, they raise moral questions of what property *ought* to be. By saying "it's ours," activists challenge the legitimacy of other claimants, worry about the ethical consequences of those private claims, and imply that a collective claim has an inherent value. The redevelopment of the inner city, here and elsewhere, concerns contending moral visions. Many of these implicate land and property. It is to these moral dimensions and their geographies that I now turn.

CHAPTER 3

The Moralities of Land

Under all is the land. Upon its wise utilization and widely allocated ownership de-pend the survival and growth of free institutions and of our civilization. . . . [T]he interests of the nation and its citizens require the highest and best use of the land and the widest distribution of land ownership. . . . Such interests impose obligation beyond those of ordinary commerce. They impose grave social responsibility and a patriotic duty to which REALTORS® should dedicate themselves.
     —from the preamble of the U.S. National Association of Realtors "Code of Ethics"

[R]esidential real estate as speculation, no. I really and truly think that should be illegal. . . . What, you can speculate on someone else's life? . . . You know, there's always talk about getting the government out of the people's bedrooms. How about getting the fuckin' land pimps out of people's bedrooms!
                                    —Downtown Eastside Residents Association

[T]he first place to which the inhabitants are entitled is surely the place where they and their families have lived and made a life.
                                    —Michael Walzer, *Spheres of Justice*

Introduction

A discussion of land and property entails more than questions of definition. "Choices of property rules ineluctably entail choices about the quality and character of human relationships," argues Singer "and myriad choices about the kind of society we will collectively create."[1] In this chapter, I want to draw on the struggle in Vancouver's Downtown Eastside to reflect on these moralities. Yet the question: What ought property to be? is hard to separate from the question we have already posed: What is property? Given the widespread presumption that property is *private* property, as noted above, it is not surprising that most moral evaluation has similarly focused on private property's moral value. In so doing, however, other forms of property are by no means ignored. In fact, one can argue that they provide a vital foil, both in the sense that dominant understandings of property rely upon them as a constitutive outside, against which to justify private ownership, and—as I shall show later—because dominant forms of ownership are subject to creative critique by those interested in sustaining alternatives.

Given the material and symbolic significance of property in the Downtown Eastside, especially in light of the community claim identified in chapter 2, the moralities of property are particularly controversial. The effect is to construct a moral divide, or frontier, between contending constituencies. To make sense of opposing arguments, I shall argue, it helps to again draw on the category of landscape, recognizing at the same time the entanglements of landscape in a particular place.

Ethics in Geography

Normative political theory has been criticized as "sociologically and spatially naïve."[2] However, a growing body of scholarship attests to the ways in which space and ethics are entangled.[3] Andrew Sayer and Michael Storper note that ethics frequently rely upon "geographical imaginaries" given that the establishment of a normative principle often implies some kind of spatial organization, such as Locke's "enough and as good" principle.[4] David Smith has also written on the spatial scope of beneficence, in an attempt to think through the relation between an ethic of care, which privileges our obligations to our "nearest and dearest," and an ethic of spatial justice, which places principles of universality at the center of moral deliberation.[5]

Material spatial arrangements and representations can also reflect moral judgements and inform moral deliberation. There have been numerous attempts to create a moral order through conscious forms of spatial engineering, for example. But social action can also create spatial arrangements that are "a palimpsest of past rights and wrongs."[6] These can be remarkably durable, Sayer and Storper note; the bantustan system no longer exists in name, but it continues to trap many black South Africans in its effects. The neoliberal project of spatial cleansing by removing the undesirable—such as beggars and the urban homeless—from public space relies upon moral deliberations concerning who should be where.[7] Everyday transgressions and disturbances, as well as more formalized political actions (such as "take back the night" marches), can destabilize these moral rules and the spatial imaginaries they are associated with.[8]

The ethics of urban spaces have also received attention. Early experiments in urban planning, which saw the creation of English model towns such as Saltaire or Port Sunlight for industrial workforces, saw the attempt to instill moral goals, such as religiosity, hard work, and sobriety, through the organization of urban spaces.[9] Social science in the nineteenth century also assumed a relationship between the conduct of urban populations and their habitat.[10] Subsequent urban scholarship, such as the Chicago school of sociology, was fascinated with the "moral order" of the city. Robert Park saw the spatial division of the city as a reflection of a moral order, where the "natural areas" of the city are occupied by groups that organize themselves, in part, according to a shared "moral climate." To the Chicago school, slums were imagined as one of the "moral regions" of the city that, through dynamics of demoralization and sociospatial pathology, create "unadjusted, psychopathic personalities . . . that serve to shut the person off from the rest of the world."[11] Planning, as an intervention into urban space, has also been called inescapably normative. Constance Perin has argued that "[l]and use planning, zoning, and development practices are a shorthand of the unstated rules governing what are widely regarded as correct social categories and relationships—that is, not only how land uses should be arranged, but how land users, as social categories, are to be related to one another. . . . [T]he land use system [is] a moral system that both reflects and assures social order."[12]

Landscapes also have a moral dimension: "[T]hey speak to notions of how the world *should* be, or more accurately how it should *appear* to be."[13] An obvious example is the monument, which seeks to materialize the moral. This can occur in highly organized and didactic ways—such as the Christian cathedral, designed to imbue religious values—or it can occur in more coded and even oppositional ways—such as monuments to victims of male violence.[14] The category of landscape, again, enjoins us to think about both the material and representational. For example, in a reading of "antihomeless" laws in the United States, Don Mitchell suggests that a central motivation has been to enhance "the exchangeability of the urban landscape in a global economy of largely equivalent places." In other words, the goal is to ensure that the homeless population does not threaten the exchange values concretized in the material landscape. However, this intervention is simultaneously an aesthetic one, as urban spaces are rendered in morally charged ways (as dangerous, threatening, and "dark," prior to a "clean up" of the homeless, for example).[15] But landscape, as noted earlier, can be a site of contestation, perhaps, in part, because of its relation to moral meanings. A park can be read as a public amenity that celebrates the values of "nature," or it can be interpreted as a hard-won community site that affirms localized values of struggle and ownership.

Places, as well as landscapes, "are inescapably normative . . . normativity is not so much something to be added onto place as to be teased out of it."[16] Moral deliberations and contests in other words, need to be localized. Michael Walzer's distinction between thin, universalistic morality, and thick, particularized, and local moralities is useful here. The former can be localized with particular inflections and thickness: when people took to the streets of Czechoslovakia in the late 1980s with calls for "Truth" or "Justice," for example, they signaled moral claims that everyone, everywhere recognized in general terms. Yet the particular meanings of these demands were inseparable from a particular place, at a particular time— Prague, in 1989.[17] Similarly, struggles over the ethics of land development in the Downtown Eastside, as we shall see, are both shaped by and productive of the historical geographies of the neighborhood.

The Ethics of Gentrification

The political and ethical battlelines have become sharply drawn on Vancouver's gentrification frontier. Developers, merchants, and residential "pioneers" call increasingly for the need to "clean-up" the area, responding to and helping to constitute relentless media images of "skid row's" welfare dependency, transience, and crime. For those contesting displacement, developers are cast as predatory, and those taking up residence in the new lofts are frequently labeled yuppie outsiders. Conversely, proponents of gentrification cast area activists who oppose new condo developments, as exclusionary and willing to see "the Downtown Eastside continue its descent [rather] than become a market area for newcomers."[18]

These ethical contests are not unexpected, but reoccur in other urban settings. For one constituency, gentrification must be seen for what it is: class warfare, the extermination and erasure of the marginalized. Concealed by the optimistic language of "revitalization," gentrification in fact constitutes an unjustified "invasion" of viable, working-class neighborhoods. "Pioneers," such as artists, attracted to life on the cultural margins, for example, are criticized as failing to recognize their pivotal role as agents of change. As one New York activist suggested: "the best thing the artists of this city can do for the people of the Lower East Side is to go elsewhere."[19] There are many examples of low-income areas that have contested gentrification, arguing for the rights of community members to remain within their neighborhood.[20] The moral vision is clear: "moving people involuntarily from their homes or neighborhoods is wrong":

> Regardless of whether it results from government or private market action, forced displacement is characteristically a case of people without the economic and political power to resist being pushed out by people with greater resources and power, people who think they have a "better" use for a certain building, piece of land, or neighborhood. The pushers benefit. The pushees do not.[21]

We need to recognize the "right to stay put," it is argued. Local control over housing and communities is needed: "not by outsiders looking to maximize their profits, but by the people who live there."[22]

Conversely, others have a more sanguine, even enthusiastic reading of gentrification, celebrating the agency and creativity of the urban "pioneer." One academic commentator condemns the "unsentimental ideological vigor" of those who would have gentrifiers "read their Gramsci and mend their ways." Rather than being engaged in the "class project of keeping the workers down," they should be celebrated as agents of a critical urban movement, engaged in an emancipatory project that carves out a "space of freedom and critical spirit."[23] Long-term residents have much to gain from new arrivals, on this account. Nonacademic discourse contains many examples of explicitly progentrification arguments or, at best, assertions that such a "natural evolution" is ultimately for the good, despite the social cost. State interventions distort the free market and threaten property rights. Thus, prodevelopment interests in the Sixth Street area of San Francisco oppose city intervention as a usurpation of "property owners' rights and control," and a "slap in the face to all property owners or commercial leaseholders, to our rights, and economic development and investment."[24]

In an important series of essays, Neil Smith has revealed the significance of similar frontiers to the moral and political terrain of gentrification. He notes the manner in which the inner city has become discursively constituted as an urban wilderness of savagery and chaos, awaiting the urban homesteaders who can forge a renaissance of hope and civility.[25] At the same time, Smith reveals the material politics of the frontier, as the shifting margins of profitability and revalorization map out the physical process of gentrification on the ground. The mythic frontier of gentrification is undergirded by an economic frontier, in other words.[26]

But such frontiers, of course, are also borders: despite ideological appearances, they are not simply imposed on empty space, but mark out a line of conflict between two antagonistic spaces. To that extent, frontiers can be sites of struggle and violence.[27] There are, of course, two sides to every frontier and it is necessary to map both. What I aim to do here is to try and make some sense of how the ethical frontier is drawn by area residents, activists, developers, politicians, and others engaged in debates over gentrification. These moral conflicts, whether in Vancouver or elsewhere, implicate many issues, including the ethics of poverty, race, globalization, and neoliberalism. I shall suggest that the ethics of property—in all its economic, political, and social dimensions—also play a very important role. Different readings of rights, property, time, and space combine to create opposing constellations of arguments relating to gentrification and residency. Such polarities mark out a sharp divide between opposing moral visions of property. In

Vancouver, at least, opposing constituencies in the gentrification "wars" have a very different reading of real property. This does not only entail different renderings of what property is, as we have seen above. It also leads to struggles over what property ought to be. For one constituency, private property ownership—imagined as relation between owner and land—is a good thing, to the extent that it fosters responsible citizenship and the highest and best use of land. This is especially important in the Downtown Eastside, it is argued, given the prevalence of a mobile population of renters and transients who, by their very presence, compromise the telos of property. For local activists, private property is understood in more relational terms as a vector of exclusion and displacement that threatens a valuable collective property relationship. "Good" property relations, put simply, are threatened by "bad" forms of ownership.

Second, I will argue that these readings are intrinsically geographic, in several important ways. At its extreme, they entail the mapping of a frontier that is simultaneously ethical and spatial. Different "geographies of property"—contesting readings of space, occupation, and entitlement—are very much at issue here. Not only does a property regime entail a specific set of spatial assertions (in part, turning on landscape, as discussed in chapter 2), but contending property narratives are inseparable from the places in which they are deployed. They both speak to the designation and characterization of certain places (as "skid rows," for example, or as "vibrant communities") and are formed within localized material conditions.

But borders are not just spatial: they also have histories.[28] My third concern will similarly be with the way in which histories of property are evoked, both through narratives of the past and projections of the future. However, I will also seek to recover alternative and oppositional histories. As with space, different histories can serve contending social purposes. As we shall see, dominant property discourse in Vancouver relies upon certain assumptions of the "natural evolution" of the land market; this contrasts with a denaturalized and politicized reading of the histories of property advanced by opponents of gentrification. Such histories, of course, are inseparable from local geographies.

These opposing arguments about residential change seek to answer a series of questions, such as: What is a place like prior to gentrification? How should change occur? and What are the broader dynamics of change itself? In making sense of these questions in Vancouver's Downtown Eastside, I shall focus in particular on three polarities that roughly coincide with these questions. First, a characterization of an inner-city population as mobile and transient is counterposed with a claim to residency and citizenship. Calls to increase "social mix" to revitalize the neighborhood are answered by the argument that "mix," in the context of prevailing property arrangements, will translate into social exclusion. Finally, a dynamic concept of "highest and best use" is countered by a claim of "community use."

Prodevelopment Interests and the Property Frontier

You cannot have a free society without private property.
—Milton Friedman, quoted in Tom Bethell's *The Noblest Triumph*

I argued for the existence of a collective property claim in chapter two; however, a cadastral map of the Downtown Eastside would reveal that though some parcels are held by nonprofits or the state, the majority of the land is privately held, including most of the residential hotels. The private property owner thus plays an inevitably important role in the history and future of the Downtown Eastside, as do the ideologies and practices surrounding private property more generally. However, the issue is further complicated by the importance attached by the state to property, the effect of which has been to create significant tensions with the collective property claim outlined above. We can see this clearly in relation to the development of Gastown, an enclave within the Downtown Eastside (fig. 2.1).

The original nucleus for European settlement, Gastown emerged as a self-identified neighborhood in response to a sweeping plan in the 1960s to build a freeway through much of the area and to create a massive office development on the waterfront. This threat to the built landscape was met by a successful grassroots campaign to secure protection for the site. Advocates presented the physical landscape of Gastown as valuable heritage, and as a repository of social memory. Initially, they imagined a site of inclusivity, predicated on identity, choice, human dignity, and integration.[29] Combined with a shift in political sensibilities, this campaign caused the city to finance infrastructural developments and then, in 1974, to create special purpose historical area zoning. However, the use of zoning, which relied upon the actions of the owner to maintain and sustain property, created an inevitable conflict, the effects of which have only intensified in the ensuing decades. By placing the ownership of private property at its core, a planning regime is created that encourages owners to enhance the value of their properties through acts of exclusion and policing of the urban poor, many of them long resident in Gastown. Although property values have increased in Gastown, many merchants, commercial owners, and loft-livers worry at the seepage of drugs, decline, and destitution from the surrounding Downtown Eastside. A political culture of property has also developed in which local citizenship is predicated on ownership (despite the fact that a large population of renters has long lived in Gastown). Despite being a creation of the state, the zoning constraints under which property owners have worked, combined with its imagined frontier location on the boundaries of skid row, have also fostered a culture in which owners imagine themselves as rugged pioneer individualists, suspicious of state intervention and the nonprofit sector.[30]

Stories of Highest and Best Use

Given the faith in private property, how then to explain an apparent failure in the market: the deepening decline of the land market in the streets adjacent to Gastown? "[P]roperty needs a tale, a story, a post hoc explanation," it has been suggested.[31] And dominant interests in Gastown, and Vancouver more generally, tell what has become a familiar story of land and loss. In the beginning, we are told, the area *was* Vancouver, to the extent that white settlement and the development of the land market took off in Gastown. Hardy masculine pioneers felled the mighty trees and carved out the blocks and lots that became the basis for land speculation. While the locus for development may have moved westward, landowners and businessmen worked hard to create the modest homes and commercial developments that made the area productive and vibrant. By World War II, however, this story of modest success ends, as "decline" sets in. For reasons that are not rendered explicit in the story, the area is increasingly "taken over" by a decay that is simultaneously moral and physical. As the land market flattens and properties undergo devalorization, so the colorful pioneers give way to the dependent and disabled fishermen and loggers of Hastings Street. Owners and business people give way to renters and dependents. Growth becomes decline, which deepens as we move to the present. Boarded up properties, apparently abandoned, are seen as symbolic of a "lost" neighborhood; "taken" from Vancouver society by the nameless, alien, and scarred bodies of the urban underclass. "A big mistake was made," argues one Gastown resident, "when we gave up the downtown eastside. . . . It's my city too."[32]

The closing of the Woodward's department store, in particular, a few blocks away on Hastings Street figures in this nostalgic story of the decline of property. Mythologized as a happy, familial place that united Vancouver society (remember the window displays at Christmas! the busy and happy crowds of shoppers!) the dark and boarded up store, and the threatening streets and people that surround it, has come to crystallize this sense of dispossession (fig. 3.1). Woodward's is remembered as a productive place, "when the streets bustled with people working, living, and shopping in the area." Woodward's is also memorialized as a shared, friendly site: we "remember how nice it was, how good it felt, how safe it seemed, how clean and upbeat it was when we all mixed together: on Hastings at Woodward's."[33] But this has all been lost: "My neighborhood has been slowly

Remembering Woodward's

Earnest jingles and cowlicked grocery boys made it our own

Figure 3.1 Remembering Woodward's. *Georgia Straight,* September 3–19, 1993. Reproduced with the permission of Rod Filbrandt.

sliding down hill," "Look what has happened to the surrounding area since the Woodward's closing." The presence of poor people, drug dealers, addicts, prostitutes, and social agencies, all of whom "have their own reasons to keep the status quo here in the downtown eastside,"[34] are not just signals of decline. It is implied that they have also caused this downward spiral.

But Ahgtai's proposal for Woodward's marks a new chapter in this story. As a private developer, he and other likeminded entrepreneurs are welcomed as ushering in improvement and revitalization. This is the logic and telos of the property market. Interventions by the state or local antigentrification activists are thus imagined as just that—"public" incursions in a "private" process with its own objective momentum that can be explained only as wrongheaded and politically driven.

Such narratives decry the present and project an optimistic future through the redemptive power of property and class relations. Such melioristic historical geographies are invoked in relation to more general narratives of change. The story—and it is a familiar one—is that of the progression to "highest and best use," the inexorable telos of the land market. Progress is inevitable (and usually beneficial), and entails the valorization and intensification of the land. Gentrification is thus defined as a process that "seems to depend on the inscrutable whims of an invisible hand" as New York's housing commissioner put it.[35] Describing his imagined future for Woodward's, one observer's account was titled "[U]rban Evolution Eventually Will Drop Its Blanket over Downtown's Decay." While recognizing the "human toll of forced relocation," he went on to assert that gentrification "inevitably encroaches." "Like it or not," such "natural urban evolution" appears as inevitable as Vancouver's winter rains, or the spawning of the salmon.[36]

The concept of highest and best use is frequently invoked in discussions around urban redevelopment. It appears to have originated in jurisprudence relating to the condemnation or appropriation of private property by the state, the courts holding that equity to the owner was the price set by the highest and best use, defined as the "reasonable and probable use that supports the highest present value."[37] Present uses, or the owner's abilities as a developer, for example, are thus ignored—rather it is the market potential of the site under reasonable conditions that is definitive.[38] While the highest present value may be the present use, in general the expectation is that of new development. Highest and best use, in this sense, is the ultimate end of a parcel of land, left unchecked. This is not just a prediction, it is a prescription—highest and *best* use, in other words. The highest and best use of urban land is a moral imperative and a necessary expectation. It is inevitable, natural, and beneficial. From this perspective, "intervention" that constrains or denies highest and best use—such as planning—are presumptively suspect.

Highest and best use is not dissimilar to many other economic talismans, such as "economic development," "market stability" and so on in which "growth" is equated with "development." Contemporary urban neoliberalism, some argue, has increasingly embraced the principle of highest and best use as a metric for urban land use and planning decisions, abandoning a logic of community and neighborhood.[39] Urban land is expected to undergo sequential "improvement," premised on private ownership, in which rents are maximized. The Chicago school, perhaps, frames the telos of highest and best use in the principle of "succession" which "represents something more than a mere temporal sequence. It represents rather an irreversible series in which each succeeding event is more or less completely determined by the one that preceded it."[40]

The concept, in slightly different forms, insinuates itself into many academic analyses of urban land. For example, neoclassical economic analyses of the land market hold that land has value based on an expectation of future rents, the expectation being that any parcel of land will "adopt the system making the highest use of its soil."[41] Critically, this is not simply a dispassionate prediction. The *highest* use, put crudely, is usually the *best* use.[42] This is made explicit in Richard Hurd's treatise *Principles of City Land Values,* originally published in 1903, that proved a foundational text in neoclassical urban analysis. His aim was a "science of city real estate" which could be used "in judging [land] values." However, running throughout this "science" we find constant ethical judgements, with the identification of "bad" and "good" uses of land, based upon the rents extracted. Salt Lake City, with blocks 660 feet square "furnishes an aggravated case of loss of value in land by bad platting." The Union Railroad Depot in Toledo offers "an exceptional case of nonutilization of frontage . . . Many thousands of dollars of income thrown away."[43]

Such accounts are not only *about* property. Property itself becomes a story, with its own immanent logic. The prevalence of highest and best use, and its taken-for-grantedness, I want to suggest, reflects its roots in the master narratives of liberal property, such as that of Locke, which rely on a "story line": "beginning in a plenteous state of nature, carrying through the growing individual appropriation of goods, then proceeding to the development of a trading economy, and culminating in the creation of government to safeguard property."[44] William Blackstone unfolds a similar narrative, beginning with God's grant to mankind, where "all is in common," to the development of rights not only to "the temporary *use* of the soil," but "a permanent property in the *substance* of the earth itself," and concluding with a state of maximal property whereby everything capable of ownership has been assigned "a legal and determinate owner."[45]

Accounts such as Locke's are storied in at least two ways. First, like any academic argument, there is a sense of progression, of narrative momentum, as claims and facts are marshaled sequentially in pursuit of a self-evident conclusion (with phrases such as "And thus, I think, it is very easie to conceive without any difficulty"). Second, the momentum of this intellectual story is undergirded by a teleological story of property's beginning, middle, and end. In part, this is a story about the privatization of the divine commons, in which an almost alchemical mixing of human labor with the soil creates private property: "As much Land as a man Tills, Plants, Improves, Cultivates, and can use the Product of, so much is his Property. He by his Labour does, as it were, inclose it from the Common."[46] In narrativizing property, a conditional, exclusionary, and often contradictory treatment is rendered inevitable and natural; a powerful narrative like Locke's can "make the contingent seem determined and the artificial seem natural."[47]

Locke's enclosure is not simply inevitable, given the unfolding telos of property, it is also normatively *good,* to the degree that it expresses divine will. Locke is equally descriptive and prescriptive. As Richard Ashcraft reminds us, "Lockean natural rights are always the active fulfillment of duties owed to God."[48] Although God gave the earth to man in common, "it cannot be supposed that he meant it should always remain common and uncultivated." Rather, he gave it "to the use of the industrious and rational." "God . . . commanded Man also to labour [and] subdue the Earth, i.e. improve it for the benefit of Life. . . . God, by commanding to subdue, gave authority so far to appropriate." Conversely, land that is not enclosed and used productively is termed "waste" (Locke goes so far in his condemnation of waste as to argue that waste land, even if enclosed, might be seized by another).[49] It is this claim that allows him to justify the enclosure of aboriginal lands by European colonizers, given the increased benefit to mankind that the latter produce. Locke does not simply seek to justify private property, "he is also concerned to defend certain *kinds* of property as being more beneficial to mankind than others."[50]

This is a story in which the past is imagined only as a precursor to the future, and urban space is located within the grand narratives of progress, growth, and "improvement." Processes of urban development, such as gentrification, must therefore be seen not only as material, but also as undergirded by powerful metaphors and narratives that naturalize and justify.[51] And as Saskia Sassen shows, this entails not only an affirmation of "improvement," encoded in narratives of growth, but also a devaluation of certain "spatialities and identities" (despite the degree to which the "margins" may be central to the dominant economy).[52] The conversion of low-income housing into up-scale yuppie lofts, the prevailing "highest and best" use for many inner-city areas, is not only part of the "natural" evolution of the area, but actively embraced as marking an "improvement" or a "revitalization" of formerly "depressed" (or "wasted") areas. Consequently, any argument that low-income residents have a right to occupancy is to spit in the wind of "natural" inevitability. The best that can be hoped for is some mitigation of the costs of such change. A narrative that traces "improvement" toward a "highest and best use" thus appears to have attained an ideal ideological invisibility; rather than a contestable story, it has become a doxic truth.

If gentrification entails progress, it follows that urban space that has not been "improved" is somehow nonprogressive. And indeed, many characterizations of the Downtown Eastside and its residents position them as "outside" the time of progress. For example, one account compares the gentrifying "pioneers of the new urban frontier" with those that are "just killing time."[53] Another commentator looked forward to the day when "the future will arrive" for the Downtown Eastside.[54]

Another spin on this, repeated to me several times in interviews, was to see change as not only inevitable, but equitable. One former city councilor saw any social housing in the DES as "merely putting off the inevitable":

> Neighborhoods change over time and land values change. . . . In Dunbar [a middle-class Vancouver neighborhood], I would have trouble buying in there if I had to; certainly my kids can't. So middle-class people have to commute. They go to Tsawwassen or Surrey [suburban areas]. Why shouldn't the poor? Why should the poor be guaranteed to live downtown, right in the middle of what is becoming a high rent district. . . . [If displaced, the poor will] move around, just like everyone else does.[55]

But local developers express similar narratives of advance—playing more particularly on the quest for "world-class" city status. Nat Bosa, builder of the Citygate condo complex, on the western edge of the Downtown Eastside, shed no tears at the displacement of long term residents in an interview with a business magazine: "Whenever you build something new, a lot of the people that frequent those sort of pubs and hotels . . . [i]t's not their setting anymore. They move away. As far as I am concerned, all that is going to be gone anyway. It's lived its life." Bosa sees this as part of an evolution, the sweeping away of the industrial wastelands. "I always maintain that . . . the city . . . was not beautiful. Now it's becoming beautiful. Because the rot is going. I like to call it the Cinderella city."[56]

Owners and Renters

These stories are consequential, and are put to work at both an ideological and a practical level. In the past they have been justification for attempted programs of urban "renewal" and slum "clearance" in which ambitious reworkings of space were imagined as solutions to social failures. More recently, the rather tentative arrival of new urban pioneers—inner-city loft dwellers and property developers—in places like the Downtown Eastside have been applauded. For many, the influx of more affluent and propertied residents is to be encouraged, to the extent that they will provide both a moral example—a form of uplift through osmosis—and bring about physical improvements in the neighborhood. As property owners, they are assumed to have a particular interest in their surroundings. One local property owner argued that: "[I]f the market-housing people aren't going to yell about poor conditions, I don't think anyone is."[57] A recent newspaper article maps this divide in stark spatial terms, distinguishing the space of a named owner from the anonymous fauna of the street:

> There's a world of difference between the inside and the outside of Alison Harry's world. Inside, the walls are painted deep teal. The high-gloss wood furniture gleams in reflected lamp and candlelight. Music hums from the CD player. . . . Outside, at the corner of Princess and Hastings, the nightlife is just beginning. . . . The dazed, drugged, and drunk are walking slowly in and out of the bars. Harry can hardly wait for the middle class to invade her neighbourhood. "My choice is gentrification or ghettoization. . . . The area is being left to rot. . . . *We need to show them there's a better way. They need to see people in action.*"[58]

"Social mix" or "social balance" has become a commonplace in neoliberal planning discourse: the assumption being that a "socially mixed" community will be a "balanced" one, characterized by positive interaction between the classes.[59] Such optimism has a long pedigree. The Garden City movement, for example, sought a social mix with a paternalistic rationale that foreshadowed its later application. The departure of the "well-to-do" from the "heart of our cities" it was argued:

> robs each community of the citizens whose duty it is to maintain the standards of administration and refinement, and leaves them to become hopeless and more dingy still . . . The wealthy middle-class deserters must take up again their civic responsibilities.[60]

Postwar housing policy in Britain also promoted social mixing, but now in the name of universal state provision and national reconstruction. Social mix has since reappeared in a neoliberal guise. Britain's Urban Task Force was strongly in support of a mixture of activities, uses, and tenures. This became a guiding principle for the Blair Government's proposals for urban renaissance.[61] While this is partly motivated by a desire to improve a neighborhood's social capital and thus reduce social exclusion, social mix has also developed "a parallel discourse centred on the eviction or exclusion of certain members of the community."[62]

There are presumably a variety of qualities of the middle class that render them desirable as vectors of urban renewal, but their tenurial status seems particularly significant. An influx of the middle class, one presumes, would be less welcome were they renters, rather than homeowners. And indeed, British housing policy has consciously sought to promote owner-occupation in an attempt at combating what is curiously termed "tenure segregation." This has occurred through encouraging tenants of state housing to exercise their "right to buy" or through the sale of development sites, facilitated in some cases by grant aid to private developers.[63]

Similar logics are at work elsewhere. For example, San Francisco's Sixth Street has also been targeted as insufficiently "mixed." One advocate argues that the concentration of poor people leads to ghettoization: "Property owners and families say they have a right to live in a normal neighborhood. The concentration of SROs on Sixth Street is at odds with economic rehabilitation."[64] Similarly, many commentators have called for social mix in the Downtown Eastside. Proposals to develop Woodward's as nonmarket housing are derided as a "warehousing" of the poor, or as creating a "ghetto." This perhaps echoes the widespread agreement among many policymakers that urban social pathologies are related to the spatial concentration of the poor.[65] Almost universally, a mix of social groups and tenurial forms in Woodward's is welcomed by a group of experts as contributing to a resurgent vibrancy to the building and its surrounds.[66] One Gastown architect looked forward to a time when the neighborhood encompasses "people from all backgrounds living together, from those who need to eat at soup kitchens to those who buy their coffee from Starbucks."[67] Fama's original proposal for the building was seen by another observer as bringing "a balance between lower- and middle-class families [that] will clean up the hardened domain physically, socially, and criminally [and] lift spirits, hope, and ambition."[68]

Embedded in these claims, I think, are some important ethical conceptions of property. Real property has long had a special significance in governmental discourse, given its supposed value in the formation of desirable social and political identities. Its stationary condition, supposedly, ensures that the owner has a special interest in his or her immediate community and a stake in a property-owning democracy. As noted earlier, within the stream of "self-developmental" theory, the ownership of private property is seen as a means by which the self becomes constituted as a "free actor." "To attain freedom," for Hegel, "it is necessary that I have property, for in my property I become an 'object to myself.' Not to have a sphere of property that is one's own is to fail to attain self-conscious knowledge of oneself as free."[69]

It follows, then, that those who do not own property (or, more importantly, those who are imagined as nonowners) are not only incomplete citizens, but partial or deformed subjects. Perhaps it is this that partly explains the enduring suspicion toward, and devaluation of, renters.[70] Our very language suggests the distinction; thus we describe owners of private property as living in "homes," located in "residential communities," while renters live in "units of housing," "apartments," or "projects" that are, if anything, a threat to "community."

The manner in which property and community are linked in the case of urban areas undergoing "renewal" or "gentrification," then, is significant. Programs of renewal often seek to encourage home ownership, given its supposed effects on economic self-reliance, entrepreneurship, and community pride. Gentrification, on this account, is to be encouraged, because it will mean the replacement of a marginal anticommunity (nonproperty owning, transitory, and problematized) by an active, responsible, and improving population of homeowners. By virtue of their relation to property, owners will fashion and improve a community, both physically and morally, stabilize it through their fixity and presence, and serve to represent it given their supposed interest in responsible citizenship.

These views are not just articulated by the affluent. A political refugee from Zimbabwe, Ntombi Mayaba, was quoted as arguing that more social housing in the Downtown Eastside:

will only promote what are called ghettoes and that will breed ugliness. We want to be mixed with other people. These could be rich people or middle-income people, but we want to be mixed with them. They have a right to choose where they want to be without us standing in their way. . . . Our area will improve because people who have money have the power to improve areas. . . . And if we live together we may rub shoulders and it may rub onto us.[71]

Social mix is an immensely persuasive concept. Who, after all, notes Neil Smith, could be against it?[72] In its housing plan for the Downtown Eastside, the reader is reminded of the City's resolution to "foster the social development of Vancouver as a home to a wide variety of people with many different racial, ethnic, cultural backgrounds and social, economic lifestyles."[73] Left-leaning academics also argue for the importance of spaces in which encounters with diversity are possible, seeing them as critical to the inculcation of "civil deportment."[74] Yet as we shall see below activists challenge social mix, pointing out in essence, that it is not an innocent concept. Differences in tenurial status, they remind us, are differences in power.

Ghetto Talk

If those with money and property improve the neighborhood, those without contribute to its decline. A sustained stream of ghetto rhetoric marks out the Downtown Eastside as a zone of marginality and moral deviance. "We all know what happens . . . when ghettos become established," claims one observer. "The only law is the law of the concrete jungle. *Ghettos are the universities of immorality.* You can graduate in crime, disease, dissolution, and death."[75] As noted, the poor are themselves imagined as causal agents of decline—a decayed built landscape and damaged bodies are locked together. The visual decay of the landscape—the boarded-up buildings, the disorder of the street, the pervasiveness of "lowest and worst use"—are both cause and effect of the feral population of the "dazed, drugged, and drunk." Ipso facto, the removal of this population is a precondition for neighborhood improvement. Describing the area around Woodward's, one observer argued that the relocation of the "unfortunate denizens of the inevitably fading welfare culture" must be undertaken in a "brisk manner to save from utter decay these once-noble blocks of Hastings [Street]."[76]

But more than ghetto talk is used to characterize the people of the Downtown Eastside. The Downtown Eastside, for some developers, appears to be *terra nullius,* devoid of people who could have any claim to that space. In describing his loft project in the heart of the neighborhood, a developer averred that the new residents would revitalize the area, given that there was presently "no population down there."[77] Similar assertions, often somewhat more implicit, have been made by other commentators. To characterize a dense, inner-city neighborhood—containing several thousand people—as "empty" seems a striking claim. A related argument is that, if there is a population in the area, it is a highly mobile, itinerant one, geared to the rhythms of the resource economy. A transient population, by definition, is a rootless population. As such, they could not be thought of as having any attachment to the place. One local commentator described the historical geography of the area in these terms:

> So a lot of guys down here were in that sort of revolving door thing: they were down here drinking off their paychecks. Then they'd leave and they'd go back upcountry and work for four months and then they'd be back for four months. And it was quite different, there was no tensions that I'm aware of. . . . [T]he guys coming down and drinking off their paychecks, they didn't have any pretensions about where they were living . . . . they were living down here because it's where they could afford to live. . . . Again there was [sic] no pretensions about the thing being a neighborhood and all this jazz.[78]

There are interesting echoes of Robert Park's characterization of the hobo as one who engages in "locomotion for its own sake." Although there is a perverse freedom here, locomotion is ultimately deemed pathological and antisocial. In order that there be "permanence and progress in society the individuals who compose it must be located . . . [A]ll forms of association among human beings rest finally upon locality and local association."[79] Nomads, "so the modernist story goes, head nowhere."[80]

Another extension of this "mapping" is to suggest that the retired resource workers have given way to a socially marginal and criminalized population made up of sex trade workers, criminals on the lam, mentally ill people "released into the community," and substance abusers of all types. Again, these stigmatized populations are deemed mobile, attracted only to the neighborhood by virtue of its concentration of social services or with the acquiescence of the police.[81] However, they are also characterized as "outsiders" with little stake in the neighborhood:

> there are a whole bunch of people now living down here who weren't living here ten years ago. This is primarily the Riverview crowd [a mental hospital]. And the drug dealers and whatnot. . . . And I to this day resist considering them *part of the community.* I mean they're either out and out criminals or they need serious help. . . . They should be somewhere else as far as I'm concerned. Either help them or put them in the clink. One or the other. They don't deserve to live down here, they do not have the God given right to live down here. . . . In ten years *they don't become indigenous species as far as I'm concerned.*[82]

To that extent, displacement not only would be relatively benign (given the presumption that area residents have no real identification with the place), but it would mark the "improvement" and "revitalisation" of the area, as property owners with an "obvious" stake in the quality of life of the neighborhood move in and the marginal and dangerous move out.

The similarities with the ideologies that undergirded the colonial dispossession of native peoples are striking. Deemed mobile, native peoples could not be seen as enjoying any legitimate entitlement given the supposed conjunction of permanence and possession.[83] This does not mean, of course, that native peoples did not—and do not—claim forms of entitlement. However, those property claims were not communicated in a language that was legible to the dominant society. But the postcolonial geographies of property are evident in other ways. In social mix, the Victorian assertion of moral improvement through property is still with us. Commentators on colonial land policy took it as a given that the acquisition of landed property was a prerequisite for stability, progress, and prosperity. Indigenous populations were to be civilized through principles of private property, in distinction to primitive forms of land acquisition.[84] However, there was a simultaneous recognition that too much property— particularly in a land-rich colony such as Canada—was dangerous to the maintenance of social hierarchies. Herman Merivale's influential theory of "systematic colonization" preached the necessity of the cautious dispersal of Crown lands to ensure the continued proletarianization of a segment of the population and thus guarantee economic advance.[85]

Antidisplacement and the Ethics of Property

> *[W]e must bring principles of social justice and human rights into the picture. . . . If the central conflict is one of land use and land ownership; of property rights vs. people's right to decent housing, this raises questions of social ethics. Does a low-income community have a right to occupy the land its members have lived on for decades? Or is it the unlimited right of landowners and developers to make the best profit on the land that the free market can give? The situation of Downtown Eastside SRO hotel tenants facing evictions because of conversion to upscale uses is similar to that of tenant farmers whose land is wanted to expand the cash crops of a landowner.[86]*
> —Marg Green, *The Downtown Eastside*

For those resisting gentrification, a very different reading of the historical geographies of property rights emerges. The rights of low-income residents to remain within the neighborhood, it is argued, rely upon the simultaneous affirmation of a localized collective entitlement to a space, noted in chapter 2, and the moral condemnation of a predatory, profit-driven property regime. Gentrification threatens not only displacement, but also dispossession. A moral boundary—between the poor and the "yuppies"—and a propertied boundary—between positive forms of collective entitlement and negative forms of individualized speculation—

presuppose a geographic boundary—between the space of the neighborhood, and predations from "outside."

Terra Populi

Considerable energy has gone into challenges to the dominant view of the neighborhood as an "unpropertied," empty space. Long-standing alternative geographies of the area map it out as both *occupied* and, more importantly, as *settled* by a viable community of residents with an historic stake in the neighborhood. Area activists counter claims of mobility by an emphasis on the remarkable stability of the area's residents, many of whom have occupied the same hotel rooms for many years.

At the same time that Gastown formed in the late 1960s, groups of young, politically radical organizers began working in the skid road area. They pursued a new agenda that challenged the dominant rendition of the area as the haven of derelicts and transients, seeking instead to articulate a vision of inner-city residents and citizens whose biggest problems were poverty, deteriorating housing, unemployment, and a lack of access to services. Increasingly explicit was a claim of occupation and residence. Contrary to characterizations of the population as shiftless and mobile, activists reminded outsiders, "of the district's stability, of the loyalty of many elderly men to it, of the small minority who were transients and alcoholics."[87] The place, in other words, was a neighborhood and a community to which residents could claim some collective attachment and entitlement. This provided the conditions for the development of an indigenous organizational base capable of mobilizing local "citizens" in alliance with other groups, including the city, to address these problems.

Central to that mobilization was a self-conscious mapping strategy. Organizations like the Downtown Eastside Residents Association (DERA) played a formative role here, struggling to rename skid road. The name, the Downtown Eastside, derives from these remappings, originally delineated in a 1975 newspaper article by a prominent activist and future member of Parliament. The boundaries of this space were drawn to be deliberately wide and inclusive, encompassing a broad swathe of the low-income area to the east of the downtown. Note the references to shared poverty and permanent residence:

> The area designated as the "downtown eastside" stretches along the harbour from Clark Drive to Burrard Street (except for the Strathcona neighborhood, which maintains its separate identity). It contains downtown businesses, waterfront industries and a newly developed Gastown commercial-entertainment area which has pushed Vancouver's Skid Road eastward. The residents of the area include many single people who live in rundown hotels and rooming houses, the

most visible of whom are the transients, alcoholics, and social outcasts on the streets. However, the majority are permanent residents who have lived downtown for many years and include a number of Japanese and Chinese families in the eastern section.[88]

As noted in the previous chapter, this space was also invested with political meaning: parks, streets, hotels, and commercial spaces were all enrolled into a deeply charged landscape of memory. However, this landscape is seen as legible only to those versed in local understandings. The landscape, activists argue, is not silent, but speaks to a history of struggle, occupation, and use. This representation of space is far removed from the tendency of some external interests to treat the Downtown Eastside as *terra nullius,* devoid of any viable claim to place. Activists, of course, see this as facilitating the reoccupation of the area by frontier-minded developers and residents, echoing Simon Ryan's discussion of the close links between the "blank spaces" on colonial Australian maps and the processes of dispossession and land expropriation.

> In the erasure of land, not only is prior . . . occupation and ownership ignored, but the land itself is inserted into a particular narrativization of history. A blank sheet, of course, intimates that there has been no history, but also constructs the future as a place/time for writing.[89]

In a helpful reading of struggles over gentrification in Cincinnati, John Davis notes the saliency of differing clusters of ideas that not only offer particular accounts of the history of a neighborhood, but also map its geography—its buildings, socioeconomic diversity, and so on—in particular and consequential ways. Such opposing historical geographies (Davis terms them accounts of "property and place") entail contending readings of community, pluralism, the market, home ownership, and low-income housing. For those opposed to gentrification, for example, the concept of "community" is understood not as a disaggregated bundle of physical artifacts, but as a localized set of relations that is:

> conceived exclusively in terms of social interaction and affective bonds among the indigenous population. . . . Buildings are important, but only as a means of securing a cherished future, where reciprocity and mutual aid are made possible by an abundance of social property. The built environment . . . presents an opportunity to preserve the last remnants of a social community ripped apart by urban renewal and threatened with extinction by gentrification . . .[90]

Yet as in Gastown, progentrification interests construe "community" as a physical inventory of local heritage buildings, threatened by the inappropriate forms of property use by low-income residents who appear not to value heritage as a good. The fear is that "[u]nless something is done immediately, this structural 'community' of aesthetic and historic significance will be irretrievably lost."

Similarly in the Downtown Eastside, argue many community activists and commentators, hegemonic accounts imagine the neighborhood as buildings, not people, as an empty, speculative site, rather than a viable community space. The two are fundamentally incompatible.

> [W]hen people come up with an argument like that [highest and best use], what they're doing is they're not looking at human beings. Clearly what they're looking at is a product, a product called housing. . . . The thing is that housing is an aspect of a community, and is an aspect of a human being. . . . And all these people who have the attitude that poor people can live in a little box anywhere who obviously . . . have two standards. One for themselves and one for the rest of society. . . . [C]ommunity networks . . . are as valuable as the housing.[91]

> Well, I think this is, this is the main argument, is that a neighborhood isn't just buildings. . . . Is that what you call a neighborhood, a collection of houses? That is a very warped perception of human life, I'd say. Is this what you call a community? The real estate? Whose definition is that? . . . It certainly isn't a traditional definition of community. And it certainly isn't even a traditional definition of heritage to say save the buildings and get rid of all the real heritage, the history and the culture and the actual human beings who live that history and that culture.[92]

While the communicative markers by which local residents map their collective "property claim" may be invisible to outsiders, they are integral to the local geography of possession:

> [T]he condo industry acts as if no one else is living in the neighborhood, and they are homesteading an urban wilderness. . . . [T]his is already a vital community. It was made that way by residents, not by developers or others who patronize and insult poor people. Carnegie Centre, CRAB park, the network of decent and affordable social housing, improved safety in the hotels, the drugs driven out of Oppenheimer Park—these are the real signs of revitalization.[93]

Bad Property/Good Property

In early attempts to carve out the Downtown Eastside as a viable community, the iconic figure of the retired resource worker played a central role. Such claims still have political purchase. However, rather than a mobile sojourner, the "old timer" is seen here as a long-term occupant and, moreover, one with a particular attachment to his locale, rather than rootless. The narrative here celebrates the dignity of masculine labor, and the pioneer spirit that underpins the province's resource economy. "Frontier" mythology is at play here, but in a reconfigured form. Devoting his life to pushing back the provincial resource frontier, the resource worker is now cast as settled quietly in the neighborhood, organically connected to his hotel and his community.[94] Perhaps implicit here is not only the claim of dignified rest, following an active life, but that of Lockean entitlement. By mixing his labor with the land, he has made the province "ours"; it is only appropriate that we respect his modest claim to his home.

As we have seen in the previous chapter, the story of such residents and their dispossessions has entered into a counternarrative of property. But as noted, the entitlement of working-class residents is said to extend beyond the individual hotel units. The neighborhood itself is imagined as in some ways "owned" by area residents. In part, this relates to the argument that the neighborhood has been intensely used and physically produced through local struggle and collective agency, thus vesting a claim to this space in its low-income residents. Moreover, the physical landscape—the community centers, hotels, service agencies, co-ops, and streets—itself speaks of successful working-class resistance to attempts at community erasure through displacement.

Local histories also subject prevailing property relations to critical scrutiny, particularly given the precarious tenurial status of many of the hotel residents, and concerns for the actions of "slum landlords" and, more recently, unscrupulous developers. Groups like DERA have long sought to defend the rights of marginalized hotel residents to secure, clean, and safe accommodation. For some observers, this reflects "a socialism with a pragmatic face, confronting real issues oppressing real people, and offering real strategies to resolve them."[95] That pragmatic socialism, given the material realities of the neighborhood, is necessarily entangled with deeply charged moral visions of class, law, and property rights, including a critique of the contradictions of prevailing relations.

The collision between the localized entitlements of the poor and the manifest inequality of prevailing capitalist property relations became increasingly visible, as noted, during the run-up to the Expo '86 fair. As far as many local activists were concerned, it was not the "joyous human event which inspired a sense of optimism," as some developers would have it.[96] The immanent logic of highest and best use was locally recast as one of dispossession and immoral commodification, as hotel owners kicked several hundred residents out of their hotel rooms. For the then leader of DERA, it was an attempt to "annihilate [community] history, to annihilate that talent, it was like ethnic cleansing. . . . It was perverted, incorrect, economically wrong."[97]

Given the tightening encirclement of the neighborhood by development, community activists contest the material inequities of dominant property relations, and prevailing narratives of "revitalization" and highest and best use. Assertions at the inevitability and naturalness of prevailing property relations, and the unfolding logic of highest and best use are directly challenged. Responding to the teleology that saw Woodward's redevelopment as a "natural urban evolution," one activist responded by arguing that there was nothing natural about gentrification: "It's a conscious act of market development and urban planning, laced with moralistic, ideological, and cultural preferences."[98] As a DERA leader noted: "[W]ell, murder happens everywhere too, so does this mean we should support it? Displacement isn't like the weather. It's not a force of nature. It's done for very specific reasons." Along with many others in the neighborhood, she also savaged benign assumptions of neighborhood "improvement" and "revitalization" through the logic of highest and best use:

> Highest and best use for who? Highest and best use for who? . . . People in this neighborhood want the neighborhood cleaned up. We'd like some help with that. But we don't consider getting rid of the whole stinkin' lot of us as cleaning up the neighborhood. We could always bring in the neutron bomb, I guess, and it would be pretty clean in the end.[99]

More practically, representations that link a decayed local landscape to its disordered inhabitants are also challenged. Thus, while the closure of Woodward's is lamented, taking "a large chunk from the heart of the community and out of Vancouver's history," this is blamed not on the poor, but on private developers and speculators who "have been turning the once lively West Hastings Street into a boarded up and bleak American style inner city. The dark empty buildings are a testament to their indifference and greed."[100]

In this sense, property rights are seen as socially relational. They do not reside in the narrow nexus between owner and thing owned; rather they must be seen as contextual and potentially inequitable. Any property developments that would "get rid of the real heritage" is deemed an immoral act of violence given the historical and spatial embedness of those "actual human beings."

> [T]here's a huge human cost to relocating or fracturing any community, and I think we need to recognize that as a social value if we want to have a better place to live. . . . I don't think it's right to displace people from their land base, even if it's rental units.
>
> Q: What's important here? Why is that something worth defending?
>
> A: I think that we relate to our environment and to our history together as a community, and to places. . . . [I]t's only the poor who are ever dislocated.[101]

Oppositional property narratives reject the individualization and reification of property that would cast property as the benign relation between *persona* and *res*. At a city meeting to discuss a proposal to build "micro-suites" for low-income residents, one activist demanded "one [additional] square foot for every man and woman murdered in the Downtown Eastside, for every disabled person, for every child gone hungry, for every addict and alcoholic." The detached "square foot" of the developer is here clearly set against local relations of power, exclusion, and violence. Private property implicates others in relations of power, it is argued, in ways that legal realism acknowledged long ago:

> Whatever technical definition of property we may prefer, we must recognize that a property right is a relation not between an owner and a thing, but between the owner and other individuals in reference to things. . . . [T]he essence of private property is always the right to exclude others. . . . *[D]ominium* over things is also *imperium* over our fellow human beings.[102]

Property relations *are* individualized by activists, however, but are done so in a much more politically charged manner. Thus, a long-standing tactic is to personalize the development process. In other words, the target of community organizing against a condo proposal is never the legally fictional corporate individual, but is always a named chief executive of that corporation.[103] As noted in chapter 2, activists insisted on identifying the Woodward's developer. This refusal to mystify the individualized corporation also serves to make the point that property development not only entails the displacement of real people, but is also caused by real people.

This does not necessarily mean that private property is the problem. Certain formal property rights—such as those of the hotel resident, or even the area resident who owns his or her own home—are acceptable, even morally valuable, as long as they are localized and noninvasive:

> I think property rights are important . . . if they're associated with your, you know, a place to live and feed and clothe yourself and, but then, they are limited where they impinge on your neighbor's right to do the same thing. So I don't see how you can say anyone has the right to acquire money, or acquire more money when they already have a lot of money and by taking away other, other people's lives, their right to do whatever with private property does impinge on other people and they don't recognize that.[104]

This relational and localized reading of property receives another twist, with the argument that local material conditions of deprivation and disadvantage have bred a local "property" tradition of inclusivity and sharing, which contrasts with that of "outsiders":

> The Downtown Eastside is tolerant and quite inclusive, and I think that's why they rail against the private developer who's saying "this is my sandbox and I'm going to do anything I want here," where people will say, "I don't have much to offer, but do you want a share of it?" You see it with cigarettes, you see it with lots of things in the community, where people are social, and they meet and share things, and it might be a bottle, it might be anything. . . . It's their area, it's where they live. And I think that's why private property and the rights of private property are as foolish to them as they are to me. Because it *doesn't make any sense*, because it's exclusive. . . . I don't think it's even necessarily a politic; it's a philosophy of life that has meaning with people.[105]

Thus, some activists argued that their goal in developing Woodward's—as with CRAB Park—was not to exclude others, but to create a development that would ensure that the site "could once again be a central gathering and meeting place for people from the community and the whole city." They sought a "model development that reflects the historical sharing of Woodward's."[106] Responding to Gastown interests who claimed they felt excluded by activist's plans for the building, one activist stated that he wanted Woodward's to be shared by everyone: "Historically it was a building that was shared. This is an opportunity for people to come together."[107]

Yet, despite a language of shared space, local activists have opposed the development of market housing in Woodward's and elsewhere. Loft dwellers in Gastown are viewed with suspicion. Condo sales offices have been picketed, and potential buyers urged to go elsewhere. The arguments of antigentrification activists can thus easily be taken as an unethical form of exclusion. One Gastown homeowner, in a "dispatch from the 'gentrification' wars," as he put it, went to so far as to claim that he was "a casualty of the politics of exclusion. Not because of the color of my skin. Nor my religious affiliation. Nor my sex. But because of my (relative) affluence. I am a homeowner."[108]

Social Mix/Private Exclusions

And this brings us back to "social mix." As noted, the concept is morally persuasive, with its implied claims to inclusivity, tolerance, and social "balance." The problem with "social mix" however is that it promises equality in the face of hierarchy. First, as often noted, it is socially one-sided. If social mix is good, argue local activists, then why not make it possible for the poor to live in rich neighborhoods? Why are concentrations of the rich not deemed "ghettoes?" To the planner or politician, however, social mix is said to work one way, "bringing 'back' more of the white middle classes [to] retake control of the political and cultural economies as well as the geography of the largest cities."[109] Second, the empirical evidence suggests that it often fails to improve social and economic conditions for renters. Interaction between owner-occupiers and renters in "mixed" neighborhoods seems to be limited. More importantly, it can lead to social segregation and isolation.[110] Some critics even point to social mix as a conscious instrument of residential purification, designed to exclude "anti social" elements.[111]

Activists point to the actions of Gastown property-owners as an example of the exclusionary effects of "social mix," where property-owners have deployed a language of balance in the service of exclusion, and where developers promise condo buyers a lifestyle that is theirs "for the taking."[112] As noted, state mappings initially called Gastown into being, and in so doing, institutionalized certain forms of localized identity as congruent with the production of "heritage"-designated properties. Subsequently, legitimized "Gastown" representatives have engaged in their own mappings, designed to distinguish Gastown from its more dubious neighbor and to solidify zoning boundaries that are highly fluid with respect to the movement of people.

Thus, the presence of the poor in Gastown, who actually constitute the great majority of the residential population, is explained by Gastown representatives in terms of the siting of social service facilities and subsidized housing rather than their pre-existent residency. "There is," one analyst claims, "a fiercely competitive economic struggle between market and nonmarket interests . . . for finite and shrinking numbers of development sites."[113] As a consequence of the "subsidies" they receive from state and charitable sources, such facilities threaten to crowd out the market interests because the latter are not subsidized and, hence, noncompetitive vis-à-vis development costs. They also, apparently, attract the poor to Gastown, creating problems for everyone else. "Advisory" groups established by the local state in the 1970s have emerged as key proponents of these claims:

> Gastown has experienced an influx of facilities targeted to clientele at the lower end of the socioeconomic scale, which cater to the *socially disabled* and consequently have been known to attract an undesirable element. Ironically, there is a dearth of facilities for *Gastown residents*.[114]

One interesting example of the struggle over space concerned the developer who persuaded the city to let him fence off a section of public space adjacent to his Gastown condominium development. Named the Van Horne, the project honored the late-nineteenth-century President of the Canadian Pacific Railway (a far cry from the proletarian origins of Solheim Place and Tellier Towers). For community opponents, the closure entailed not only the unjustified loss of public space to a private developer, but a clash over the meanings of that space, where an area deemed active, community space was regarded as threatening by new residents.

Poor people are thus represented as interlopers who are present only to utilize services that are not required by authentic locals. A heritage area, it seems, is not a place for the poor. They must, then, belong elsewhere. In comparing itself to the image of a deteriorating, burnt-out "ghetto," Gastown has been successfully able to claim the status of a neighborhood and community and, in so doing, inscribe onto the landscape a space where the poor are outsiders and property-owners are those with rights of representation and voice. The Downtown Eastside was also successful in making this claim, of course. However, such is the relative power of the ownership model that the poor now find their collective claim eroded by those whose entitlement is state-sanctioned. Exclusionary social relations are legitimized in the language of social balance.

The landscapes of collective property, then, are threatened by "social mix." Landscapes can be represented and used in the "wrong" way. For those moving into the neighborhood will not only contribute to the material displacement of many residents. It is feared that they will also facilitate their cultural dispossession in an "eviction of memory."[115] As one activist noted, "there is more than one way to lose a neighborhood. You can lose it through homelessness, but you can also lose it by just outnumbering people, just pouring in."[116] Residential hotels—that speak to a complex history of working-class marginalization, struggle, and survival—can easily be converted into private lofts, displacing history by "heritage," and replacing one narrative with that of "highest and best use." One activist poignantly suggested the perils of effacement through this communicative translation when she imagined the Carnegie Community Centre—often referred to as the neighborhood's living room—as a yuppie coffee bar.[117] The concern is that "outsiders" will simply not read the landscape appropriately, and will fail to acknowledge the property claim that it embodies. For some commentators, if the area continues to gentrify, "it'll be the lucky ones at least [that will] have decent housing but no community."[118]

This point is made powerfully in a cartoon in a community newsletter, showing DERA's Four Sisters Co-op, built in response to the Expo evictions, renamed as the "Four Winds Condo Apts—Under new management; enjoy our narrow view. Lofts for sale starting at $190,000" with former residents shown being bused out to suburban Surrey.[119] It is not only the physical displacement that is objectionable, in other words, but also the cultural effacement of a collective and locally embedded entitlement (fig. 3.2).

Conclusion

In the summer of 2002, Jennifer Clarke, the mayoral hopeful for the incumbent municipal party, gave a campaign-opening speech in which she promised to retake the DES "one block at a time."[120] Downtown Eastside poet Bud Osborn has made clear that these and other reclamations would be met with opposition: "we resist /Person by person /square foot by square foot /room by room /building by building /block by block."[121]

Property is not the only ethical cleavage line in the Downtown Eastside. Issues relating to governance, gender, and racialization all play an important role. However, if one wishes to make sense of the ethical and political divisions that gentrification is associated with, the contested terrain of property discourse seems one important site. I have tried to suggest that dominant property narratives engage in a complex set of moral moves, including the erasure of an existent population (via renaming, presumptions

Figure 3.2 Cultural displacement. Cartoon by Garry Gust, Carnegie *Newsletter,* 1994. Reproduced with the permission of Garry Gust.

of mobility, and so on), subjectification (casting gentrifiers as moral "improvers") and teleology (through the logic of highest and best use). At an extreme, the effect is to render displacement natural, inevitable, and beneficial. Conversely, those opposed to gentrification engage in a denaturalization of gentrification, through a conscious attempt at rendering property as potentially inequitable. Drawing upon bittersweet local histories of dispossession and successful resistance, a moral distinction is drawn between the rapacious, individualized property claim of the developer, and the collective, embedded entitlements of local residents. These claims and the resultant conflict are enacted through a variety of means, including narratives, representations, and material interventions. All are entangled with a local landscape. Thus it is, that the same empty building—Woodward's—can be claimed and read in radically different ways.

But at the same time, it is dangerous to think of the frontier as necessarily fixed and naturalized. To the extent that the frontier is necessarily a border, both conceptual and material, it can be a zone of crossing, a contact zone where transculturation, relationality, and hybridity can occur.[122] Again, the terrain of property discourse and rights is no exception. However, as the crossings at so many political borders are predicated upon certain power relations, so is this crossing. Clear battle lines are established between poor tenants and unscrupulous developers, only to be dissolved as the exigencies of the land market oblige community representatives to negotiate and compromise. The inner-city property frontier is an ambiguous and somewhat fluid one. Movements across the property border, I shall suggest, often presuppose and reproduce the dominant property regime.

Indeed, the gentrification frontier has become increasingly fractured in recent years. While many homeowners and merchants in the slowly gentrifying neighborhood of Strathcona (like Gastown, part of the original Downtown Eastside—see fig. 2.1) have been sympathetic to many of the concerns of the urban poor, its shift from incipient upgrading to speculative infills may foster a shift in attitudes. Chinatown, also an enclave with the Downtown Eastside, is another interesting case. While shared histories of poverty, sharply inflected by racism, encouraged solidarity with groups such as DERA, some merchant interests (though not all) began to be less sympathetic toward their poorer neighbors, hiring private security guards and opposing the embrace of a harm reduction–based drug policy. With Gastown, and some interests from Strathcona, Chinatown merchants formed a "Community Alliance" in 2000 in opposition to these policies. Similar claims, as above, concerning heritage, decline, and poverty reoccur in this opposition, as do claims to "community" and histories of residency. Local activists, however, see such opposition as a war against the poor, and a form of displacement by other means.[123]

Property turns out to be a site for moral conflict and struggle. For activists, however, this struggle is not simply predicated on a condemnation of the negative ethics of property but a defense of property's potential and promise. This requires, of course, a reworking of what actually counts as property, such that the collective claim of local residents may also be acknowledged as "property." What property *is,* and what it *ought* to be, are inseparable questions. There are two sides to every frontier; opposing historical geographies of property create a sharp moral and political cleavage between two dialectically related encampments. However, this division is not inconsequential. It has been noted that the maps we make of the social world are not disinterested. Rather, they shape the way in which we are invited to constitute that world, and the actions that we take therein.[124] Similarly, dominant "property maps" of the inner city—as empty, as un-named, as "undeveloped"—play a critical role in making possible (making invisible, even) material dispossessions.

I opened the previous chapter with the poetry of Bud Osborn, who along with others has "raised shit" in the Downtown Eastside in opposition to the "urban cleansing" of gentrification. Osborn's poem, however, links the violence visited upon the Downtown Eastside by "friendly predators," and the organized resistance to this violence, to other struggles. His poem is prefaced by a quotation by the sixteenth-century scholar and priest, Bartoleme de la Casas, describing the violences of colonialism, including the ways in which "towns, provinces, and whole kingdoms have been en-tirely cleared of their native inhabitants." Osborn is careful to link the poli-tics of dispossession and resistance in Vancouver to a global process that has driven the populations "from land they have occupied/in common/ and in community/for many years," naming the Zapatistas in Chiapas, Mexico, the Ogoni in Nigeria, the Dalits in India, and a long list of other indigenous populations.[125] This linkage between colonialism, gentrifica-tion, and the politics of land is worth dwelling on. In the following chapter, then, I explore the unsettled politics of urban land in relation to indige-nous entitlements. In a concluding chapter I return to consider the link be-tween colonial violence and the displacements of gentrification.

CHAPTER 4

Land and the Postcolonial City

*It was disturbing, that: to have unknown country behind you as well as in front. . . .
Out here the very ground under their feet was strange. It had never been ploughed.
You had to learn all over again how to deal with weather: drenching downpours
when in moments all the topsoil you had exposed went liquid and all the dry little
creek-beds in the vicinity ran wild. . . . And all around, before and behind, worse
than weather and the deepest night, natives, tribes of wandering myalls who, in
their traipsing this way and that over the map, were forever encroaching on boundaries that could be insisted on by daylight—a good shotgun saw to that—but in
the dark hours, when you no longer stood there as a living marker with all the glow
of the white man's authority about you, reverted to being a creek-bed or ridge of
granite like any other, and gave no indication that six hundred miles away, in the
Lands Office in Brisbane, this bit of country had a name set against it on a num-
bered document, and a line drawn that was empowered with all the authority of
the Law.*

*Most unnerving of all was the knowledge that, just three years back, the very
patch of earth you were standing on had itself been on the other side of things, part
of the unknown, and might still, for all your coming and going over it, and the sweat
you had poured into its acre or two of ploughed earth, have the last of mystery upon
it, in jungle brakes between paddocks and ferny places out of the sun. Good reason,
that, for stripping it, as soon as you could manage, of every vestige of the native; for
ringbarking and clearing and reducing it to what would make it, at last, just a bit
like home.*

—David Malouf, *Remembering Babylon*

*The matter of the Indians runs deep in Vancouver, and does something to under-
mine the cool of the place. It is queer to remember, looking out upon this city's
prospects . . . that not so very long ago all this country was the domain of another
culture altogether.*

—Jan Morris, *City to City*

Colonial Cities

To talk of land and displacement, particularly in a place like Vancouver's Downtown Eastside, and not to consider colonialism is to commit an unforgivable, but not unprecedented oversight. Colonial dispossessions and displacements cast long shadows that, as we shall see, are still with us. For the making of a settler city, like Vancouver (or New York, or Melbourne) was predicated on significant remaking of property. Yet those colonial dynamics are all too easily elided. Take, for example, the city of Victoria, on Vancouver Island, once the province's preeminent staging post for colonial settlement and economic expansion. Although it has long since been overshadowed by Vancouver, it remains the province's political center: an ornate legislature gazes out onto its famous Inner Harbor, also fronted by the Canadian Pacific Railway's Empress Hotel. Now marketed as a tourist center, it trades vigorously on its historical and colonial connections. It is not named after a queen and an historic era for nothing. "[L]ashings of fake Victoriana and chintzy commercialism" notes one mainstream travel guide, "tearooms, Union Jacks, bagpipers, pubs, and ersatz echoes of empire confront you at every turn."[1] However, these "echoes of empire" have local resonances. The travel guide reminds us that native people originally inhabited the site, living in what is described as "a virtual paradise." When he first glimpsed this part of the world, we are told, the English explorer George Vancouver declared it a "perfect Eden." "The serenity of the climate, the innumerable pleasing landscapes, and the abundant fertility that nature puts forth," he declaimed, "require only to be enriched by the industry of man with villages, mansions, cottages, and other buildings, to render it to the most lovely country that can be imagined."[2] "Man" arrived, the travel guide tells us, in 1842, when Victoria received its earliest white visitors who went on to fulfil George Vancouver's mandate. No further mention is made of the original inhabitants of Paradise.[3]

In direct response to the selectivity of these accounts, an alternative tour of Victoria has been created that alerts visitors to their "historical amnesia." The re-enactment of the "glory days of the 'West Coast Raj,' " it is claimed, serves to "erase a part of our past that could help us to come to grips with the collective colonial hangover."[4] Arguing that this erasure forgets the violent displacements of aboriginal people, tourists are asked to consider Victoria's Bastion Square, the fortified site that held the cannons of the Hudson's Bay Company, now replete with craft stores and cobbled walkways, as a site for the organized display of violence, directed at aboriginal people.[5] Visitors are also invited to look over the Inner Harbor, to what is now the Ocean Pointe Resort, a five-star hotel and condo complex. This, we are told, was the land that was settled by Lekwammen Indians (known as the Songhees by white society) after Fort Victoria was established. Under a treaty, signed in 1850, they surrendered their traditional territories to the Hudson's Bay Company on the condition that certain sites were assigned to them. Almost as soon as this and other treaties were signed, a concerted campaign was launched to physically remove the Lekwammen. Their lands had grown increasingly valuable, or were deemed an impediment to "orderly" urban development, and their presence offended white sensibilities. "How much longer," asked one letter writer, "are we to be inflicted with the intolerable nuisance of having hundreds upon hundreds of hideous, half-naked, drunken savages in our midst?"[6] Finally, in 1910, the federal and provincial governments brokered a deal that finally "got the Indians out of town and out of sight."[7]

A relatively liberal provincial policy gave way, in 1864, to the assertion that native people had never owned land, thus rendering extinguishment irrelevant. This "white myth" declared "that British Columbia had been in essence an empty land, devoid of society, government, or laws. . . . [A]ll land in the colony was not only under British sovereignty but also directly owned by the Crown."[8] With land ownership vested in the Crown, reserves were simply a gift from a generous government. Federal policy was somewhat different. Native people were construed as wards of the state, with reserves defined as land held in trust for their benefit. The Royal Proclamation of 1763 acknowledged native land ownership, except where it was extinguished by voluntary cession.

For Edward Said, the relation between imperialism and land is a fundamental one: "At some very basic level, imperialism means thinking about, settling on, and controlling land that you do not possess."[9] The alternative tour of Victoria similarly describes the city as a fully imperial space, created through acts of colonial dispossession. But if those dispossessed are erased from the official account of Victoria under the white logic of "highest and best use," the postcolonial tour of the city, while remembering their historic presence, also now places them "out of town." In both cases, the city has become a white space, it's aboriginal presence apparently confined to the past.

Yet while native dispossession is complete, land in British Columbia remains profoundly unsettled. For over a century, First Nations in British Columbia have sought recognition of their rights to land through delegations, legal petitions, and direct action. It was not until 1991 that the province of British Columbia gave partial acknowledgement of aboriginal title, and began treaty negotiations with native peoples, that continue, often proving fractious and controversial. Even the historic treaties in and around Victoria continue to be contentious. In August 2001, in a wonderful piece of political theater, two First Nations filed a lawsuit claiming ownership of the 4.2 hectares of land—estimated as worth around $46 million—on which the British Columbia Provincial Legislature sits. The Esquimault and Lekwammen base their argument—which accuses the Crown of trespass—on an 1850 treaty that guaranteed them a parcel of land known as the James Bay Reserve. The bands are sueing the federal government, claiming they illegally transferred the land to the provincial government in 1876 who then built the provincial legislature, completed in 1898. They continue to seek a court declaration affirming their treaty rights, the award of damages, and the payment of rent. The state has not only unjustly dispossessed, they suggest. Even on its own terms, it is a trespasser.

The Esquimault and Lekwammen base their claim on history and geography, noting their relation to those who signed the treaty in 1850. Signatories such as See-sachasis, Hay-hay kane, and Tsatsulluc, who made their marks at Fort Victoria on the 29 April 1850 are claimed as direct ancestors of contemporary plaintiffs, such as Chief Andrew Thomas and Chief Garry Albany. However, they also ground their claim in cartography, noting that the reserve was formally surveyed and recorded as such by the colonial surveyor in 1854, appearing on the Victoria town map in 1855. In 1859, however, the land is identified as "Government Reserve," the year before the first legislative buildings were erected.[10]

Postcolonial Cities

The end of the twentieth century saw the emergence of a flourishing postcolonial literature "concerned with the impact of colonialism and its contestation on the cultures of both colonizing and colonized peoples in the past, and the reproduction and transformation of colonial relations, representations, and practices in the present."[11] However, there is a striking absence in this scholarship. With a few important exceptions, the recognition of the city as a postcolonial space has been limited.[12] Although urbanists have registered the contemporary ethnic diversity of the city, "blockages restrain recognition of the cultures, bodies, and economies of those who inhabited the lands on which those cities now stand."[13] This is an important oversight, given the continuing effects of colonialism in contemporary life. Historic injustices continue to resonate and provide a basis for contestation over the histories and geographies of settler societies.[14] But such conflicts are also rooted in ongoing tensions, as colonial practices and representations are reproduced and contested. As noted above, the colonial encounter continues even within the city. Historic conflicts over land continue to have a contemporary relevance to urban settlers and indigenous peoples alike, shaping "a very specific local politics deeply marked by the historical legacy of the colonial dispossession of indigenous peoples."[15] Indeed, the terms of history (and geography) are themselves contested.

It is this local politics that I seek to consider here. In this chapter I make some preliminary comments on the city as a postcolonial space. By drawing from the sparse literature that does exist (much of which is based on the Australian experience), I hope to make some sense of the colonial politics of Vancouver. My account is deliberately but necessarily broad, both historically and geographically. In so doing, I run the risk of underplaying the undeniable spatial differences (in law, colonial consciousness and practice, indigenous histories, and so on) between settler societies, as well as the historic differences between the contemporary city and its earlier manifestations.[16] However, given the undeveloped nature of scholarship in this area, these seem inevitable and necessary compromises.

In so doing, several important points emerge. To the extent that the lands upon which colonial settlements were established were held, in some form, by indigenous peoples, the settler city requires their dispossession. It is easy to assume, however, that the creation of the colonial city led not only to the dispossession of indigenous people, but also to their continued erasure from city-space. Contemporary aboriginal geographies can easily appear as indistinct "scratches on the face of the country," especially in the city, which as a visible and naturalized space of modern settlement, appears hostile to an enduring native presence.[17] I want to contest this: while dispossession is complete, displacement is not. Physically, symbolically, and politically, the city is often still a native place. In this, I make a distinction between dispossession and displacement, such that the former refers to the specific processes through which settlers came to acquire title to land historically held by aboriginal people.[18] Displacement, while related, refers to the conceptual removal of aboriginal people from the city, and the concomitant "emplacement" of white settlers. Both dispossession and displacement *were,* and still *are,* vital to the making of the settler-city. Place making and the enactments of claims to land are social and political projects. They are both immensely powerful but also, to the extent that they are enacted, are partial and incomplete. For a settler society, displacement is a social achievement, but also an aspiration; it is an accomplishment, and also an assertion. To that extent, displacement is open to contestation and remaking.

Dispossession and displacement as active projects are very much about land as property. Property is both the point of these struggles and the medium. Struggles over the meanings and moralities of property have been central. Law, in this sense, must be conceived not simply as an instrument of colonial domination but as a means through which colonialism has itself been produced.[19] In order to understand the historic dynamics of colonialism and its contemporary echoes, it helps if we attend to the geographies of land. The meanings and practices associated with land as property have proved critical, yet are inseparable from its spatialities. In particular, I wish to consider the difference that *urban* property makes to this local politics.

Urban Dispossessions

The creation of a settler society usually requires the dispossession of others. Dispossession has occurred (and continues to occur) in many ways, including military violence, forcible removal, legal fraud, state expropriation, forced extinguishment, treaty abrogation, and the nonenforcement of protective legislation.[20] However, the tendency has been to ignore or underplay the role of the city in colonial dispossession. Yet the "urban frontier," as Hamer puts it, has played a critical role, both economically, politically, and symbolically.[21] Early Canadian cities, for example, have been described as scattered "outposts of empire."[22] Inevitably, these outposts were frequently located on lands used and occupied by native peoples. The city was not so much settled, as "resettled."[23] More particularly, towns were often located on sites that were of special native significance. It seems that in the United States white settlers took this as a good omen.[24] The area surveyed for the City of Melbourne had also been an important meeting ground for the Kulin, the original Aboriginal inhabitants, but was soon denied them.[25] Johnson offers a history of the establishment of Melbourne as a story of dispossession and spatialization, predicated on the powerful combination of surveying, land acquisition, and aboriginal expulsion and geographic containment.[26] Vancouver was also superimposed upon a network of ancient native villages, resource sites, and symbolic landscapes.

The town also emerged as a vital economic and political node in a broader colonial network, directing flows of capital and command that opened up resource frontiers in the colonial interiors. All of this, of course, was pivotal to the process of colonial dispossession. But colonial towns also quickly emerged as speculative spaces. Layout was designed so as to facilitate the acquisition and transfer of urban land. Vancouver's initial expansion, it has been argued, was largely a product of land speculation, rather than expansion in the production of goods and services.[27] Boosterist publications marveled at the leapfrogging of prices, and the fact that areas of "wild land" could become "first-class property" in a matter of months.[28] Vancouver "is a purely business town," noted one observer, "a land of speculation . . . above all, in city lots."[29]

Louise Johnson insists that any account of urban land "must recognize the significance of its prior occupancy and revisit the colonial past to retell some of the histories of initial dispossession."[30] For urban lands were not unowned lands. The lands upon which Vancouver was carved out, for example, had been occupied for millennia, in complex, seasonal rhythms, by native peoples, settling in seasonally used village sites.[31] The beaches "gave us shellfish, crabs, and eel grass," note two Squamish elders. "The forests and flatlands provided deer, large herds of elk, bear, and mountain goats. Food plants were harvested, and the trees supplied the wood for our houses, canoes, weapons and other ceremonial objects."[32] Native trails, patterns of use, and landscapes of ritual crisscrossed the area.

While some colonial notions of property may have seemed strange to the established residents, the latter were not people without property. Indigenous relations to land, though diverse and varied, are distinct. Although indigenous conceptions of property entail rules for the allocation and conveyance of rights of access and use, and developed concepts akin to title and possession, it has been argued that these differ ontologically from nonnative forms of ownership.[33]

Property appears to have had a central role in precontact Squamish culture, shaping social standing and regulating access to economic resources.[34] Property relations defined access to personal items such as canoes, slaves, and hunting and fishing sites, and also regulated rights to use personal names, songs, spirit powers, and magic. Clan and kinship relations structured access to particularly scarce resources, so that deer, duck and fish nets, bird rookeries and so on were owned by extended families, while access to other sites, such as clam beds or fish dams was open to all village members. Personal property was also recognized; builders and their descendants owned houses for example. However, most forms of property, including resource sites, were not alienable from the family.

At the same time, property appears to have been a central means by which relations with others were defined, particularly in the context of significant events: "To assume a family name, . . . to commemorate a change in status growing out of a life crisis, or to publicize any event having a bearing on social status demanded a public distribution of goods."[35] Such distributions of property "were integral elements in the social fabric, and cannot be discussed apart from it."[36] The circulation of property reached its apogee in the klanak, or potlatch. In sum, this was a legal polity, the Squamish claim:

> Social and political relations and the distribution of power within our society was circumscribed by a complex body of rules. Through our system of laws and customs, we defined the rights and duties of our citizens. In exercising our political and legal power, we defined ourselves, our culture, and our values.[37]

So if the arrival of Europeans marked the creation of a capitalist, liberal property regime, it did not signal first ownership. Yet despite the centrality of law and property to the Western imagination, dispossession occurred under the sign of both. The irony is not lost on at least one observer: "law, regarded by the West as its most respected and cherished instrument of civilization, was also the West's most vital and effective instrument of empire."[38] While different legal arrangements were deployed, "in all cases, the end result was the same: the legal form of colonization . . . effected the translation of newly acquired territories into exploitable property."[39] However, it has been argued that the legal system not only facilitated dispossession but also concealed, legitimized, and depoliticized that process, attributing "to the new land arrangements an aura of necessity and naturalness that protects the new status quo and prevents further redistribution."[40]

But if this process entailed law, it also required the making of space.[41] "[I]t was by appeal to a specifically legal sensibility that the geography of colonies was mapped, transforming the landscapes of others . . . into territory and real estate; a process that made spaces into places to be possessed, ruled, improved, protected."[42] Maps and map-making played a critical role here. Surveyors have been termed "the point men of British imperialism"[43] for good reason, given their role in the "imposition of a new economic and spatial order on 'new territory,' either erasing precapitalist indigenous settlement or confining it to particular areas."[44] The survey, moreover, served more than instrumental ends. The survey arbitrated between an acknowledged regime and those forms of property deemed to lie "outside" its frontier. If colonial possession was dependent upon dispossession, the survey serves as a form of organized forgetting.[45] Johnson reads colonial cartography, in part, as an instrument through which a space of imagined emptiness is sequentially filled with European entitlements. Absent from these maps, of course, are prior entitlements, as well as the "ongoing processes of regulation, dispossession, containment, and resistance."[46] I return to the role of the map below.

The creation of Vancouver saw native geographies and property relations obliterated by a cadastral grid that provided the template for colonial land speculation and urbanization. The mainland north of the forty-ninth parallel became a Crown colony in 1858, and British law began to be enforced.[47] The establishment of a land policy, although rather tentative in practice, was a priority. By the 1860s, a regiment of Royal Engineers began laying out and subdividing lands in the area. Given that the land was seen as unowned, it was a short step to vesting ownership in the Crown. Land was thus divided into alienable sections, to be distributed, through sale or preemption, to white settlers. Small, scattered reserves were set aside for native people in the area that became Vancouver (fig. 4.1). Once inaugurated, the land system itself "became the most powerful single agent of disciplinary power." It mapped out rights, and their denials, and sustained them with sovereign power.[48] The creation of a Western property system, then, entailed dispossession; thus established, it itself operated as a disciplinary regime.

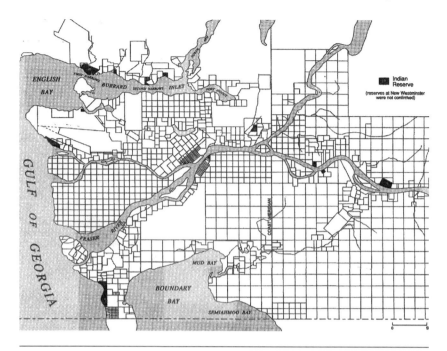

Figure 4.1 Land surveys, Lower Mainland to 1876. Originally published in Harris, Cole (1993) 'The Lower Mainland, 1820–81.' In Wynn, Graeme and Timothy Oke, editors. *Vancouver and Its region.* Reproduced with the permission of Cole Harris.

The link between dispossession and the settler-city endures today, although in different ways. For example, the growing population of native people within many settler-cities speaks to the effect of nationwide colonial dispossessions. In Canada, endemic poverty and a lack of a land base on the reserve compel the relocation of many native people to the city. By 2001, half of all Aboriginal people in Canada were urban, one-quarter of them living in ten urban areas.[49] The United States pursued an explicit policy of native relocation in the 1960s, driven by an assimilationist Indian policy and a suspicion of Indian political structures, including land-holding status. These were seen as a violation of American principles of individual property rights and private enterprise. Relocation was also motivated by a desire to ease private access to Indian trust lands. Large numbers of native people were encouraged to relocate, although they often did so more from desperation than free choice. As in Canada, many ended as part of the urban poor. However, as we shall see, the result was not always assimilation. Rather, pan-Indian social institutions developed in cities that provided a nucleus for native activism.[50] Joan Ablon documents the emergence of a pan-Indian orientation in the San Francisco area, claiming that many Indians more forcefully identified as such after moving to the "white world" of the city.[51]

Displacement

While indigenous peoples were quickly dispossessed, they were not entirely displaced from the city. If the making of property requires sustained enactment, so does its denial. Dispossession is not necessarily complete and secure at the moment when title changes hands. The important point to note is that displacement, in this sense, depends upon iteration. *Terra nullius*, it has been pointed out, is a "most unstable foundation for the nation" given its tenuous empirical purchase. It requires shoring up by a range of "spatial technologies of power" such as surveying, planning, naming, and mapping.[52] Colonialism, put another way, "is not something that occurs at one time or in one place, but is an ongoing process of dispossession, negotiation, transformation, and resistance."[53] The creation of the city requires active place making that relies upon certain forgettings of the past, as well as some creative reconstructions. This is a positive and negative project of effacement and of production. Urban displacement, in the sense I use it here, seems to entail two related maneuvers. First, native people must be conceptually *removed* from urban space. If located anywhere, native people are frequently imagined in the past or in nature. In either case, they are placed outside the city. Second, displacement requires the concomitant *emplacement* of a settler society: This place is to be made into a white place through physical settlement and occupation.

This is a complicated process. All I can do for now is to take some tentative cuts at it in relation to the themes already broached. I want again to emphasize the importance of spatial narrative—stories told about a place—that order and legitimate native dispossession in the city. Entangled in those stories, and offering physical and representational justification for them, are landscapes that are both material and representational. I focus, in particular, on the urban built environment, and the map. These enact prevailing property arrangements and relations as natural, appropriate and inevitable. Yet at the same time, counterstories and mappings complicate the certainties of the settler-city in intriguing and unsettling ways.

Spatial Narrations

As far as I am concerned there is nothing to claim. The war between cowboys and Indians ended some hundred years ago.

    —Bill Homburg from a letter to the *Terrace Standard*

For most of us, colonialism happened elsewhere, and the recognition of it here, and of ourselves as its agents, suddenly qualifies our fulsome accounts of the progress and development of an immigrant society while connecting us with a much less comfortable past . . . [C]olonialism is not only about gunboats and economic domination, but also about cultural assumptions and agendas that have long outlived the gunboats.

—Jean Barman and Cole Harris, "Editorial"

As noted in previous chapters, the enactment of property entails, in part, story telling. Narrative appears central to the master stories of property, such as those of Locke and Blackstone, as well as to more everyday enactments of property. Scholars have also pointed to the importance of settler stories, characterizing them as "self-justifying accounts, told by a colonial people." Yet "ongoing doubts and insecurities about the moral legitimacy of their occupation of Indigenous lands," Dara Culhane suggests, "require that these stories be told, and retold."[54] Social memory in Australia has been said to entail the "recalling and forgetting, selecting, ordering, and erasing [of] memories."[55] But these frontier stories are also about places and spaces. The positive characterizations of Perth as sunny, bright, and clear, for example, require the forgetting of its "darker geographies."[56]

In part, these stories are of property and the West: of the transition from Edenic nature to improved settlement; from common to private entitlements. We have already considered the power of this story in relation to the *telos* of highest and best use. We should also acknowledge, however, that the start of these stories is as important as their conclusion. Many begin with an unsettled and violent world before time, and before private property. For Hobbes, this was a time where "there can be no propriety, no dominion, no *mine* and *thine* distinct; but only that to be every man's that he can get, and for so long as he can keep it."[57] A world of uncertain entitlements, it is for Locke a violent world of "fears and continual dangers."[58] The absence of government and private property, Hobbes argued, underpins a life of "continual fear, and danger of violent death; And the life of man, solitary, poor, nasty, brutish, and short."[59]

But these worlds without private property are also located in space that is before History. This is a strikingly geographic exercise, in which as Burke put it, "[t]he great Map of Mankind [is] unroll'd at once."[60] "In the beginning," claims Locke, "all the world was *America*."[61] The space of the savage, for many classical European writers on property, is one devoid of law and property. In that sense, Western notions of property are deeply invested in a colonial geography, a white mythology, in which the racialized figure of the "savage" plays an anchoring role:[62]

> Disorder on law's part cannot . . . be located in law itself. The sources of disorder must exist outside of law—in the eruptions and disruptions of untamed

> nature or barely contained human passion against which an ordering law is intrinsically set. The savage was the concentration of these dangers and the constant and predominant want of the savage was order.[63]

Peter Fitzpatrick documents the ways in which the law of the European Enlightenment reduced the world to European universality: "That which stood outside of the absolutely universal could only be absolutely different to it. It could only be an aberration or something other than that which it should be."[64] European legal identity, he argues, entails the mapping of the colonial subject as purely negative ("ni foi, ni loi, ni roi") from which the positivity of Western law is derived. Law, as set of culturally rooted presumptions and understandings, has thus been characterized as a thoroughly Eurocentric enterprise.[65]

Locke, it should be remembered, was deeply implicated in the colonial project in North America, and wrote widely on colonial affairs.[66] He imagined Amerindian government and relationships to land as at an earlier stage of development than Europe and therefore akin to the state of nature, the starting point for his story of private property. Appropriation may thus occur without consent. Native lands (with some exceptions) were deemed unimproved, and could thus be justly expropriated by those who were capable of reclaiming the "waste." Indeed, this is a divine imperative: the story also invokes God's command to Man to render the earth fruitful, ordering him to "multiply and replenish the earth, and subdue it."[67] Indigenous peoples in New England were said to "inclose noe Land, neither have any setled habytation, nor any tame cattle to improue the land by, and soe have no other but a Naturall Right" (a right, that is, to the products of their labor). Thus cleared of preexistent entitlements, the enactment of European claims is straightforward: "he that taketh possession of it, and bestoweth culture and husbandry upon it, his right it is."[68]

While we must acknowledge their historic specificity, these classical tales have more recent echoes. For example, Turner's frontier thesis is predicated on a story of improvement that begins with "savagery."

> The United States lies like a huge page in the history of society. Line by line as we read this continental page from West to East we find the record of social evolution. It begins with the Indian and the hunter; it goes on to tell of the disintegration of savagery by the entrance of the trader. . . . [W]e read the annals of the pastoral stage in ranch life; the exploitation of the soil. . . . the intensive culture of the denser farm settlement; and finally the manufacturing organization with city and factory system.[69]

The essential relation operative in this story is that between God, white man, and Land.[70] Cronon's commentary on Turner's story is telling: "If ever there was a narrative that achieved its end by erasing its true subject, Turner's frontier was it: the heroic encounter between pioneers and 'free land' could only become plausible by erasing the conquest that traded one people's freedom for another's."[71] Similar stories also insinuate themselves into other legal discourses. Shamir describes the dispossession of the Bedouin under Israeli law as reliant on structured narratives that "order the story of the Bedouins" at the same time as they complement Zionist stories of the control and redemption of the land.[72]

From savagery to settlement; from no property to private property; from waste to improvement. It is easy to find accounts in Vancouver of native people that echo this colonial story. Vancouver's first archivist, J. S. Mathews, portrayed the place that would become Vancouver prior to European contact as "a vast amphitheatre of virgin solitude," "sleeping away the silent centuries" in a "primeval paradise of stillness." "Our" Indians, he assures us, were then "a scattered few in an empty land."[73] However, the potential of the land would "fire the envy of people as yet unseen, rouse this fairyland from its trance of centuries, and herald the doom of an ancient race." Similarly, prior to European "discovery," the place that became Victoria was imagined as "the perfect Eden," you will remember. George Vancouver imagined the day when men would uncover its immanent potential. But these stories continue to be told. British Columbia's Lieutenant Governor approvingly quoted Vancouver's words in a speech in 2000, to the disgust of invited native leaders. Squamish Chief Joe Mathias expressed understandable dismay that "the Queen's representative would be using an explorer's words to say that the land was ripe for the taking. It's empty, there's nobody here, its bounty is available to us, the discoverers."[74]

But there is another dimension to colonial storytelling, revealed above. In a form of anticonquest, dispossession is itself written out of the story.[75] Scholarly accounts of North American urban settlement, for example, routinely displace dispossession. Thus, John J. Macionis and Vincent N. Parillo trace the development of North American cities in the "colonial era" (which ends in 1800) by briefly noting the presence of indigenous populations. While some lived in permanent settlements, most are characterized as mobile, living in "small societies." European urbanization begins unproblematically in the seventeenth century, apparently in empty spaces.[76] Another author explains early North American urbanization by the spatial logic of mercantile capitalism, premised on the "opening" of the "hinterland." Yet scant mention is made of the first occupants, or their active and often creative role in this process.[77] A history of Vancouver describes the unproblematic absorption of its prior occupants "into a community that from the start was gloriously polyglot."[78] These urban stories are, to borrow from Christine Chivallon, a form of "wounded memory." Her focus, on the remembering of slavery in the urban West, marking a "scratched out" history, or "nonhistory" surely also applies to the aboriginal experience.[79]

Yet even when that history is acknowledged and even regretted the narrative momentum of the dominant story encourages a view of dispossession as a necessary and inevitable transition. A children's book published in 1968, for example, describes the creation of colonial Vancouver from the perspective of a white boy, Dave Henderson. Superficially *Red Paddles* is redolent with Trudeauesque claims to inclusivity. Dave befriends a native boy, Little Bear, from the Squamish settlement at Xwayxway, in what is now Vancouver's Stanley Park. Relations between settlers and native people seem mutually amicable, with promises of "peace and goodwill between the Indians and the white men." Yet at one telling moment, the Henderson family reflects on the future:

> "Sometimes I wonder what they really think of this invasion by white men. Or do they realize that slowly and surely they are being asked to give up their rights in this beautiful country? And they are not always asked".
>
> "But things wouldn't go ahead", Mrs. Henderson said, "if we didn't make changes. . . ."
>
> "What will happen to them?" Dave asked.
>
> Mr. Henderson looked serious. "No one seems to be giving much thought to the native race we are pushing back so we can build a city . . ."
>
> For awhile there was silence. Then Mr. Henderson said, "It will be a big day when the first transcontinental train comes through to Vancouver."
>
> And Dave cried, "I'm glad I'll be here to see it. I'm glad that I'll see Vancouver grow to be a big, important city."[80]

Ironically, Vancouver's Stanley Park offers a powerful example of this "pushing back." It was in the adjacent waters that George Vancouver arrived in 1792. Once colonial settlement began in earnest, dispossession quickly occurred. In 1862, for example, a local mill owner proposed to build a sawmill on Little Bear's home at Xwayxway. Colonial officials noted that the mill owner "had no objection to their (the Squamish) remaining where they are. They can at any time be removed. The Ground does not belong to their Tribe."[81] After a smallpox epidemic in 1888, the authorities ordered the burning of the village. The same year, the land was designated parkland (proclaiming that it was to be enjoyed by all, regardless of race or creed). The native presence was literally paved over, with the ancient midden from Xwayxway used in the construction of a park road. One park historian has also claimed that two-dozen skeletons from the village site, turned up in construction in 1962, were "thrown in the woods to rot or put in museums."[82] Designated state property, its inhabitants' collective claim was illegible to the dominant legal imaginary. Some native and "mixed-race" residents, now deemed squatters, lingered in the park, until the city brought a successful action to dispossess them in 1923.[83]

Urban Settlement

As the Henderson family recognize, one crucial way in which such narratives of improvement is made obvious is in their urban materialization. Colonial cities, put simply, cannot be conceived as native spaces because they have so obviously been occupied, built upon and "improved." In her exploration of European conquests in the Americas, Patricia Seed explores the culturally diverse ways in which the possession of the New World was justified and rendered natural. English claims to territory, she shows, were enacted through apparently "mundane activity," where the placement of objects—houses, fences, gardens—signified ownership: "Englishmen occupying the New World initially inscribed their possession . . . by affixing their own powerful cultural symbols of ownership—houses and fences— upon the landscape."[84] Locke's insistence on the material marking of property, Seed argues, reiterates these deeply held cultural beliefs. If so, the city, as a materially "improved" space, marked with "symbols of ownership," surely qualifies as an obvious space of colonial ownership in a way that nonurban spaces might not, at first.

Perhaps in part because of this, settler cities have also long been imagined as spaces of civilization, set against a world of savagery.[85] Representing order and good government, the colonial town was imagined as an outpost within the wilderness.[86] The town was seen as a center that would radiate "knowledge, enterprise and civilization," as one American writer put it. The influential nineteenth-century colonial thinker, Edward Wakefield, urged the early establishment of towns in colonial space in order to facilitate this transference. The founder of Melbourne saw towns as "centers of civilization and Government" which can "extend the power of order and social union to the most distant parts of the wilderness." When John Simcoe, the Lieutenant Governor of Upper Canada, formulated plans for settlement in the 1790s he emphasized the town's ability "to give power & energy to civilization."[87] Town life, he claimed, induced "habits of Civilization and Obedience to just Government."[88]

To the extent that native peoples are seen as outside, or even a threat to civilization, it becomes harder to imagine them as urban. Observers frequently juxtaposed the "two worlds," with the assumption that the savage was giving way before civilization and settlement. An observer of Detroit in 1810 imagined it as "the point of contact, between the aboriginal inhabitants of the wilderness, and the civilized people, who are pressing these natives of North America back, by the double force of physical and moral weight."[89]

Put another way, if the Lockean narrative of the West begins with the anomic "natural" world of the native, it ends with the city, a space of secure, private, nonnative entitlements. The colonial landscapes of North

America, Bentham claimed, offered a striking contrast between the domain where property and security coexist, and its antithesis—the violent spaces in which property is absent:[90]

> The interior of that immense region offers only a frightful solitude; impenetrable forests or sterile plains, stagnant waters and impure vapors; such is the earth when left to itself. The fierce tribes which rove through these deserts without fixed habitations, always occupied with the pursuit of game, and animated against each other by implacable rivalries, meet only for combat, and often succeed only in destroying each other. The beasts of the forest are not so dangerous to man as he is to himself. But on the borders of these frightful solitudes, what different sights are seen! We appear to comprehend in the same view the two empires of good and evil. Forests give place to cultivated fields, morasses are dried up, and the surface, grown firm, is covered with meadows, pastures, domestic animals, habitations healthy and smiling. Rising cities are built upon regular plans; roads are constructed to communicate between them; everything announces that men, seeking the means of intercourse, have ceased to fear and to murder each other.[90]

And yet, as David Hamer notes, indigenous peoples often continued to use colonial towns for their own purposes: "the town was a European form of settlement, and indigenous peoples seldom manifested any desire to 'live' in it in the European sense. But for some time they continued trying to use the land as *they* had traditionally used it, and the two forms of land use overlapped and intersected in complex ways." In general, their presence was soon seen as incongruous and intolerable by European urbanites. It was common to object to their transgressions of privacy and private property, such as looking into windows. In Adelaide, for example, the Aborigines caused offence by cutting down trees and by the noise of the corroborees. There were also complaints that native people did not respect European conventions regarding the use of streets: "A town," it was soon claimed, "was a European form of community. Aborigines, Indians, and Maori did not 'belong' there."[91] Robin Fisher documents pressure for removal of Indians from the vicinity of towns in British Columbia, such as Victoria, justified by the stated desire to prevent harm to European morals but also, more importantly, by the desire to access Indian lands.[92] Authorities in Perth also sought to eliminate, remove or, at best, contain the aboriginal presence. The Native Administration Act ensured Aborigines were officially banned from the Perth metropolitan area until 1955.[93]

Some colonial commentators were romantically nostalgic for the passing of the native, while others were celebratory. Thus, the settlement of upstate New York was described in 1849 as one of improvement and progress. We are invited to marvel at how "the noble enterprise of the white men has so changed the aspect of this region" and how the "aboriginal forest has lost its charms of savage wildness."[94] The centennial of Nashville in 1880 was commemorated by the placing of fourteen printed placards indicating where and when Indians had scalped pioneers. The figure of the Indian is thus used for didactic purposes to reveal how much progress has been achieved within the city, as the "shriek of the locomotive" replaces "the howl of the wolf and the whoop of the red man."[95]

Similarly in Vancouver, a native presence, once removed, could be reinserted on the terms of the dominant society. Stanley Park, imagined now as a place of nature and visual contemplation, was the ideal location. Thus, an account published in 1929 celebrated the "quaint little habitations" of the Stanley Park "squatters," noting with approval the picturesque touch they added.[96] Untouched by development, the park was a space deliberately insulated from the dynamics of highest and best use. Its carefully contained forest reminded viewers of the land from which the city grew. It is no accident that the park currently contains an aquarium and, until recently, a zoo. Perhaps for those reasons, the park was also chosen as a site in which to locate other artifacts located in nature and the human past. During the 1920s, the Art, Historical, and Scientific Association of Vancouver proposed to build a "model Indian village" in Stanley Park. They initially proposed that an "old, deserted village" from elsewhere be purchased and relocated. As this proved impossible, a member of the AHS was sent North to secure information from first hand sources, and hopefully engage native people to build lodges. The village and totems were designed to represent the work of the Haida and Kwakiutl in particular, and Coast Indians in general.[97] Standing on the "verge of the 'forest primeval,' " the poles were seen as "the marks and relics of other days."[98] In this landscape of colonial contemplation, the observer was asked to acknowledge "the shades of a forgotten people."[99] The totem poles remain an iconic feature of today's Stanley Park.[100]

Chivallon notes the way the built form of the city tends to militate against the acknowledgement of alternative memories, given its role in the materialization of dominant self-conceptions. Urbanity, memory, and national heritage are brought together, given that the landscape of the past is considered necessary to the construction of an ordered and settled social memory.[101] There are echoes here of Jennifer Nelson's discussion of the selective remembering of Africville in Halifax, Nova Scotia. Settled by "free slaves," Africville became a space of troubling blackness for Haligonians. In the 1960s, urban renewal forced the resettlement of the population and the destruction of the neighborhood. Following sustained protest and pressure from those dispossessed, the city subsequently created a municipal park on the site. Although there is a provisional acknowledgement of the injustice of the destruction of Africville, Nelson also points to the ways in which such social remembering, as concretized in a park, can serve as an "act of burial—indeed, a monument seeks to 'put to rest'—and of forgetting, which forms a poignant link in the chain of ongoing evictions of

Africville from its own space. . . . Like the proverbial lie, once told, the story necessitates the telling of a chain of 'maintenance fictions,' complete with the management of space in such a way that the fictions prevail intact and that oppositional stories remain buried."[102] Similarly, perhaps, the totem poles in Stanley Park memorialize at the same time as they forget.

Maps

The cover of an atlas of Vancouver, published in 1992, maps the colonial transition.[103] At the top of the page we see a map labeled "The First Nations: 'Vancouver' in the 1850s," depicting the space that is to become Vancouver prior to sustained European contact. Although rendered using Western cartographic conventions, the map documents the many villages, middens, and trails of the Coast Salish peoples. Native topologies are also displayed— thus a camp site in what will become the Downtown Eastside is labeled "q'emq'emel'ay," translated as "big leaf maple trees." Villages and campsites stud the area that will become Stanley Park. At the bottom of the cover we see a map of contemporary Vancouver. The native presence is literally erased from the map, replaced by a cadastral grid. Native place names have been replaced by names celebrating the British imperial project and corporate capital. This is a striking example for my purposes. While it is helpful in reminding us of colonial dispossessions, it suggests that native displacement is complete. I want to question this. Although the act of dispossession can perhaps be traced to a particular moment, the process of displacement continues to be enacted and, as we shall see, contested. Second, the map appears as a backdrop to this process—as one that records a transition. I want to point to the role of spatial representations of land as integral to both displacement and dispossession, both then and now.

In 1885, Lauchlan Hamilton was charged, as it were, with making the second map. He was employed by the Canadian Pacific Railway (CPR) to survey and lay out the cadastral grid for the area that became Vancouver's downtown core. The CPR had been deeded 6,300 acres of land in return for the designation of the site as the western terminus of the transcontinental railway. The province confidently assured the CPR that "squatter's claims have been otherwise disposed of, there are no known claims against the land."[104] When the first train arrived in 1887, Vancouver's population had jumped to five thousand; by 1892 it had reached fourteen thousand. Property assessments increased in value from $2 million to $20 million in the same period.[105]

We have already noted the practical significance of such spatial visualizations in colonial dispossession. However, maps and maplike visualizations may also play an important persuasive role in displacement, both by conceptually emptying a space of its native occupants, and by reassuring viewers of the unproblematic and settled occupation of urban space by a settler society.[106] The map, in the sense that Orlove uses it, tells a proleptic story, oriented firmly on the future.[107] Hamer notes the intense preoccupation with the future in early frontier towns in the New World. The unfinished and often squalid reality of such settlements was overlooked, as visitors and residents were encouraged to imagine the future potential of a city. Spatial organization and representation, he argues, played a critical role in this project. Vast grids were created for new towns, far larger than was immediately necessary. These plans, "being future-oriented and making little sense in the present, . . . forced people to 'see' and indeed to live in the future . . . Plats were essentially maps of the future."[108]

Similarly, Hamilton was lauded not only for his technical skills, but also to the extent that his survey opened up this space of futurity, turning a space of passivity into one of action. When the city bestowed the freedom of the city upon him in 1938, the city's archivist, J. S. Mathews, commended him in these terms: "You first saw this great metropolis and port as a silent wilderness of forest; then, deep midst towering trees, and with your own hands, marked its place; planned its streets, and named them."[109] Mathews played a leading role in the commissioning of a plaque, commemorating Hamilton's survey, installed at the site at which he drove his first stake. The inscription reads: "Here stood Hamilton, First Land Commissioner Canadian Pacific Railway. In the silent solitude of the primeval forest he drove a wooden stake in the earth and commenced to measure an empty land into the streets of Vancouver."[110]

Bird's-eye views of settler-cities, widely produced in the late nineteenth century in this boosterist embrace of the future, similarly imagine "an empty land." A view of Vancouver, published in 1898 demonstrates this tellingly. The cadastral grid of the new city is laid out before the viewer who is invited to marvel not only at its present accomplishments (the busy harbor, the fine buildings, the effacement of wilderness), but also at its possibilities. Its cadastral spaces, now empty, invite improvement. In so doing, existing uses that detract from those imaginings must be effaced. Thus, we see nothing of the native encampments that continued to cluster on the urban margins (fig. 4.2).[111] Contemporary mappings of the city, of course, do this even more thoroughly. In his *Conscience of the Eye*, Richard Sennett characterizes the North American urban grid as "a Protestant sign for a neutral city." The grid "neutralizes space," he suggests, in a number of ways. It invites us to imagine space as boundless, allowing the grid to "extend block after block after block outward as the city grew." The grid strips "away the character of a place," ignoring and effacing the natural environment and, one might argue, any pre-existing property claims. Space simply becomes "a void to be filled up."[112]

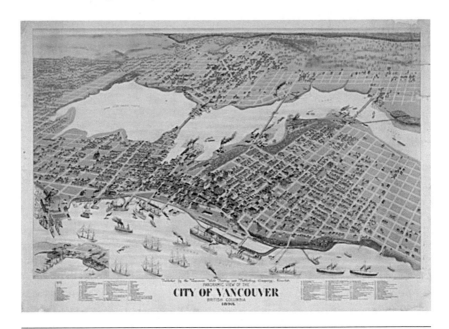

Figure 4.2 Bird's eye view—Vancouver, 1898. City of Vancouver Archives, Map 547.

Contestations

The map as story, and its link to material settlement, is nowhere clearer than in the children's book, *Red Paddles,* mentioned above. At one moment, Dave and his Squamish friend take a trip to the CPR lands. They travel through the dark of the forest, encountering wild animals, then burst into the light of a clearing. They find Hamilton's first survey stake, and then meet the surveyor himself. In ringing tones, he describes how in time, "this city will stretch out to the east and to the west and to the south. . . . Hills will be leveled and swamps drained." Dave looks around the clearing, "wonder still in his eyes," and fills the space, now conceptually emptied of nature and its native past, with urban futures: "Can't you just imagine," he cries, "big, tall buildings here, and there, and there? A big store over there, maybe. And a bank on the corner of that street."[113]

Yet just over a hundred years later, the space imaginatively carved out by Hamilton was the site for a very different intervention, powerfully challenging these maps and stories. Cheyenne and Arapaho artist Hachivi Edgar Heap of Birds has placed provocative art pieces in cities across North America, including New York, Santa Fe, and Denver, designed to remind "the city's current residents that they are guests of people whose land they oc-

Figure 4.3 Day/Night, 1991, Seattle. Hachivi Edgar Heap of Birds. Reproduced with permission.

cupy."[114] This has included public art in Minneapolis, commemorating the forty Dakota executed by Abraham Lincoln in the 1860s. This was located in the city's Grain Belt, in an attempt at highlighting the cost of economic "progress" to native people. An installation in Seattle's Pioneer Square, next to a preexistent bust of Chief Seattle, announces in Lushootseed and English: "Chief Seattle Now The Street Are Our Home" and "Far Away Brothers and Sisters We Still Remember You" (fig. 4.3). The intent is to "proclaim that for many transient intertribal people the streets of Seattle [including the area around Pioneer Square] are home," and also to acknowledge the link between these people and their traditional territories.[115]

Heap of Birds' 1991 installation in Vancouver was similar to a project entitled "Native Hosts New York." Using authoritative signage, an inverted "British Columbia" is advised that "Today your host is Musqueam." The ambivalent language of hospitality is intriguing. On the one hand, it echoes the legal fiction that access to property is conditional on an invitation from the owner. However, it perhaps also signals the oft-stated (and oft-ignored) Native argument that their claim need not be exclusive. Land can be shared. But the placement of the Vancouver display, on the lawns of the Vancouver Art Gallery, is also significant, given that the building used to serve as a law court (fig. 4.4).[116]

Figure 4.4 Native Hosts, 1991, Vancouver. Hachivi Edgar Heap of Birds. Reproduced with permission.

Indigenous people like Heap of Birds have always contested the enactments of colonial property. Yet recent years have seen added impetus to these challenges, driven by indigenous organizing and radicalism, as well as some important, if partial, legal acknowledgements of native land claims, such as the *Mabo* decision in Australia, and *Delgamuukw* in Canada.[117] As in Victoria, native litigants have also expressly targeted parcels of urban land in some cases. A partial list, as of early 2002, include treaty protests in Victoria (as noted above), a Metis legal action relating to the land now occupied by Winnipeg, and a Chippewa claim to 2,500 acres of residential and industrial land in Sarnia, Ontario. In Australia, claims for native title have been made in relation to the town of Alice Springs, the township of Broome, parts of Kununnurra, Darwin, Tennnant Creek, the Perth metropolitan area, and parts of Sydney. In New Zealand, treaty rights have been used for claims to land in Wellington, Orakei, and the township of Turangi. Recent legislation (such as the 1993 Native Title Act in Australia) or judicial decisions have obliged urban decision makers to consult with native titleholders.[118]

As noted, a growing number of native people also live in cities, although many are both socially and politically disenfranchised. Vancouver, for example, is host to native people from at least thirty-five different Nations. Yet this population continues to be treated as "out of place." Evelyn Peters has documented the multiple ways in which "urban" and "aboriginal" continue to be regarded as mutually contradictory within Canada.[119] This can often have deleterious consequences for urban natives, affecting native treaty settlements, service delivery, and cultural identity.

Native struggles for justice and land unfold in varied ways across all settler spaces. However, if we accept that the city is a site of particular ideological, material, and representational investments on the part of a settler society, native contestation has a particular valence here. Indigenous people continue to enact their own claims to urban places, in part through other mappings and other stories designed to challenge both dispossession and displacement: these can include challenges to white emplacement, the remapping of an enduring native presence, and the contestation of dispossession. While such contestation can be gestural, indigenous claimants "can and do unsettle the colonial authority of cities."[120]

Native activism located outside the city can have undeniable urban consequences, disrupting the imagined divide between urban and rural. The early 1990s, for example, saw a wave of native blockades across British Columbia. Given the continued dependence of the urban economy on flows of resources extracted from traditional native territories, it was appropriate that these blockades began to register within the city. Of special significance was a blockade that cut off the towns of Lillooet from the west and Pemberton from the east, and a rail blockade by the Stó:Lo on the main Canadian National rail line into Vancouver, which cost CN around $3 million a day.[121] But even the contemporary service economy can be threatened when the picturesque Indian becomes political. The high-stakes campaign by corporate and state interests to host the 2010 Winter Olympics in Vancouver and Whistler, though receiving some native backing, has also been complicated by native land claims. For example, a coalition of aboriginal people lodged a formal complaint with the International Olympic Committee in Lausanne, Switzerland in June 2002. For Rosalin Sam, a member of the Lil-Wat band at Mount Currie and the St-at-imc Nation, at issue were "the title and rights, our aboriginal title and rights to the land. Whistler is part of our St-at-imc territory."[122]

But that which is located outside the city can also erupt within it. Many of these challenges seek to contest dispossession, by insisting that the creation of the settler-city entailed an unjust dislocation of others. We have seen this in the case of Victoria, for example, where the land upon which the legislative buildings, the symbolic center of power and state authority, were built, is reclaimed using the very maps and texts of the colonial power itself. Other challenges to dispossession have occurred in Vancouver. The website of the Squamish Nation, for example, offers a creative mix of images, text, and maps in its exploration of the politics of dispossession in an ancient Squamish settlement (Sun'auhk) on the southern shore of Vancouver's English Bay.[123] In 1869, a reserve was laid out around the Sun'auhk village site. In 1913, however, the occupants were relocated to North Vancouver, perhaps because their presence was an affront to the dynamics of displacement.[124] A series of sequential maps show the "death by a thousand cuts" that this space then suffered (see fig. 4.5a, b).[125] The land then became a park and site, ironically enough, for the city's museum and

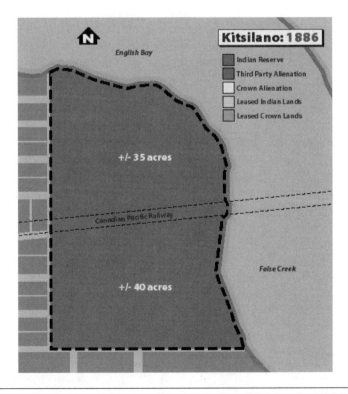

Figure 4.5a Resisting dispossession. Indian Reserve 6, Kitsilano, 1886. From Squamish Nation website (*www.squamish.net*). Reproduced with the permission of Chief Gibby Jacob, Squamish First Nation.

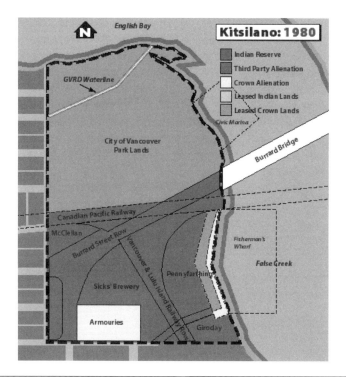

Figure 4.5b Resisting dispossession Indian Reserve 6, Kitsilano, 1980. From Squamish Nation website (*www.squamish.net*). Reproduced with the permission of Chief Gibby Jacob, Squamish First Nation.

archive. One set of images juxtaposes the museum, built to resemble a traditional Coast Salish hat, with some of the original occupants (fig. 4.6). But this is not an exercise in memorialization: historic dispossessions are presented as an enduring injustice.

Jane Jacobs provides a helpful account from Australia that illustrates other indigenous challenges to urban dispossession. In the atmosphere of "reconciliation" following the *Mabo* ruling, the city of Melbourne commissioned an Aboriginal and non-Aboriginal artist to produce the "Another View Walking Trail" to wind through central Melbourne, passing seventeen sites with newly installed artworks, as well as existing colonial monuments. For Jacobs, this entailed a powerful unsettlement: the trail "takes symbols of dominant culture . . . and destabilizes their authority by presenting oppositional narratives of the events they set in train. It reclaims city space."[126] Precisely for this reason, the trail generated controversy. Most unsettling was a mosaic which was to be located outside the Supreme Court, attacking foundational principles of justice. Law was cast

Figure 4.6 Resisting displacement. Chief Andrews and his son. From Squamish Nation website (*www.squamish.net*). Reproduced with the permission of Chief Gibby Jacob, Squamish First Nation.

as implicated in colonial dispossession, with an aboriginal head impaled on the sword of justice. As Jacobs shows, the concern was not only with the telling of these alternative truths, but with the location of their telling. The authorities sought to police "the geography of the 'other' view which ensured that at least some of the grand sites of colonial authority remained pure."[127]

But such postcolonial challenges need not be purely symbolic. They can also entail material occupations and reworkings that similarly unsettle the material landscape of the settler-city.[128] In 1969, a nineteen-month occupation of the former prison of Alcatraz, set in San Francisco's bay began. It was initiated by Native American students from various California universities, as well as other urban natives, relocated to San Francisco under the native relocation policy of the 1960s, and received support from Bay Area Indian organizations. It proved the first of a series of Indian protests and occupations in the United States directed at government installations or historical sites of double-edged meaning. These included, for example, the attempt at liberating Ellis Island; the occupation of Fort Lawton, an abandoned military installation north of Seattle; and the symbolic retaking of Plymouth Rock. Behind these protests were urban-based Indian organizations. A relocation program that moved rural natives into the city in the name of assimilation fostered instead a radicalization, that brought together the urban and the native in unexpected ways: "Everywhere the government's relocation program had sent Indians, groups began to boisterously and aggressively complain about the conditions they found themselves living in."[129]

The motivations for the "retaking" of Alcatraz were various and overlapping, but protests at dispossession were central. The fact that the island prison had held many native people, including two Modocs from northern California, Slolux, and Boncho, who had resisted dispossession made it a logical target for some.[130] Resistance to native dispossession and treaty abrogation (notably the 1868 Black Hills Treaty, signed with the Sioux and Arapaho) also motivated the retaking. The island, for one, "symbolized the contempt with which the government regarded native claims."[131] At the same time, an ironic appeal was made to colonial enactments of dispossession in a native proclamation that reclaimed Alcatraz "by right of discovery." Given the desire to be "fair and honorable in our dealings with all white men," the proclamation offered to purchase the island for twenty-four dollars in glass beads and red cloth.[132]

Native people have not only resisted historic dispossessions, they have also, as with Heap of Bird's art, remapped a continuing native presence, reminding observers that the settler-city not only *was,* but still *is,* native land. Displacement, in that sense, is directly challenged in powerful and unsettling ways. The "Another View Walking Trail" challenges not only historic injustices, but also contemporary law. Jacobs notes the productive effect of such claims in relation to dominant notions of reconciliation, which prefer "resistance to be something which happened *then* but is remembered *now.* . . . [t]here is far less comfort with reconciliatory performances which unsettle the sacred infrastructure of colonial history or remind modern Australia that it is far from postcolonial."[133]

The enactments of displacement are denaturalized and occasionally reworked by such interventions, which offer different stories and different maps. The Squamish Nation seeks to re-inscribe an historic native presence in order to advance an enduring contemporary claim. The Squamish continue to insist that their "use and occupation of the traditional territory has *continued* uninterrupted since the arrival of the Europeans. . . . The Squamish people *continue* to occupy their traditional territory. . . . The Squamish people *continue* to harvest fish. . . . The Squamish people *continue* to take game from the land. The Squamish people harvest timber and other resources from the forests. The Squamish Nation has also established its place within the modern economic infrastructure by relying on its historic rights. Despite the intense pressure of massive urban development, the Squamish Nation has never ceded or surrendered their aboriginal title."[134] Unjust dispossessions may have occurred, in other words, but displacement is not complete. The city remains unsettled. Even sites, such as Vancouver's Stanley Park, which supposedly "put to rest" native dispossession, have been creatively "re-excavated" by the Squamish. In 1984, for example, plans to enlarge the Vancouver Aquarium's whale pool were opposed as a "desecration" of native remains from the Xwayxway village site.[135] Similarly, with Alcatraz, "a dramatic outcropping out in the middle of the bay," the fact that the occupation occurred in the heart of a large city and port was not incidental.[136] The native proclamation held that it would be "fitting and symbolic" that ships entering the Golden Gate "would first see Indian land, and thus be reminded of the true history of this nation. This tiny island would be a symbol of the great lands once ruled by free and noble Indians."[137]

Self-confident narratives of unproblematic urban settlement are thus compromised by alternative stories and geographies. Native people, supposedly excised from urban space, are shown to endure: "the desired 'purity' of the colonial city has . . . always been productively compromised by the continuing presence of the colonized."[138] Affrica Taylor describes the film "The Coolbaroo Club," set in Perth, which relies upon a double movement of "deconstruction and reinscription" of urban space, by "simultaneously exposing some of the technologies of power through which Perth has been inscribed as a 'naturally' white place, even as it reinscribes the city with aboriginal cultural memories." The film reveals the mappings that prohibited the area around the city center for aboriginal peoples under section 39 of the Aborigines Act, yet documents the presence of aboriginal people in this forbidden space.[139] The Squamish website also includes a striking and provocative graphic, showing a bulls-eye centered over downtown Vancouver, the area of most intense "improvement" (fig. 4.7). For one

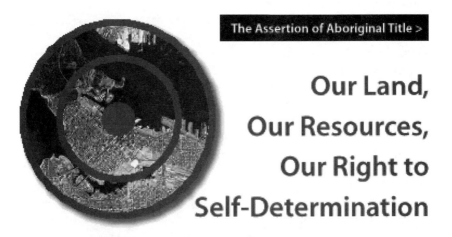

Figure 4.7 The continuing native presence. From Squamish Nation website (*www.squamish.net*). Reproduced with the permission of Chief Gibby Jacob, Squamish First Nation.

former Musqueam Chief: "We can claim downtown Vancouver. It is ours. There is nothing in anybody's laws saying that it is no longer Musqueam or Squamish or Capilano or Tsawwassen."[140]

But native people have also carved out more sustained material spaces of settlement within the colonial city. One interesting example is that of Redfern, in Sydney. Forged around a utopian Black cooperative, it was also motivated by a concern at aboriginal land rights and discrimination in the housing market. Sparked by a police crackdown on aboriginal squatters, a settlement grew that was soon labeled by one aboriginal leader as "Sydney's Aboriginal Embassy"—"we are making a stand for aboriginal land rights."[141] Ultimately, the federal government released funds to purchase forty-one houses for aboriginal residents. Not only did this mark one of the first land rights' victories for Australia's Aborigines, it also successfully claimed "an entitlement at the metropolitan heart of White Australia."[142]

A handful of aboriginal families and activists from Redfern formed the nucleus for another significant urban settlement. In 1972, an encampment was established directly opposite Canberra's old federal Parliament buildings. It was reportedly prompted by the announcement of assimilationist government proposals that, while acknowledging aboriginal demands for land rights, set clear constraints on state recognition. The concern was at their unsettling effect: aboriginal claims would lead "to uncertainties and possible challenges in relation to land titles in Australia that are presently unquestioned and secure."[143] Arguing that this effectively made them aliens in our own land, so like other aliens, they needed diplomatic standing, the protestors named their encampment the aboriginal tent embassy. The authorities objected that this implied aboriginal sovereignty. Given prevailing assumption that the land was *terra nullius,* prior to European settlement, this possibility was out of the question.[144] The growing encampment was also seen as an eyesore and "a blight on the national capital."[145] Using a hastily enacted bylaw that forbade camping in a public place, police moved to clear the site. Violent confrontation, clearance, and successive re-occupations ensued. The embassy has now become a permanent fixture, even achieving recognition by the Australian Heritage Commission.[146] However, successive governments have sought to negotiate for the removal of the embassy or the creation of more appropriate spaces, including the creation of the nearby Reconciliation Place, a museum and memorial to aboriginal peoples, criticized by some as presenting a whitewashed picture of history.

The embassy made conscious use of symbolic protest, acting as a "comment on living conditions in aboriginal Australia, on the question of land ownership (of this particular piece of ground as well as other parts of Australia) on the relative status of indigenous people in a city dotted with embassies, and on the avenues of protest open to the otherwise (often) silent minorities in Australian society."[147] The protest thus has an undeniable geography. Its very location, in a federal capital, and an urban site, reinscribes an indigenous presence in the colonial landscape in ways unsettling to the urban imagination. And clearly the injustice of dispossession, and the ongoing attempt to reclaim lands are also at the core of the protest. But perhaps the embassy also challenges the spatial enactments of property in other ways. One observer, for example, has suggested that the tents themselves enact a claim to land in ways that mimic, and thus question, colonial modes of settlement. Their ephemerality and collapsibility represent "an opportunistic occupation of space" that remind us of the tents that housed the first Europeans to settle in Australia at Port Jackson in 1788.[148]

Despite its enduring and undeniable permanence, the embassy itself has become nomadic. It was reconstructed in the Hague, in an aboriginal appeal to the World Court. In July 2000, a tent embassy appeared in Victoria Park, South Sydney, in advance of the Sydney 2000 Olympic Games. This concluded a three thousand kilometer Peace Walk, under the banner: "Walking the land for our ancient right." Its route took it through the traditional territories of many aboriginal nations, following a path determined by sacred song-lines, that connect the living to the dreamtime, the focus of aboriginal law and beliefs. The act of walking—which disqualifies native people from ownership, according to dominant tropes—becomes the means of enacting an alternative claim to land. Bruce Chatwin's comments on Australia are relevant: white Australians, he notes, often assume that "because the aboriginals were wanderers, they could have no system of land tenure. This was nonsense. Aboriginals, it was true, could not imagine territory as a block of lines hemmed in by frontiers, but rather as an interlocking network of 'lines' or 'ways through.' "[149]

Entanglements

There is a significant gulf between recognizing Aborigines' rights to something like Ayers Rock [sic – Uluru] and . . . encouraging militant aboriginal groups to lay claim to sites such as the heart of Collins Street in Melbourne or Bennelong Point in Sydney.

—from an editorial in *The Australian*

As I write this, aboriginal students are contesting proposed developments of lands on the main campus of my suburban university, arguing that First Nations have not been adequately consulted or included in the planning process. The university lies on unceded aboriginal lands, claimed by the Musqueam, Squamish, Stó:Lo and Tsleil-Waututh First Nations.[150]

The response to such unsettling claims to the city has been diverse and complicated. For many years, of course, the institutional response has been dismissive. "Not an inch to the Indians," trumpeted one Vancouver columnist, arguing that their claims are "insupportable in law and untenable in reason."[151] Indigenous claims to land are simply dismissed as "not-property," given their failure to accord to the settled definitions of the ownership model. Thus a university representative counters native opposition to redevelopment by claiming that the university obtained the land from the city of Burnaby and holds clear title. But the growing acknowledgement, albeit provisional, of certain native claims to land, has given some urbanites pause. A case involving private land in Vancouver in which homeowners were refused a building permit due to the existence of a protected midden caused one journalist to note that "[h]omeowners in urban areas are sure to be frightened, wondering how secure their own land titles are if native Indian groups can make claims based on nothing more than oral evidence."[152] Another media report reflected that "[o]nce considered important mostly to rural British Columbia, the native Indian land claims issue is now beginning to hit home in the big city."[153] The *Mabo* decision in Australia generated anxiety around the possibility (unlikely in practice) that claims could be made to urban lands. Increased First Nations' militancy in British Columbia makes some city dwellers worry that the land itself, like the proverbial carpet, may have been pulled from under them (fig. 4.8).

However, the unsettling nature of indigenous claims may also relate to the geographies of the ownership model itself. Richie Howitt's description of Australians as ill equipped to deal with the complexities of an emergent "edge politics" that trades in "ambivalence, uncertainty, change, overlap, and interaction," seems to be of more general relevance. The ownership model is similarly predicated on the concept of the bounded individual, encouraging monological and insulated encounters.[154] The ownership model encourages the bounding of property into spaces of "certainty, identity, and security," such as aboriginal reserves, urban areas purged of indigeneity, national parks, and freehold estates.[155]

A striking example of the hegemony of this "spatial order" occurred in 1995, when the *Vancouver Sun* hired a cartographer to map out the spatial extent of all extant land claims across the province (fig. 4.9). A map of the Vancouver region was shown, carved up by several native claimants. The immediate effect is to threaten the city: native claimants, previously imagined as outside the city suddenly unsettle a space of secure title and white settlement.[156] The map suddenly compromises a colonial claim, rather than underwriting it: "On the map they are just colorful lines drawn over

Figure 4.8 Unsettlement. *Vancouver Sun,* February 4, 1998. Reproduced with the permission of Graham Harrop.

the surface of British Columbia, carving the province into puzzle pieces of all shapes and sizes. But these lines are no game. . . . [they] divide the province into odd-shaped mini-states."[157]

But the objective geographies of the ownership model also reassure the settler-city. In the newspaper's mapping exercise, the authority and objectivity of cartography was used to demonstrate the absurdity of these claims. For the map shows that the claims overlap. Given the presumption that property must be clearly and exclusively delimited, this is a powerful counter. These are not real boundaries, but a "criss-crossing mess of colored lines." Statistics are also invoked to ridicule a native claim—the article ran under the headline: "Native's wish list takes in 111 per cent of B.C.'s land mass." First Nations' claims, apparently a threat, are ultimately presented as incongruous given their mismatch with dominant geographies of property.

Figure 4.9 Colonial maps and the settler city. *Vancouver Sun,* April 1, 1995. Reproduced with permission.

Yet despite this, the power and persistence of native enactments to land is such that unsettlement endures. Boundaries become uncertain. Colonial distinctions between self and other, yours and mine are no longer determinate. Boundary drawing occurs, but dissolves. Aboriginal claims "turn what seems like 'home' into something else, something less familiar and settled."[158] Drawing from psychoanalytical theory, Ken Gelder and Jane Jacobs characterize the postcolonial world as uncanny: "An 'uncanny' experience may occur when one's home is rendered, somehow and in some sense, unfamiliar; one has the experience, in other words, of being in place and 'out of place' simultaneously." In the uncanny city, "one's place is always already another's place and the issue of possession is never complete, never entirely settled."[159]

This can, of course, be deeply challenging. However, it can also be productive, compelling us to recognize other spaces and other modalities of property. In so doing, a relational politics is forced to the surface, where the city, to borrow from Homi Bhabha, is "in the process of the articulation of elements: where meanings may be partial because they are in media res; and history may be half-made because it is in the process of being made."[160] Evelyn Peters also urges us to acknowledge the link between First Nations' people and the city as part of a broader project "of learning to see the other landscapes which inhabit our taken-for-granted spaces."[161] Howitt urges the decolonization of the dominant spatial imaginary, given the prevalence of an "edge politics" of uncertainty and overlap.[162] These calls, of course, are far from easy if we accept the dominance of the owner-ship model and its associated geographies. A just settlement thus requires an act of imaginative reworking. Never easy, the challenge is even harder in the city, given the particular ways in which colonial claims to land are en-acted here. Precisely for those reasons, however, the city is one crucial place to begin.

CHAPTER 5

Back to the Land

[T]he notion that the city speaks for itself conceals the identity of those who speak through the city.

—Rosalyn Deutsche, *Evictions: Art and Spatial Politics*

Disquieting the Land

Some years ago, I was walking through the Downtown Eastside with a camera, as I had to prepare some photographs for a lecture. On Cordova Street, I came upon what, at first sight, appeared to be a conventional sign, announcing a development application. However, closer inspection revealed that someone had carefully superimposed text and graphics over the official signage. This was not commonplace graffiti, but entailed considerable creative energy. In my mind's eye, I see the artist working in the city archive, researching the history of the site and then, early one morning, slipping down to Cordova Street and quietly rearranging the text and map. Perhaps a passerby questioned the artist; likely not. Unlike the confident permanence of a municipal sign, the supplication, as I shall call it, has a transience and a lightness of touch. Rather than spray paint, Letraset was used. Even now, some of the letters were peeling away. Yet at the same time, the neat black letters and lines of the supplication appropriated the iconography of official signage, and its implied authority.

The supplication quickly disappeared. Yet, several years later, its "metaphorical wit" continues to engage, baffle, and provoke me.[1] Its potential meanings are many. Its emphasis on dispossession and the materialities of land speak to the violences embedded within and constitutive of law.[2] The politics of social memory and the role of the monument are also foregrounded.[3] As I suggest below, it mediates between political possibilities, rather than foreclosing on them, or constructing binary choices. Its blend of narrative, graphics, and text, and its reliance on and inversion of an official vocabulary gives it a semantic fluidity that creates space for a variety of possible meanings. Nick Couldry's suggestion that new genre public art, such as the supplication, should be read not so much for its determinate "intentions and messages" that reflect "underlying social patterns" but more as a "strand in debates about those very social conditions" is useful here, as is his recognition that such debates, and the contexts within which they occur, are deeply spatialized.[4]

One set of social conditions that the supplication invites us to debate, it seems to me, relates to the enactment of land and property. Like conventional enactments of property, the supplication also draws (or redraws) maps and tells stories, though in a somewhat more explicit, yet still subtle way. It reanimates and reoccupies this apparently inert space, confronting and reworking the official stories and maps of property. The effect, in part, is what David Pinder terms a subversive cartography—that is, one that both subverts existing cartographic conventions, and yet seeks to create maps outside these framings.[5] Most immediately, the supplication breaks down the consequential distinction between maps and stories. Indeed, it consciously mingles the two, placing stories on maps, and maps on stories.[6]

Figure 5.1 Supplication on Cordova Street. Photograph by author.

This creative reworking is immediately evident in the sequence reproduced below:

- 0—*Dove down to the ocean floor to get mud for the land*
- 46—*Walked the paths of the land*
- 62—*Divided the land*
- 63—*Built, born, fought, loved, died on the land*
- *One level of underground parking for 19 car spaces*

Normally, this section of an application notice would include text like that which is retained at the end of the sequence, listing the dimensions and attributes of the development. The artist has transformed this flat spatialized rendering, with its hopeful claims of the "highest and best" use of the site, into what appears to be a sequencing of the past. Now the numberings of the development are turned into dates, beginning with zero, suggesting some original moment.

But who is it that dives and walks, in this story of the land? I suspect that the story being narrated here is that of the original occupants of this land; the Coast Salish peoples, including the Musqueam and Squamish Nations, who have used the area, adjacent to the rich marine life of what became Burrard Inlet, for millennia. The zero with which the supplication begins must signal some originary moment at which time begins. Indeed, the phrase "dove down to the ocean floor to get mud for the land" is echoed in at least one Squamish story of divine creation:

> In the beginning there was water everywhere and no land at all. When this state of things had lasted for a long while, the Great Spirit determined to make land appear. Soon the tops of the mountains showed above the water and they grew and grew till their heads reached the clouds. Then he made the lakes and rivers, and after that the trees and animals. Soon after this had been done, Kalana, the first man was made.[7]

If we treat the numbers of the supplication as marking time, what seems to follow from this act of creation is an extended period in which humans, if they are present at all, touch only lightly on the land and do not permanently settle ("Walked the paths of the land"). Perhaps this signals the nomadic rhythms of Native life, in which settlements were used seasonally as resource availability shifted. But while walking plays an important role in aboriginal realities, it also figures in Western renderings of native life. Despite the complex and layered relations of tenure that characterized Coast Salish life, a propensity to move has been read as an inability to own. Fixity and stasis are required in Law's lands.

But as the supplication reminds us, walking gives way to something else. Suddenly, and recently, the land was "divided," as Royal Engineers begin platting and surveying a land that now becomes parceled into private properties. As noted in the previous chapter, the combination of cartography, private property, and colonial violence underpinned the rapid displacement and dispossession of native peoples, particularly on this land, so close to the rapidly expanding settlement that became Vancouver. For better or worse, land is now used much more intensively, becoming a space for building, birth, fighting, loving, and dying. While that fighting and dying include native people, it also involves other dispossessed peoples.

What is served by this story? As we shall see below, it is not simply an exercise in wistful nostalgia. One immediate effect is to complicate and politicize the story of highest and best use, and reveal the white mythologies from which it draws. As noted, dominant narratives imagine native forms of land use as akin to a state of nature, characterized by mobility and communal ownership, which inevitably gives way to higher and better uses. Native lands are deemed unimproved, and can thus be justly expropriated by those who were capable of reclaiming the "waste." As Hamilton's monument noted, these are imagined as "empty" lands.

But the supplication reinscribes a native presence. While the Musqueam and Squamish may not have "improved" the land in a form intelligible to Western property narratives, they are still present. The Native chronology does not stop with the dividing of the land, despite powerful mythologies of their inevitable and natural "disappearance."[8] We are also reminded of a continuing native presence by the sinuous lines superimposed over the map, perhaps signaling tracks and trails. While these could be read as ecological features, they could also signal the ways in which people, including native people, traverse and cross cut the cadastral grid. Given dominant framings of land and property, reinserting a contemporary native presence is important. For the Downtown Eastside turns out to be place in which many native people from across Canada reside, displaced from their traditional territories by colonial dispossession. But this is also space in which formal native claims have become more visible. Consequently, nearly all land in British Columbia is contested, associated with over a century of native activism. Dispossession may have been achieved, but not displacement. Despite the dividing of the land, native people still "walk" it, in other words.[9]

With their future orientation, the stories and maps of highest and best use efface past uses and occupations. As the supplication insists, those occupants include the anonymous native peoples who used, and use, this space. But named people who occupied the various houses on the site are also chronologically listed, superimposed over the map.

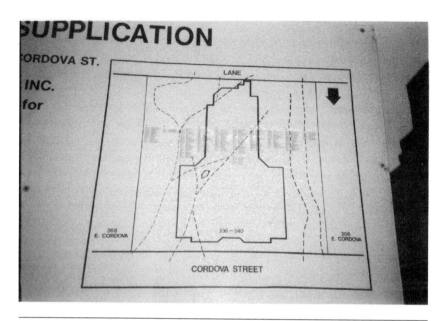

Figure 5.2 Supplication—detail. Photograph by author.

For Number 336, for example, the artist lists the following:

1986–88	*Lin Bo Xian*
1985	*Hsu Ti Hong*
1980–82	*Lee Yeung*
1978–79	*Kin Kui Kwong*
1976–77	*Sien Richard*
1974–75	*Mah Mai*
1956–66	*Wong shack*
1947–55	*Longworth J*
1946	*Wong J*
1942–45	*Orientals*
1936–41	*Shinkosha Theatre*
1935	*Japan Info Bureau*
1935–41	*Tsuyuki K*
1923–34	*Orientals*
1914–18	*Chinese*
1911–13	*Fakahira R*
1910	*Senior John*
1909	*Percy Thomas V*

This retrospective story also reworks and quietly critiques the dominant maps and narratives of property. First, in looking backwards, it reminds us that the story of property is not simply the story of the present, projected into the future. Rather, the chronology now reads back from the present, tracing a story of previous occupations. To that extent, it reinscribes those who "Built, born, fought, loved, died on the land," effaced by the bulldozing narrative of improvement, reminding us of the dense vernacular histories embedded in everyday urban landscapes.[10] In so doing, the master narratives of property are rendered contingent. Rather than simply a space of potentiality, awaiting "improvement," we are reminded of layerings of past use and occupation. Again, this is not an exercise in nostalgia. As we shall below, the location of this site—an area and a population collectively threatened by the material and cultural displacements of development—make this politically important. Further, the buildings that were occupied appear not simply as empty speculative shells but sites rich with nonmonetary value. Although previous occupants may have had speculative intent, they likely were renters, with a particular "investment" in their immediate landscape. Radin argues that while this "investment" does not conform to dominant fungible norms of property, it nevertheless may constitute a morally valuable and defensible property claim.[11]

In addition to the animation of the map's inert, abstract space with overlapping personal histories, the supplication also includes a layering of names. In so doing, it reminds viewers that the narratives of property—whether they concern the past or the future—implicate individual persons. Property relations are not simply between an owner and a particular space, but also between people. In capitalist society, those relations are generally skewed in favor of those who own. Thus it is a critical gesture to reframe property in relation to people. Most immediately, it politicizes property. Put another way, the supplication publicizes that which is usually regarded as private, re-framing a neutral issue of *dominium* to a more obviously political question of *imperium*.[12]

As we shall see, a close inspection of the names remapped onto Cordova Street is instructive when situated within this place. But there is another dimension to the naming that is also unsettling. Nearly all the occupants listed by the artist appear to be men. This is not surprising, given the tendency of street directories, from where the artist likely derived the records, to list only the male head of household. Where women are named, they are widows, and are thus always assigned a status relative to men (as "Mrs."), thus appearing as provisional occupants. The "Mrs." also appears to preclude mention of women's first names. While this is not surprising, given patriarchal codings of marriage, it does raise some important questions concerning the gendered enactment of property in stories and maps.

That women and men stand in an uneven relation to property is clear.[13] Women are not only often denied access to ownership, but can become objects of ownership themselves.[14] More particularly, women's access to property seems largely conditional on their relation to men; "women just don't seem to be as 'propertied' as men, except insofar as they happen to be located in families that are headed by men."[15] This patriarchal relation is also evidenced in property discourse more generally. And the "land," referred to in the supplication, is also very much at issue. Most immediately, the master narrative of property is deeply gendered, reliant upon certain tropes of Woman, especially in relation to nature.[16] Laura Brace explores the seventeenth-century discourse on "husbandry," deeply implicated in "improvement" and emergent conceptions of private property, which imagine landed property as "invested with men's most generative capacities."[17] But similar conflations also occur in acts of colonial dispossession. The Americas, of course, were also imagined as female potentiality, awaiting masculine domination.[18]

As commentators such as Gillian Rose and Anne Bottomley argue, such masculinist accounts rely upon certain spatializations. Bottomley, for example, describes the attempts of property law to disembed itself from the lived spaces of the land as a means of enshrining a masculine legal mastery reliant on a positioning of Woman as "the unrepresentable, that-which-does-not-fit."[19] For these reasons, Rose and Bottomley seek to create ways of seeing, which "while working within a phallocentric economy of meaning, nonetheless refuse to sanction its codes."[20] Bottomley seeks to recuperate women's own experiences of law through creative "acts of mapping" that can give "body to law, land to land law, landscape to text."[21] Similarly, by problematizing dominant spatializations and by highlighting the gendered absences in the historical record of ownership, the supplication also quietly remaps women in their relationship to the spaces and stories of property.

The development application, altered by the artist, also appears to have nothing to say about place; indeed, it appears to efface it. In this sense, the geocoding ("No. 215878, 336 E. Cordova St") is spatial, rather than placial, directing us to a cadastral and institutional gridding that pulverizes space, assigning each parcel and proposal to an abstract surface in which spaces and actions only have meanings according to apparently fixed and enclosed governmental categories, such as planning. As has been noted, one immediate effect is to make possible action at a distance, such that the uses and disposition of multiple parcels of land can be regulated and organized from afar. Space becomes actionable. The map itself detaches the space, viewing it in abstraction. The same gridding can easily be relocated to another space, without any loss of meaning: "There is nothing you can dominate as easily as a flat surface of a few square meters: there is nothing hidden or convoluted, no shadows, no *double entendre*."[22]

But if the application effaces place, the supplication reinscribes it. The artist's choice of this place was surely a conscious act. Property is not only remapped and renarrated, it is also "re-placed."[23] In so doing, the maps and stories circulating in dominant accounts of property, embedded within the application, are also consciously located in this place.[24] As we shall see, this is important. "This place," however, is far from self-evident. Several places can be invoked, the choice of which enacts property in particular ways, rendering other stories and maps invisible. Spatial scale, it seems, is also political.[25]

Placing Cordova Street

Let us begin with Cordova Street. What is its story? Cordova used to be Oppenheimer Street, named for David Oppenheimer who, with his brother Isaac, bought three hundred acres from the Hastings Mill in 1884. In 1886, they established the Vancouver Improvement Company, cleared the land and sold off lots. Although these were close to the original nucleus for what would become Vancouver, the arrival of the Canadian Pacific Railroad shifted the locus of development westward; early on it was clear that the area would be Vancouver's industrial and working-class neighborhood. The buildings demolished by the bulldozer on Cordova Street were likely the small houses, shacks, and lodging rooms of the fisherman, mill workers, and longshoremen who were employed in the area. Reportedly, they were originally built for railway workers, many of them Chinese.

This story of speculative growth, much of it centered on residential development, is very much the story of Vancouver. As a place, Vancouver has long defined itself in terms of the logic and metric of real estate and real property and their dynamic interplay.[26] Katharyne Mitchell notes that property's stories continue to resonate within Vancouver, particularly in light of its globalization, alerting us to the ways in which, for example, local understandings of race and racism are caught up in dominant and oppositional narratives of property development. These narratives, in turn, are implicated in competing constructions of Vancouver as a place and its openness to extralocal flows. The politics of property prove complicated: proponents of globalized development position local opponents as reactionary, small-minded, and even racist in their defense of place.[27]

But these stories of growth and ownership have also been crosscut and complicated in other ways. Ownership entails dispossession; growth has gone hand in hand with decline. As the supplication reminds us, these displacements have included aboriginal peoples. However, other dispossessions have also ensued, as revealed by the shifting names on the supplication. Until 1941, Japanese names predominate (Nagawa, Fakahara, Imai, Kojina, or just "Japanese"). In 1943, different names emerge. K. Imai gives way to B. E. Brewer. Henry Unruh replaces Imae Tarakita.

Cordova Street is a block away from Powell Street, the nucleus of a Japanese-Canadian settlement that grew up in the 1890s, and a few blocks away from Vancouver's long established Chinatown. Both of these sites speak to the generalized racism operative within Vancouver society that curtailed, both informally and formally, the spaces within which racialized groups could locate within the city. At the same time, the way in which such communities were obliged to live (often at high densities, in substandard housing) was itself seen as further proof of the undeniable alienness of "Orientals," when juxtaposed with the ways in which the white population used propertied space. Such urban racisms implicate not only property, but also stories and mappings. As noted, Western notions of property are deeply invested in a colonial geography, in which the racialized figure of the "savage" play a central role, as Peter Fitzpatrick has convincingly demonstrated.[28] That the Japanese could be regarded as "aliens" while Scots and English were placed as "natives" surely depends on complicated stories of colonial destiny. With echoes of Locke, this was "British Columbia," empty, unsettled, and unimproved, awaiting the arrival of white, British men who would improve and make it theirs.

But such mappings were also at work more locally. Kay Anderson alerts us to the ways "imaginative geographies" were constructed on the part of the dominant white society in early Vancouver, so that "Oriental" residential concentrations, such as "Japantown" as it was known, served to reify racial categories, and naturalize the "superiority" of dominant groups.[29] Such places were ascribed an ontological stability and facticity from which one could "read off" racial characteristics. Her treatment of "Chinatowns" would seem to apply equally to "Japantown."[30]

> "Chinatown," like "Chinese," has been a historically specific idea, a cultural concept rooted in the symbolic system of those with the power to define. From this vantage point, Chinatown says as much about the frames of mind of the West as it does about the ethnic attributes of the East.[31]

The power to define a place can often mean the power to decide the destiny of that place. Precisely because of the ascription of otherness to Japantown and its occupants, it was possible to imagine the erasure of this place from the map. And thus, following the declaration of war between Canada and Japan in 1941, people of Japanese descent were formally identified as "enemy aliens" and the residents of Powell and Cordova Street were "evacuated" to internment camps in the interior of the province.[32] In 1943, the Custodian of Enemy Properties began selling off confiscated properties in the area at low prices. As the supplication reminds us, thus it was that T. Okano's home (from 1934) became W. J. Campbell's in 1942.[33]

While this story was repressed for many years, it has been reinstated with the struggle for redress, most notably with Joy Kogawa's searing *Obasan*.[34] And in retelling this story, the place in which it was most powerfully evidenced is also reinscribed:

> Powell Street has taken on a somewhat mythical significance, idealized as a symbol of collective loss. Its violation was the violation of the presence not only of those who actually lived there, but of all those Japanese Canadians for whom the past is a displacement of freedom. We therefore attach ourselves to its memory as though only through the assertion of a sense of place can memories become redemption.[35]

Oppenheimer Park, a few houses away from 336 Cordova Street, is now the site of the annual Japanese-Canadian Powell Street Festival that provides a celebratory focus for that sense of place in "a landscape of memory and hope."[36]

Placing Skid Row/Downtown Eastside

But there are other "places full of time," to borrow from Richard Sennett, that we need to attend to here.[37] If we step back a few more blocks, we would locate Cordova Street in Downtown Eastside, the symbolic heart of which, at Main and Hastings, is just two blocks away. Long a place for Vancouver's working class, and racialized populations, as well as an active if somewhat down-market commercial area, the area is now seen as synonymous with criminality, marginality, and profound "Otherness." Again, it is surely no accident that the supplication was placed here. Narratives and mappings of property, when emplaced *here,* as I noted earlier, acquire another set of powerful and intensely political meanings. The threat of displacement has sparked intense struggles that center on land use, property rights, and the landscape, which pivot in turn on contending stories and representations of the spaces of property. Highest and best use, put bluntly, confronts community use. Reinscribing histories of past occupation and their relation to future developments, as the supplication does, starkly reminds us of the tension between these two stories.

The politics of land, in relation to gentrification, has tended to turn on class. We see this in Vancouver and more generally. Thus, in the Downtown Eastside, activism has drawn from a broadly socialist vocabulary, using an analytical frame that, for good reason, focuses on concepts such as poverty, social marginalization, the power of the "yuppie," and so on.[38] In some cities, of course, a class-based politics is supplemented by an attention to racialized power relations.[39] Similarly, the supplication reminds us that title to this land rests on the dispossession of Japanese-Canadians. However, it also reminds us of other "troubled entanglements of possession and dispossession, settlement and unsettlement"[40] in the settler-city. In particular, the supplication surfaces the link between colonial dispossessions and contemporary gentrification in ways that are not always made explicit.[41]

Neil Smith alerts us to the application of frontier discourse to gentrification in the contemporary city, whereby "urban pioneers" become the new folk heroes, serving to forge a revived "national spirit." The preexistent urban population, of course, is imagined, like the indigenous populations of the West, as "less than social, a part of the physical environment." Despite its centrality to the U.S. imagination, Smith also suggests that frontier mythology has become increasingly generalized, cropping up across the world. The frontier myth, Smith argues, does important ideological work, whether in the nineteenth-century dispossession of indigenous populations in the West, or the contemporary inner city, serving to "rationalize and legitimate a process of conquest," displacing social conflict into the realm of naturalized myth.[42] While Smith points to the ways the frontier has been wrenched from its historical and geographic contexts, I have argued that the settler-city is still "Indian country" in ways that complicate mythmaking. Vancouver's Downtown Eastside, as noted, contains a significant indigenous population, many of whom carry the psychic, material, and bodily scars of continued colonial oppression. This is also space claimed by several First Nations, yet the off-reserve natives of the city are not necessarily included in those claims. Legally invisible, the situation of urban natives is particularly challenging, given the presumed mismatch between indigenous identity and urban space.

As we have seen, native claims to land do, occasionally, figure in contemporary struggles over gentrification. Thus, for example, the campaign to secure CRAB Park involved native activists, and linked a community claim with historic native uses of the site. The park now contains a number of sites of particular native significance (fig. 5.3). On the other side of the conflict, media accounts of the Downtown Eastside as a space of anomie and emptiness occasionally mention native people (usually in negative terms). But that said, the tendency, from all quarters, has been to render native people invisible; perhaps because the categories "city" and "native" appear inherently opposed. Partly because of tactical necessity, but partly, perhaps, because of lingering racisms, the stories and mappings of the Downtown Eastside also lend themselves toward an essentialized construction of place, in which a homogeneous community with a unified story bounds itself in opposition to a threatening outside. Such stark binaries can generate ethical ambiguities. The Japanese-Canadians of Cordova Street, for example, are not always as central in community narratives as they perhaps should be; rather, the white resource worker seems to take on a mythic centrality. Also uncomfortably placed in local oppositional politics are the First Nations' people who make up a significant proportion of the local population. Even though native people are undeniably caught up in gentrification, this has all too often been ignored.[43] Yet these omissions are unsettled by the supplication that links race and displacement. Constructions of the Downtown Eastside also place men at the center of the landscape, whether as the damaged skid row denizen or the hardy resource

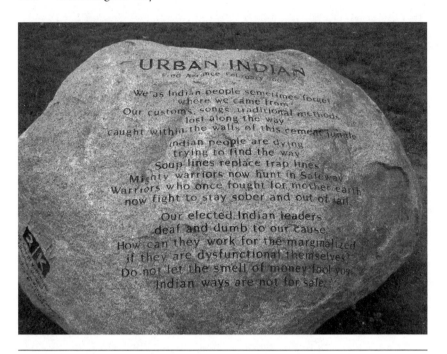

Figure 5.3 'Urban Indian', CRAB Park, Vancouver. Inscription by Fred Arrance. Photograph by author.

worker.[44] In also resituating women in this landscape, the supplication alerts us to the slippery politics of "placing."

This is important when we recognize the obvious intersections of class, race, and gender as they relate to land. The concentration of many poor, native people—many of them women—in spaces such as the Downtown Eastside is no accident. The "violent expulsions and spatial containment of aboriginal peoples," notes one observer, caught up with the remapping of colonial space, have forced many native peoples to the urban margins, in a dynamic "consolidated over three hundred years of colonization."[45] And as Evelyn Peters reminds us, these colonial processes are also gendered. She documents the ways in which the rights of First Nations' women in Canada to own reserve property were severely circumscribed by law. Combined with legislation that caused Indian women marrying non-Indian men to lose their status, First Nations' women are more likely than men to be excluded from band membership and residence on the reserve. As a result, many native women have migrated to urban areas, and are now statistically overrepresented.[46] Although Peters documents the ways in which native women have created their own support networks and laid cultural claim to urban space, others have reminded us of the violent consequences of this disenfranchisement. Driven by addiction and poverty, some First Nations' women have been forced into the sex trade, selling their one remaining alienable entitlement—their body. But the spaces in which these women often work can be violent. The Downtown Eastside offers horrific evidence of this.

In her analysis of the spaces of the sex trade, Lisa Sanchez argues that "[v]iolence needs a space, and the law provides for it."[47] The law—through property—shapes a variety of "interaction spaces" within which commercial sex is more or less tolerated. In public places, the state engages in periodic forceful displacement and harassment of women sex trade workers (partly at the behest of local property owners). The effect is to force women into concealed spaces, thus increasing their vulnerability to the sexual violence of men. While such violences are illegal, they are not radically distinct from law, Sanchez insists. Rather, law is said to effectively "create a safe space for violence—a space where violence has no witness." Hence, "law constructs boundaries between legitimate and illegitimate violence and produces sociospatial zones in which violence is tolerated."[48]

The Downtown Eastside is such a space. Driven by poverty and addiction, many women work as sex-trade workers in what is known as the "low-track." A staggering number—over sixty to date—have been reported missing. Friends and family have long feared that many of these women were murdered. Almost half of the "missing women," as they have become known, are Aboriginal. The disappearances date back to the 1970s. Despite sustained appeals from family and friends, the institutional response, until recently, has been muted at best. For years, the authorities did not appear to have acknowledged any systematic or sinister pattern in these disappearances. Finally, in the Fall of 2002, a suspect was charged with fifteen counts of murder.

I pause before saying much about these disappearances. Assuming, as now seems likely, that many were killed, the scale of violence, and the deafening institutional indifference toward their fate, beggars belief. This of course cannot be explained by the workings of property alone. However, enjoined by the subtle claims of the supplication, it seems important to consider whether prevailing property relations are implicated. Although the supplication was installed before institutional recognition of the missing women occurred, its acknowledgment of the gendered and racialized workings of property's spaces seems significant. As noted, the concentration of many aboriginal women in marginal urban spaces such as the Downtown Eastside has everything to do with colonial logics of dispossession and patriarchal power.[49] Ambiguities in prostitution law have also worked to create dangerous spaces into which many women have been driven, especially as gentrifying middle-class homeowners have put pressure on the police to remove prostitutes from residential areas in what one observer terms a "discourse of disposal."[50] As prostitutes, women are also legally imagined as objects of ownership, engaged in contractual relations.

This presents the sale of a woman's body as an entrepreneurial and willed act, rather than one borne of desperation and violence; it also, perhaps, invites the reification of that body by the male "owner." Imagined thus, such bodies can easily lose any entitlement to personhood.[51]

Colonial dispossession, the displacements of gentrification and the logic of property—my central themes in this book—here combine to locate particular people in violent spaces. The generalized indifference to their fate perhaps reflects the prevailing indifference to the urban poor: the aboriginality that makes many of the missing women "out of place" within the city may also place them "out of mind." As Sherene Razack argues in her analysis of the death of Pamela George, an Ojibway woman who was murdered while working as a prostitute in Regina, Canada; Pamela George was "considered to belong to a space to which violence routinely occurs, and to have a body that is routinely violated."[52] People have not only died *on* the land, to return to the supplication, but suffered violence *because of* the land. Aboriginal people are not alone in experiencing property's violence. However, they have perhaps felt its violences most sharply.

Conclusions

In this book, I have sought to complicate and "unsettle" property in order to demonstrate its importance to the city. As the supplication reminds us, the ownership model does not do a very good job (except, perhaps, ideologically) in making sense of the meanings and moralities of urban property. Private, individualized property is not the only form of estate. Rather than settling social life, property emerges as a site for moral and political ambiguity, contest, and struggle. Dispossessed groups voice their grievances, in part, through a language of property. The very beginnings of property are contested, as are its unfolding. Property, perhaps, even provides a ground for violence. The city, despite appearances, is an unsettled place.

Every story needs an ending. In the case of property, it's often hard to fix beginnings; similarly, endings are always contingent. However, let me offer a rather unsettling one for Cordova Street by peeling off the letters on the supplication to reveal what the development application actually sought. For the "land" on which real people "built, born, fought, loved, died" was *not* to be "improved"; it has yet to attain its "highest and best use" in purely monetary terms. The development that was subsequently built was St. James Place, developed by St. Luke's Society, associated with the neighboring St. James Anglican Church. Low-income seniors are now housed in twenty-seven units of nonprofit housing; this in an area in which such affordable alternatives are under threat from gentrification.

In one sense, it would have been easier for my story and its implied polarities if the site had been turned into yuppie lofts, rather than nonprofit housing. Yet again, the supplication is ambivalent, or perhaps multivalent. It is not a straightforward protest against gentrification. The artist would have known the future of the site: in that sense, the supplication does not conform to any neat binaries between dominant and oppositional visions of land development, but complicates and mediates between them.

Clearly, we can read the supplication as a critique of property; whether it is notions of highest and best use, the spatialized reifications of property, colonial displacements and dispossessions, property's violences, and so on. All seem close to the ownership model of property. The supplication also alerts us to those property claims that "do not make it onto our property radar screen, or appear only dimly there."[53] The ownership model enacts property, in other words, in ways that militate against recognition of these alternative possibilities, such as the collective entitlement of poor renters to inner-city space, or the claims of indigenous people to "improved" urban land.

For the ownership model does not exhaust property. Property, as Marx insisted, is not reducible to private property.[54] The city is crosscut by claims to land that are neither private nor statist. Lacking formal rights-status, these claims nevertheless are defended, articulated, and mobilized. C. B. Macpherson, in particular, notes that the meanings and political possibilities of property escape the confines of the ownership model. Moreover, the "right to exclude" has, as its necessary concomitant, the "right not to be excluded."[55] While the scope of property rights have been narrowed over time, they continue to contain within them redistributive and collective possibilities that are more than historical relics.[56]

Remembering that, for a wide range of religions, a supplication can also mean a prayer to a deity, the installation on Cordova Street also perhaps alludes to the church, the developer of the site, and to broader theological understandings of land.[57] Although Locke rests his story of property, in part, on divine revelation, the church's reading of property is far from fixed. For while Judeo-Christian principles have facilitated the ascendancy of an individualistic model of property, both Catholic and Protestant Churches contain within them appeals to a "stewardship" model of property that regards private ownership of land as encumbered with a "social mortgage," in the words of Pope John Paul II.[58]

Property rights in this sense are like all other rights; they have an expansionary logic.[59] While prevailing social relations encourage the dominance of the ownership model, this is not the only possibility. In this book, I have tried, in part, to uncover some of those other possibilities. Collective claim making endures. There are undeniable tensions, yet, the commons is not fully enclosed but always open, like private property itself, to remaking and reworking.[60] I have also tried to suggest here that the commons is not as radically dissimilar from private property as one might suppose. Collective claims can be enacted using ideological vocabularies similar to those that sustain private property, which itself has an undeniable collective quality to it. It is this that makes me ambivalent about recent calls to embrace Henri Lefebvre's notion of the "right to the city," embracing the "rights to freedom, to individualization in socialization, to habitat, and to inhabit. . . . [t]he right to the *oeuvre*, to appropriation." While such a right may be productive, it is unclear why Lefebvre insists on clearly distinguishing it from "the right to property." Although I can see that the former may be compromised by the exercise of a narrowly defined property right, I have suggested here that the "right to the city" may also be *realized* through property, when defined in more expansionary terms.[61] For far too long "property rights" have been the exclusive fief of the Right. Perhaps it is time for a reappropriation.

A supplication is also a petition to or for a person or thing. To petition for the weak is to request something of the powerful. But a petition is also a common law remedy against the Crown for recovery of property that has been unjustly seized. So when we read the supplication, perhaps we are being reminded of unjust seizures in the past, whether those of Japanese-Canadians or Musqueam. Perhaps we are also being reminded of the looming threat of dispossession that hangs over the entire Downtown Eastside. The apparent quietness of contemporary possession is shown to be layered on past and future violences and dispossessions.

The supplication not only maps these dispossessions, but makes space for those entitlements destroyed as a result. Similarly, the institutional effacement of those entitlements that do not conform to the categories of the ownership model is something I have tried to consider in this book. Our collective failure to acknowledge these property claims, it seems to me, is significant. It affects the ways we analyze urban dynamics and conflicts, for example. It makes the importance of urban property claims to indigenous politics or inner-city activism easier to overlook. An array of other urban issues, ranging from planning, community gardening, surfing, squatting, community policing, and homelessness are all, in various ways, shaped by dominant and alternative understandings and practices relating to landed property. Property provides an important political vocabulary that gives individuals and groups in the city a language for naming, blaming, and claiming. Such claims can be "private" (although even private property is a good deal more collective than the ownership model allows), but they may also be made in the names of communities, whether of interest or place. That we as scholars have sometimes failed to recognize these conversations about property speaks less to their empirical purchase, I suspect, than the power of the ownership model in closing down enquiry.

This is not only analytically significant. It is also ethically consequential. The ownership model shapes political and ethical discourse on the city. It offers a morally impoverished vocabulary for reflecting on urban affairs. Urban planning, for example, is imagined as a discourse on land use, not land rights. Issues such as gentrification in Vancouver's Downtown East-side are consequently framed in particular ways.

As a consequence, property is conceived in limited ways. That the poor could claim any sort of entitlement beyond, say, the diminished rights they might have to individual rental units, seems impossible from this perspective. That First Nations may have enduring and viable rights to urban lands seems hard to countenance. Yet to the extent that such claims are overridden or even simply ignored, a grave injustice is done. But even if acknowledged, the ownership model can often skew the moral response. Thus it is, for example, that pundits can argue for the creation of housing units for those displaced by gentrification in cheaper areas, miles from the Downtown Eastside. Thus it is that neoconservative commentators can feel that justice has been done when they advocate the settlement of native claims through individualized private property.

This raises an interesting question, beyond the scope of the present study: What would the city look like if these multiple and overlapping property claims were formally acknowledged? What would urban planning look like? How would official discourse on gentrification or native claims, for example, change? How would the settler-society reimagine the security of "its" entitlements? How would my understandings of "my" property change to acknowledge others? Put more bluntly, could the city change, given the hegemony of the ownership model? The geographies at the core of that model, I have suggested, are immensely persuasive. Can we then embrace the complexity of an "edge politics" when we live in a world of bright lines and boundaries?

The supplication alerts us to the fact that we have always lived in both worlds. While the ownership model exerts a powerful imaginative force, it is does not capture (for it cannot capture) the empirical and political diversity of property in the city. Property is enacted through sharp boundaries, fixity, and empty cadastral spaces. Yet property claims are also realized through overlap, layering, and movement. The supplication also celebrates property at the same time as it damns it. Land and its propertied spaces is the site not only for fighting and dying, but also for life, love and birth. To identify the multiple dispossessions on this site surely presupposes a normative claim to ownership of some form. Property, I have argued here, can be the problem and the solution, the threat and that which is threatened. Property relations can be configured as exclusionary, violent, and marginalizing. They can also be a means by which people find meaning in the world, anchor themselves to communities, and contest dominant power relations. To get at these multiple possibilities, we need to unsettle dominant treatments and recognize property's diverse meanings and often unsettled politics.

Notes

Preface

1. Thompson, Edward P. (1975) *Whigs and Hunters: The Origins of the Black Acts.* Allen Lane, London. Thompson mentions rural resistance in the market town of Wokingham, some five miles away. Ironically, this is now one of the richest towns in Britain, with housing prices to match.

2. In 1596, the "chief inhabitants" of the parish felt compelled to enter into a compact to "suppresse pilferers Backbyters, hedge breakers, & myscheveous persons, and all suche as be prowde, dissentious & arrogant persons." (copy with author) Discussed in Hindle, Steve. (1999) "Hierarchy and Community in the Elizabethan Parish: The Swallowfield Articles of 1596," *Historical Journal* 42:3, October, 835–851.

3. *Webster's New World Dictionary of the American Language,* 2nd College Edition, New York: Simon and Schuster, 1980.

4. Quoted in Donahue, Charles. (1998) "Property Law" *The New Encyclopaedia Britannica* Vol. 26, 15th ed., 180–205 at 191.

5. *Webster's New World Dictionary.*

6. Abramson, Allen, and Dimitrios Theodossopoulos, eds, (2000) *Land, Law, and Environment: Mythical Land, Legal Boundaries.* London: Pluto Press.

7. An important exception is neo-Marxist urban scholarship, at its heyday in the 1980s. Thus, for example, Roweis and Scott take as their point of departure "the deep structure of urban property relations." Roweis, Shoukry T., and Allen J. Scott. (1981) "The Urban Land Question." In Dear, Michael, and Allen J. Scott, eds. *Urbanization and Urban Planning in Capitalist Society,* London: Methuen, 123–158 at 140. Badcock argues that urban land and housing markets serve to distribute real income through various direct and indirect mechanisms, emphasizing in particular the distinction between renters and owner-occupiers. Badcock, Blair. (1984) *Unfairly Structured Cities.* Oxford: Basil Blackwell. Incorporation theory concerned itself with the ideology of ownership and its effects on working class militancy. Pratt, Geraldine. (1989) "Incorporation Theory and the Reproduction of Community Fabric." In Wolch, Jennifer, and Michael Dear, eds. *The Power of Geography: How Territory Shapes Social Life.* Boston: Unwin Hyman, 291–315. My goal here is not only to consider the significance of private property to socio-spatial relations, but also to acknowledge other forms of property.

8. Rose, Carol. (1994) *Property and Persuasion.* Boulder, Colo.: Westview Press.

9. See for example, Blomley, Nicholas, David Delaney, and Richard T. Ford, eds. (2001) *The Legal Geographies Reader: Law, Power, and Space.* Oxford: Blackwell.

157

10. Marx, Karl. (1976) *Capital: A Critique of Political Economy. Volume I.* Harmondsworth: Penguin Books, 713–733; 732–733.
11. Jacobs, Jane. (1996) *Edge of Empire: Postcolonialism and the City.* London: Routledge, 104.
12. Quoted in Waldron, Jeremy. (1988) *The Right to Private Property.* Oxford: Clarendon Press, at 38.
13. Macpherson, Crawford Brough. (1987) *The Rise and Fall of Economic Justice and Other Essays.* Oxford: Oxford University Press, at 77.

Chapter 1

1. Sarti, Robert. (1997) "Homeless-Advocate Hotel Evicts Tenants," *Vancouver Sun,* Oct. 14, 1997, A2; Shaw, Gillian, and Doug Ward. (1997) "Hotels Evict 100 in Face of Homeless Plan," *Vancouver Sun,* July 8, 1997, B1, B6.
2. Bromley, Daniel W. (1991) Environment and Economy: Property Rights and Public Policy. Oxford: Blackwell, 2.
3. Hoebel, E. A. (1966) *Anthropology: The Study of Man.* New York: McGraw-Hill, 424.
4. Marx, Karl, and Friedrich Engels. (1975) *Collected Works.* Vol. 5. New York: International Publishers, 32.
5. Singer, Joseph. (2000) *Entitlement: The Paradoxes of Property.* New Haven, Conn.: Yale University Press, 2–3. Underkuffler similarly notes the dominance of what she terms the "absolute approach" to property in U.S. jurisprudence (which assumes that property is objectively definable, is set apart from social context, and represents and protects the sphere of legitimate, absolute individual autonomy), which has tended to downplay an alternative understanding of property (the comprehensive approach). Underkuffler, Laura S. (1990) "On Property: An Essay." *Yale Law Journal,* 100, 1, 127–148. Clearly, the meanings of property vary within the common law world. Arguably the degree to which the ownership model is open to alternative interpretations also varies. However, I think a case can be made for its centrality as a core organizing device.
6. Singer, Joseph. (1996) "No Right to Exclude: Public and Private Accommodations and Private Property." *Northwestern University Law Review,* 90, 4, 1283–1497.
7. Singer, "No Right to Exclude," 1435.
8. I draw here from Jonette Watson Hamilton's (2002) discussion of legal categorization. She notes the importance of a spatial metaphor to this theory of categorization, such that categories are understood as spatial containers for their members, with "interiors, exteriors, and boundaries. The essential physical representation of a container in the metaphorical sense is that of a bounded region in space"; "Theories of Categorization: A Case Study of Cheques," *Canadian Journal of Law and Society,* 17, 1, 115–138 at 122.
9. See, for example, Pipes, Richard. (1999) *Property and Freedom.* New York: Vintage Books. Although common and state property are acknowledged, private property is at the core of his discussion.
10. Donahue, Charles. (1980) "The Future of the Concept of Property Predicted from Its Past." In Pennock, J. Roland, and John W. Chapman, eds. *Nomos* 22, New York: New York University Press, 28–68, at 32.
11. For surveys see, for example, Grunebaum, James O. (1987) *Private Ownership.* New York: Routledge & Kegan Paul; and Waldron, Jeremy. (1988) *The Right to Private Property.* Oxford: Clarendon. For U.S. discussions see Nedelsky, Jennifer. (1990) *Private Property and the Limits of American Constitutionalism.* Chicago: University of Chicago Press; or Ely, James W. (1998) *The Guardian of Every Other Right.* Oxford: Oxford University Press. For an analysis of property rights in Canada, see Vogt, Roy. (1999) *Whose Property? The Deepening Conflict between Private Property and Democracy in Canada.* Toronto: University of Toronto Press.
12. Macpherson, Crawford Brough (1978) "The Meaning of Property." In *Property: Mainstream and Critical Positions.* Crawford Brough Macpherson, editor. Toronto: University of Toronto Press, 1–14 at 10.
13. Geisler, Charles. (2000) "Property Pluralism." In Geisler, Charles, and Gail Daneker, eds. *Property and Values: Alternatives to Public and Private Ownership.* Washington D.C.: Island Press, 65–86 at 65, my emphasis.
14. Rose, Carol, *Property and Persuasion,* 110.
15. Macpherson, "The Meaning of Property."

16. Jacobs, Harvey, ed. (1998) *Who Owns America? Social Conflict over Property Rights.* Madison: University of Wisconsin Press.

17. Nedelsky, *Private Property,* 248.

18. Sax, Joseph L. (2001) *Playing Darts with a Rembrandt: Public and Private Rights in Cultural Treasures.* Ann Arbor: University of Michigan Press.

19. Nedelsky, *Private Property.* Bakan, Joel. (1997) *Just Words: Constitutional Rights and Social Wrongs.* Toronto: University of Toronto Press; Macklem, Patrick. (1990) "Property, Status, and Workplace Organizing." *University of Toronto Law Journal,* 40, 74. The taxonomies of property can allow for invidious distinctions; see for example Cohen, David, and Allen C. Hutchinson (1990) "Of Persons and Property: The Politics of Legal Taxonomy." *Dalhousie Law Journal,* 13, 1, 20–54. Marx also pointed to the public/private distinction as a central ideological component of capitalism. See Marx, Karl. (1975) "On the Jewish Question." In Colletti, L. ed. *Early Writings.* Harmondsworth: Penguin.

20. Nedelsky, *Private Property,* at 54.

21. Hutchinson, A. C. (1991) "Crits and Crickets: A Deconstructive Spin (or Was It Googly?)" In Devlin, R. F., ed. *Canadian Perspectives on Legal Theory.* Toronto: Emond-Montgomery, at 83.

22. For explorations and critiques, see, for example, Unger, Roberto. (1983) "The Critical Legal Studies Movement." *Harvard Law Review,* 96, 3, 320–432; or Clark, Gordon L. (1985) *Judges and the Cities.* Chicago: Chicago University Press.

23. Lefebvre, Henri. (1976) "Reflections on the Politics of Space." *Antipode,* 8, 30–37 at 31.

24. For an example, see Blomley, Nicholas K., and Joel C. Bakan. (1992) "Spacing Out: Towards a Critical Geography of Law." *Osgoode Hall Law Journal,* 30, 3, 661–690. For a discussion of "splicing," see Blomley, Nicholas. (2003) "From "What?" to "So what?": Law and Geography in Retrospect." In Holder, Jane, and Carolyn Harrison, eds. *Law and Geography Current Legal Issues.* Vol. 5 Oxford: Oxford University Press, 17–34.

25. Singer, *Entitlement,* 30.

26. Walzer, Michael. (1984) "Liberalism and the Art of Separation." *Political Theory,* 12, 3, 315–330. This is not to say, however, that the spatial boundaries of property operate, in reality, as they are supposed to. See Blomley, Nicholas. (forthcoming) "Law and Geography: Lessons from Beatrix Potter." *The Canadian Geographer.*

27. Walzer, "Liberalism," 314.

28. Quoted in McClain, Linda. (1995) "Inviolability and Privacy: The Castle, the Sanctuary and the Body." *Yale Journal of Law and the Humanities,* 7, 2, 195–242. Interestingly, she turns the masculinity of Coke's maxim around, arguing that principles of legal inviolability can productively be used to advance feminist principles.

29. Robertson, Michael. (1995) "Property and Ideology." *Canadian Journal of Law and Jurisprudence,* 8, No. 2, 275–296 at 282.

30. Bowles, Samuel, and Herbert Gintis. (1987) *Democracy and Capitalism: Property, Community, and the Contradictions of Social Thought.* New York: Basic Books, 17.

31. Hohfeld famously identified various pairings of "jural" relationships that may apply to property. Hohfeld, Wesley Newcomb. (1919) *Some Fundamental Legal Conceptions as Applied in Judicial Reasoning.* New Haven, Conn.: Yale University Press. "In Hohfeldian terms, Western law tends to ascribe to the possessor of a thing: the right to possess the thing with a duty on everyone else to stay off, the privilege of using the thing with no right in anyone else to prevent him (coupled with a right in the possessor to prevent others from using the thing), a power to transfer any and all of his rights, powers, and privileges with a liability in anyone to be the object of the conveyance (coupled with a disability in everyone else to change and an immunity in the possessor from change of those same rights, privileges and powers)." Donahue, "Property Law," 180–205, at 32.

32. See Steinberg's use of Mark Twain's fable, "Slide Mountain" and his discussion of "airspace": "a three-dimensional abstraction," airspace has become "a *thing* that could be owned and sold." Steinberg, Theodore. (1995) *Slide Mountain or the Folly of Owning Nature.* Berkeley: University of California Press, 146.

33. "Making the owner-thing relation central suppresses our consideration of the relationships structured by property rights." Singer, *Entitlement,* 30.

34. Quoted in Steinberg, *Slide Mountain* at 13.

35. The institution of private property, in this sense, appears as a natural right. Richard Pipes claims that "acquisitiveness" is universal in human and animal societies and that "claims to

exclusive use are especially emphatic in respect to land . . . Private property is not merely a legal or conventional but a natural institution. As such it is no more a subject of moralizing (unless it be for its excesses) than mortality or any other aspect of existence over which humans have at best minimal control." Pipes, *Property,* 116. For Ardrey: "He who has will probably hold. We do not know why; it is simply so." Ardrey, Robert. (1966) *The Territorial Imperative.* New York: Atheneum, 116–117.

36. Case law tends to affirm the principle that property rights are to be understood as spatially bound. See for example *Summach et al v. Allen et al.* (2003 BCCA 176) in which the British Columbia Court of Appeal ruled that a vendor did not have a duty to disclose to the purchasers of a property that the public park next door was used as a nude beach and that sexual activity occurred on a nearby dock given that "the alleged defect was occurring outside the boundaries of the property purchased."

37. See, for example, Mitchell's discussion of spatial enframing: Mitchell, Timothy. (1991) *Colonising Egypt.* Berkeley: University of California Press; and Sack's influential discussion of territoriality, noting the ways in which power can be reified such that "territory appears as the agent doing the controlling," Sack, Robert D. (1986) *Human Territoriality: Its Theory and History.* Cambridge: Cambridge University Press, 33.

38. Cresswell, Tim. (1996) *In Place/Out of Place: Geography, Ideology, and Transgression.* Minneapolis: University of Minnesota Press, 159.

39. Ibid.

40. Scott, James. (1998) *Seeing Like a State: How Certain Schemes to Improve the Human Condition Have Failed.* New Haven, Conn.: Yale University Press, 3.

41. Cohen and Hutchinson, "Of Persons and Property," 23.

42. Rose, Carol. (1998) "The Several Futures of Property: Of Cyberspace and Folk Tales, Emission Trades and Ecosystems." *Minnesota Law Review,* 83 (129), 129–182 at 132, 140.

43. Ibid., 141.

44. Pipes, *Property and Freedom,* 63, 86.

45. Bethell, Tom. (1998) *The Noblest Triumph: Property and Prosperity through the Ages.* New York: St Martin's Press, 45.

46. "Communities of individuals have relied on institutions resembling neither the state nor the market to govern some resource systems with reasonable degrees of success over long periods of time": Ostrom, Elinor. (1990) *Governing the Commons: The Evolution of Institutions for Collective Action.* Cambridge: Cambridge University Press, 1. See also Bromley, Daniel W. (1991) *Environment and Economy: Property Rights and Public Policy.* Oxford: Blackwell; Rose, *Property and Persuasion;* The International Association for the Study of Common Property (*http://www.indiana.edu/~iascp/*).

47. Gibson-Graham J.K. (1996) *The End of Capitalism (as We Knew It): A Feminist Critique of Political Economy.* Oxford: Blackwell, 258.

48. Harris, J. W. (1995) "Private and Non-Private Property: What Is the Difference?" *Law Quarterly Review,* 111, 421–444, at 438.

49. See Patton, Paul. (2000) "The Translation of Indigenous Land into Property." *Parallax,* 6, 1, 25–38. Patton notes other possible models of translation that do not privilege the Western model as the master term. John Borrows also points to the need to be more dialogical, and recognize the possibility of legal categories that are "in-between," rather than simply treating Western conceptions as the master term. Borrows, John. (2002) *Recovering Canada: The Resurgence of Indigenous Law.* Toronto: University of Toronto Press.

50. Seed, Patricia. (1995) *Ceremonies of Possession in Europe's Conquest of the New World, 1492–1640.* Cambridge: Cambridge University Press, 39.

51. Banner, Stuart. (1999) "Two Properties, One Land: Law and Space in Nineteenth-Century New Zealand." *Law and Social Inquiry,* 24, 4, 807–852 at 832.

52. Ibid., 810.

53. Ibid., 847.

54. Borrows, John. (1997) "Living between Water and Rocks: First Nations, Environmental Planning, and Democracy." *University of Toronto Law Journal,* 47, 417–468 at 430, 431.

55. Original emphasis. Royal Commission on Aboriginal Peoples (1998) *Report of the Royal Commission on Aboriginal Peoples: Restructuring the Relationship,* vol. 2, part 2. Ottawa: Canada Communication Group, 439. Settler states also tend to regard native lands as public land, which can be disposed of without native approval or knowledge, making native peo-

ples trespassers on land they regard as their own. Kedar, Alexandre. (2001) "The Legal Transformation of Ethnic Geography: Israeli Law and the Palestinian Landholder 1948–1967." *New York University Journal of International Law and Politics,* 33, 4, 923–1000.

56. Royal Commission on Aboriginal Peoples, *Report,* 458.
57. Bryan, Bradley. (2000) "Property as Ontology: On Aboriginal and English Understandings of Ownership." *Canadian Journal of Law and Jurisprudence,* 13, 1, January, 3–31 at 3.
58. Sax, Joseph. (1984) "Do Communities Have Rights? The National Parks as a Laboratory of New Ideas." *University of Pittsburgh Law Review,* 45, 499–511 at 506.
59. Dimas, Pete R. (1999) *Progress and a Mexican American Community's Struggle for Existence: Phoenix's Golden Gate Barrio.* New York: Peter Lang. Dimas situates this struggle in the context of a sustained conflict between Chicanos and the dominant culture "over land and cultural values" (145). See also Luna, Guadalupe T. (1998) "Chicana/Chicano Land Tenure in the Agrarian Domain: On the Edge of a 'Naked Knife,' " *Michigan Journal of Race and Law,* 4, 39–144.
60. Bromley, *Environment and Economy,* 2.
61. Macpherson, "The Meaning of Property," 3.
62. Laclau, Ernesto, and Chantal Mouffe. (1985) *Hegemony and Socialist Strategy: Toward a Radical Democratic Politics.* London: Verso.
63. Felstine, William L. F., Richard Abel, and Austin Sarat. (1980–81) "The Emergence and Transformation of Disputes: Naming, Blaming, Claiming." *Law and Society Review,* 15, 3–4, 631–654.
64. Williams, Patricia J. (1991) *The Alchemy of Race and Rights.* Cambridge, Mass.: Harvard University Press, 164.
65. Hale, Robert L. (1923) "Coercion and Distribution in a Supposedly Noncoercive State." *Political Science Quarterly,* 38, 470–494.
66. Cohen, Morris R. (1927) "Property and Sovereignty." *Cornell Law Quarterly,* 13, 8–30 at 12. On legal realism, see Minda, Garry. (1995) *Postmodern Legal Movements.* New York: New York University Press, 24–43.
67. Singer, Joseph William. (2000) "Property and Social Relations: From Title to Entitlement." In Geisler, Charles, and Gail Daneker, eds. *Property and Values: Alternatives to Public and Private Ownership,* Washington D.C.: Island Press, 3–20 at 5.
68. Singer, "Property and Social Relations," 6.
69. Bromley, Daniel W. (1998) "Rousseau's Revenge: The Demise of the Freehold Estate." In Jacobs, Harvey M. ed. *Who Owns America? Social Conflict over Property Rights.* Madison: University of Wisconsin Press, 19–28, at 25.
70. Nedelsky, *Private Property,* 248.
71. Grey, Thomas. (1980) "The Disintegration of Property." In Pennock, J. Roland, and John W. Chapman, eds. *Nomos,* 22, 69–85.
72. Singer, "No Right to Exclude," 1459.
73. Gibson-Graham, *The End of Capitalism,* ix.
74. Gibson-Graham, *The End of Capitalism,* ix, xi.
75. In this I am engaging in a form of "external" legal critique: that is, challenging the closures of legal understandings and categories by situating them in the world. However, unlike much legal scholarship, I will do this by paying more attention to the geographies of property than to its history. For an example of the latter, see Nedelsky, *Private Property.* I also differ from those who seek to complicate or critique liberal notions by locating property outside the West. See Hann, *Property Relations;* Abramson and Theodossopoulos, *Land, Law, and Environment.* In so doing, I also draw from "internal" legal critique that seeks to make sense of the internal contradictions of law, and reveal its "loose ends that exist as traces of resistance and insurrection" (Peller, "The Metaphysics of American Law," 1284). See Blomley (*Law, Space, and the Geographies of Power,* 14–24) for a discussion of legal critique.
76. Gibson-Graham, *The End of Capitalism,* xi, 23. For examples, see Lee's discussion of businesses that are technically suboptimal, yet able to trade on an economy of "regard." Lee, Roger. (2000) "Shelter from the storm? Geographies of regard in the worlds of horticultural consumption and production." *Geoforum* 31, 137–157; or the phenomenon of Local Exchange and Trading Schemes (LETS), Lee, Roger. (2002) "Nice Maps, Shame about the Theory? Thinking geographically about the economic." *Progress in Human Geography,* 26, 3, 333–355.

77. Grunebaum, *Private Ownership*, 8.
78. Geisler, "Property Pluralism," 65–86 at 80.
79. Singer, "No Right to Exclude," 1462–3.
80. Ibid., 1463.
81. Davis, John Emmeus. (2000) "Homemaking: The Pragmatic Politics of Third Sector Housing." In Geisler, Charles, and Gail Daneker, eds. *Property and Values: Alternatives to Public and Private Ownership*. Washington D.C.: Island Press, 233–258 at 233.
82. Abromowitz, David M. (2000) "An Essay on Community Land Trusts: Toward Permanently Affordable Housing." In Geisler, Charles, and Gail Daneker, eds. *Property and Values: Alternatives to Public and Private Ownership*. Washington D.C.: Island Press, 213–231; Davis, "Homemaking," 247.
83. Kayden, Jerold S. (2000) *Privately Owned Public Space: The New York City Experience*. New York: John Wiley and Sons, vii.
84. Jacobs, *Property and Persuasion*, 290.
85. Jacobs, Jane. (1961) *The Death and Life of Great American Cities*. New York: Vintage, 50, 35.
86. Newman, Oscar. (1972) *Defensible Space: Crime Prevention through Environmental Design*. New York: Macmillan. Newman however is adamant that these claims to public space should be essentially private, not collective. Empirical evidence suggests the existence, however, of a much more complicated and often collective set of claims. Blomley, Nicholas. "Un-real Estate: Proprietary Space and Public Gardening," unpublished paper.
87. Wilson, James Q., and George L. Kelling. (1982) "Broken Windows." *Atlantic Monthly*, 249, 3: 29–38.
88. I could go on. For example, it was clear that the "private" garden was also deeply "public," due not only to the reach of the state (for example, bylaws regulating watering, tree removal, and so on) but more clearly to the relations between neighbors and the wider community. Decisions about whether and how often to cut the grass, or what to grow where, for example, were not "self-regarding." Although the spatial markers of property were clearly in evidence (boundaries, for example) their meaning was often opaque, and always societal, rather than individualistic.
89. Rose, "The Several Futures of Property," 132.
90. William Whyte details the configurations that encourage users of public space to claim space with others.
91. Rose, "The Several Futures of Property," 132. See also Ingerson, Alice. (1997) "Urban Land as Common Property." Originally published in *Land Lines*, 9, 1. (*http://www.lincolninst.edu/landline.1997/march/commonp.html*; accessed June 6, 2002)
92. Steinberg, *Slide Mountain*, 15.
93. On counterpublics, see Fraser, Nancy. (1990) "Rethinking the Public Sphere: A Contribution to Actually Existing Democracy." *Social Text*, 25/26, 56–79.
94. Razzaz, Omar M. (1993) "Examining Property Rights and Investment in Informal Settlements: The Case of Jordan." *Land Economics*, 69, 4, 341–355 at 342.
95. Ibid., 341.
96. *http://pacificwaverider.com/surftalk/tribal_law.shtml*. (Accessed September 30, 2002)
97. Hening, Glenn. (no date) "The Stain on the Soul of Surfing," 4. *http://www.surflink.com/features/stain 4.html*. (Accessed September 30, 2002).
98. Paul Holmes, editor of *LongBoard* magazine, quoted in Campbell, Duncan. (2002) "Surf Wars Hit California." *Guardian*, March 12, 2002. Accessed online at *http://www.guardian.co.uk/elsewhere/journalist/story/0,7792,666039,00.html* (September 26, 2002).
99. Campbell, Duncan. (2002) "Surf Wars Hit California." *Guardian*, March 12, 2002. Accessed online at *http://www.guardian.co.uk/elsewhere/journalist/story/0,7792,666039,00.html* (September 26, 2002).
100. See the manifestoes of groups such as the New York–based, Green Guerillas, who claim: "It's Your City: Dig It" (*http://www.greenguerillas.org*) (September 30, 2002)
101. Schmelzkopf, K. (1995) "Urban Community Gardens as a Contested Space." *Geographical Review*, 85, 3, 364–379, at 379.
102. Gibson, Kristina. (2002) " '11,000 vacant lots, why take our garden plots?' Community garden preservation strategies in New York City's gentrified Lower East Side." Paper presented at Rights to the City conference, Rome, at 12. Copy with author.

103. Linn, Karl. (1999) "Reclaiming the Sacred Commons." *New Village Journal,* 1. Accessed online at *http://www.newvillage.net/1sacredcommon.html.* September 30, 2002.

104. *http://www.squat.freeserve.co.uk/story/ch1.html*

105. For example, see the discussion of the English–based Exodus movement, "reclaiming" underused properties which are then developed, "founded on the principles of communal ownership and co-operation, as opposed to private property and competition." Exodus Collective (1998) "Exodus: Movement of Jah People." In Wolff, Richard et al., eds. *Possible Urban Worlds: Urban Strategies at the End of the Twentieth Century.* Basel: Birkhäuser Verlag.

106. Soto, Hernando de. (2000) *The Mystery of Capital: Why Capitalism Triumphs in the West and Fails Everywhere Else.* New York: Basic Books.

107. Varley, Ann. (2002) "Private or Public: Debating the Meaning of Tenure Legalization." *International Journal of Urban and Regional Research,* 26, 3, 449–461 at 450.

108. Ibid., 451.

109. Fernandes, Edesio. (2001) "Regularising Informal Settlements in Brazil: Legislation, Security of Land Tenure and City Management." Law and Geography colloquium, University College London. See also Cockburn, Julio Calderon. (2002) "The Mystery of Credit." *Land Lines,* 14, 2, 5–8.

110. *http://www.squat.freeserve.co.uk/section6.htm* (accessed October 1, 2002)

111. Corr, Anders. (1999) *No trespassing! Squatting, Rent Strikes, and Land Struggles Worldwide.* Cambridge, Mass.: South End Press.

112. Ontario Coalition Against Poverty (2002) "Give It or Guard It!—An Open Letter to Prime Minister Chretien, Premier Eves [of Ontario] and Mayor Lastman [of Toronto]," October 8 (copy with author).

113. Locke, John. (1690; 1980) *Second Treatise of Government.* Indianapolis: Hackett Publishing Co. Inc, section 38. Kofman documents the 1994 campaign for the right to housing (*droit au logement*) in Paris to protest homelessness, which entailed a mass squat in Dec. 1994 in the 6th arrondissement. Protestors sought to force Jacques Chirac, then mayor of Paris, to use existing legislation (originally passed in 1945 to deal with wartime shortages) to expropriate unused buildings for housing. Kofman, Elenore. (1998) "Whose City? Gender, Class, and Immigration in Globalizing European Cities." In Fincher, Ruth and Jane M. Jacobs, eds. *Cities of Difference.* New York: Guilford.

114. Neuwirth, Robert. (2002) "Squatters' Rites." *City Limits Monthly,* Sept/Oct 2002. Online at *www.citylimits.org* (accessed Aug. 22, 2002). Azuela notes the ways in which extralegal property claims may incorporate certain aspects of state law in their practices, perhaps in order to persuade the authorities of their legitimacy. Azuela, Antonio. (1987) "Low-Income Settlements and the Law in Mexico City." *International Journal of Urban and Regional Research,* 11, 4, 522–542. The issue of the relation between state legality and extralegality is of long-standing scholarly interest, particularly in relation to the third world city. See, for example, Fernandes, Edesio, and Ann Varley, eds. (1998) *Illegal Cities: Law and Urban Change in Developing Countries.* London: Zed Books.

115. Robertson, Michael. (1997) "Reconceiving Private Property." *Journal of Law and Society,* 24, 4, 465–485.

116. Kirby, Andrew. (2002) "From Berlin Wall to Garden Wall: Boundary Formation around the Home." Paper presented at the Annual Meeting of the Association of American Geographers, Los Angeles.

117. Singer, *Entitlement,* 29.

118. Rose, Mitch. (2002) "The Seductions of Resistance: Power, Politics, and a Performative Style of Systems." *Environment and Planning, D, Society and Space,* 20, 383–400, at 384 and 391.

119. Bentham, Jeremy. (1843; 1978) "Security and Equality of Property." In *Property: Mainstream and Critical Positions,* edited by Crawford Brough Macpherson. Toronto: University of Toronto Press at 52.

120. "Quiet," meaning "undisturbed, not interfered with or interrupted" and "quiescent," meaning "motionless, silent, dormant," share a common etymological root.

121. Mollenkopf, John. (1981) "Community and Accumulation." In Dear, Michael, and Allen J. Scott, eds. *Urbanization and Urban Planning in Capitalist Societies.* London: Methuen, 319–337.

122. Singer, "Property and Social Relations," 6.

123. Cuff, Dana. (1998) "Community Property: Enter the Architect or, the Politics of Form." In Bell, Michael, and Sze Tsung Leong, eds. *Slow Space.* New York: Monacelli Press, 120–140 at 135.

124. "Urban Dereliction: Analysis and Aims." (n.d.) *http://ww2.phreak.co.uk/tlio//pubs.urban_de.html* (accessed October 2, 2002). Featherstone documents the occupation by protestors of 14 acres of formerly industrial land at London's Gargoyle wharf, owned by Guinness and slated for development. This was not just oppositional, he argues, but was designed to demonstrate sustainable and socially equitable alternatives (compared to the "brutal polarization" of the city). The occupation also contested norms around land and English culture: the occupation was timed to coincide with the anniversary of a post-war mass-squat by 45,000 ex-serviceman in response to housing shortages, yet "[m]ajor landowners still derive legitimacy from the production of the idea of England as a 'green and pleasant land' where the status and territory of land owners was uncontested." Featherstone, Dave. (1998) "The 'Pure Genius' Land Occupation: Reimagining the Inhuman City." In Wolff, Richard, et al., eds. *Possible Urban Worlds: Urban Strategies at the End of the Twentieth Century,* Basel: Birkhäuser Verlag, 125.

125. Ross, Warren, and J. Brian Phillips. (1995) *The Government vs. Freedom: In Defense of Property Rights.* Online at *http://pw1.netcom.com/~wsross/property/propert1.html.* (accessed October 1, 2002). See also, Pennington, Mark. (2002) *Liberating the Land: The Case for Private Land-Use Planning.* London: Institute of Economic Affairs.

126. Alberta Real Estate Association. (n.d.) "Property Rights." *http://www.abrea.ab.ca/Visitors.htm* (accessed October 1, 2002)

127. *http://www.indybay.org/news/2001/11/110791.php* (accessed June 12, 2002.)

128. Rose, *Property and Persuasion,* 11.

129. Peters, Evelyn. (1998) "Subversive Spaces: First Nations Women and the City." *Society and Space,* 16, 665–685, 679.

130. Gelder, Ken, and Jane M. Jacobs. (1998) *Uncanny Australia: Sacredness and Identity in a Postcolonial Nation.* Victoria: Melbourne University Press, 24.

131. Mitchell, Don. (1995) "The End of Public Space? People's Park, Definitions of the Public, and Democracy." *Annals of the Association of American Geographers,* 85, 1, 108–133.

132. Kahn, B. (1991) "Who's in Charge Here?" *East Bay Express,* Aug. 9, 1, 11–13, at 11, quoted in Mitchell, Don. (2003) *The Right to the City: Social Justice and the Fight for Public Space.* New York: Guilford Press, 134.

133. *http://users.rcn.com/hi-there/gerbwin.html* (accessed April 25, 2003)

134. *http://www.vonline.com/van/hojovancouver.html*

135. Krueckeberg, D. A. (1995) "The Difficult Character of Property: To Whom Do Things Belong?" *Journal of the American Planning Association,* 61, 3, 301–309 at 301.

Chapter 2

1. Kearns, Gerry, and Chris Philo, eds. (1993) *Selling Places: The City as Cultural Capital, Past and Present.* New York: Pergamon.

2. Harvey, David. (1989) "From Managerialism to Entrepreneuralism: The Transformation in Urban Governance in Late Capitalism." *Geografiska Annaler,* vol. 71, B(1) 3–17.

3. Peck, Jamie. (2001) "Neoliberalizing States: Thin Policies/Hard Outcomes." *Progress in Human Geography,* 25, 3, 445–455, at 445.

4. Smith, Neil. (2002) "New Globalism, New Urbanism: Gentrification as Global Urban Strategy," *Antipode,* 34, 3, 452–472 at 429.

5. See the essays in *Antipode* 2002, 34, 3.

6. Brenner, Neil, and Nik Theodore. (2002) "Cities and the Geographies of 'Actually Existing Neoliberalism,'" *Antipode,* 34, 3, 349–379 at 353.

7. Toronto core area office space increased by 4.1 million square feet between 1971 and 1996, for example, (Gad, Gunter, and Malcolm Mathew. (2000) "Central and Suburban Downtowns." In Bunting, Trudi, and Pierre Filion, eds. *Canadian Cities in Transition: The Twenty-First Century.* Don Mills, Ont.: Oxford University Press, 248–273 at 259.)

8. Ley, David. (1996) *The New Middle Class and the Remaking of the Central City.* Don Mills, Ont.: Oxford University Press, 84.

9. Murdie, Robert A., and Carlos C. Tiexeira. (2000) "The City as Social Space." In Bunting, Trudi, and Pierre Filion, eds. *Canadian Cities in Transition: The Twenty-First Century.* Don Mills, Ont.: Oxford University Press, 209–210 (In 1990 $.)

10. Sassen, Saskia. (2000) "The Global City: Strategic Site/New Frontier." In Isin, Engin, ed. *Democracy, Citizenship, and the Global City.* New York: Routledge, 48–61 at 52.

11. Smith, "New Globalism," 440.

12. Cf. Solnit, Rebecca, and Susan Schwartzenberg. (2000) *Hollow City: The Siege of San Francisco and the Crisis of American Urbanism.* London: Verso.

13. Smith, Neil. (1997) "Social Justice and American Urbanism: The Revanchist City." In Merrifield, Andy, and Erik Swyngedouw, eds. *The Urbanization of Injustice.* New York: New York University Press, 117–136, at 129.

14. Ibid. See also Mitchell, Don. (1997) "The Annihilation of Space by Law: The Roots and Implications of Anti-Homeless Laws in the United States." *Antipode,* 29, 303–335; Waldron, Jeremy. (1990) "Homelessness and the Issue of Freedom." *U.C.L.A. Law Review,* 39, 295–324; Wyly, Elvin, and Daniel Hammel. (2002) "Neoliberal Housing Policy and the Gentrification of the American Urban System." Paper presented at Upward Neighbourhood Trajectories: Gentrification in a New Century. University of Glasgow. Online at *http://www.gla.ac.uk/ departments/urbanstudies/gentpaps/gentpap.html* (accessed October 16, 2002). Collins, Damian, and Nicholas K. Blomley. (2003) "Private Needs and Public Space: Politics, Poverty, and Anti-Panhandling Bylaws in Canadian Cities." In Law Commission of Canada, eds. *New Perspectives on the Public-Private Divide.* Vancouver: University of British Columbia Press.

15. Keil, Roger. (2002) " 'Common sense' Neoliberalism: Progressive Conservative Urbanism in Toronto, Canada." *Antipode,* 34, 3, 578–601, at 597.

16. Grell, Britta, Jens Sambale, and Dominik Veith. (1998) "Inner!City!Action!—Crowd Control, Interdictory Space, and the Fight for Socio-spatial Justice." In Wolff, Richard, et al., eds. *Possible Urban Worlds: Urban Strategies at the End of the Twentieth Century.* Basel: Birkhäuser Verlag.

17. *http://www.space.hijackers.co.uk/html/manifesto.html* (accessed June 4, 2002)

18. Smith, Neil, and Jeff Derksen. (2002) "Urban Regeneration: Gentrification as Global Urban Strategy." In Shier, Reid, ed. *Stan Douglas: Every Building on 100 West Hastings Street.* Vancouver: Contemporary Art Gallery/Arsenal Pulp Press, 62–95.

19. See Wyly and Hammel, "Neoliberal housing policy," for an interesting mapping of the revanchist urban hierarchy in the United States. See also Choko and Harris, who identify the importance of what they label local cultures of property in Montreal and Toronto, in terms of specific patterns of urban property ownership and use. Choko, Marc, and Richard Harris. (1990) "The Local Culture of Property: A Comparative History of Housing Tenure in Montreal and Toronto." *Annals of the Association of American Geographers,* 80, 1, 73–95.

20. Unlike the U.S. Constitution, the Canadian Charter of Rights and Freedoms does not explicitly protect property rights (despite early pressure from some business groups). Canada has not seen the intense constitutional struggles around property that have been at issue in the United States, most notably, in relation to the issue of "takings" in relation to environmental regulation (cf. Feldman, Thomas D., and Andrew E. G. Jonas. (2000) "Sage scrub revolution? Property Rights, Political Fragmentation, and Conservation Planning in Southern California under the Federal Endangered Species Act." *Annals of the Association of American Geographers,* 90 (2), 256–292.) But property rights—defined broadly—have been at issue in Canada. For example, First Nations politics clearly implicates questions of access and rights to land, although overlain with culturally specific understandings of spirituality and stewardship. Recent attempts to restrict panhandling by municipalities such as Winnipeg and Vancouver raise questions of mobility rights and free speech in regard to public property. See Blomley and Collins, "Private Needs and Public Space." Discussions over water exports, forestry, and biotechnology also entail discussions over the definition, scope, and policing of Canadian property rights. See Marchak, M. Patricia. (1998) "Who Owns Natural Resources in the United States and Canada?" *Working Paper no. 20,* Land Tenure Center, North American Program, Madison: University of Wisconsin. More generally, see Vogt, *Whose Property?*

21. My observations are based on an analysis of media reports, planning documents, and other relevant publications; personal involvement in local organizing and community affairs in the Downtown Eastside; a series of extended interviews with a number of activists, developers, planners and politicians conducted in the mid 1990s; and residency from 1993–1998. I have not attempted to undertake a survey of residents of the Downtown Eastside, nor do I claim to speak for them. Rather, my analysis on popular conceptions of prop-

erty in the area is based centrally on the arguments of activists and other commentators, as well as my own direct observations.

22. Harris, Cole. (1992) "The Lower Mainland, 1820–81." In Wynn, Graeme, and Timothy Oke, eds. *Vancouver and Its Region.* Vancouver: UBC Press, 38–68, at 38.

23. See Anderson, Kay. (1991) *Vancouver's Chinatown: Racial Discourse in Canada, 1885–1980.* Montreal: McGill-Queen's University Press, for the most influential treatment of Chinatown.

24. Over 90% of the area's dwellings are rented. There are around 15,000 residents in the Downtown Eastside. In 1996, the census recorded an average household income of around $12, 500. Around 60% male, 9% of the population was aboriginal. The area contained 20% of all the city's mental health cases in 1999. 61% of the city's drug arrests were made in the neighborhood in the same year. City of Vancouver (2000) *Downtown Eastside Community Monitoring Report, 2000.*

25. Sommers, Jeffrey. (2001) *The Place of the Poor: Poverty, Space, and the Politics of Representation in Downtown Vancouver, 1950–1997.* Ph.D. diss., Department of Geography, Simon Fraser University.

26. Beers, David. (1998) "At Face Value." *Globe and Mail,* Nov. 21 1998, D1, D3, at D3.

27. Osborn, Bud. (1998) "raise shit—a downtown eastside poem of resistance," *Society and Space,* 16, 3, 280–288, at 288.

28. The assessed value of Vancouver's property has doubled in the past decade, and tripled in twenty years, to a combined value of $80 billion (*Vancouver Sun,* January 31, 2002, d4).

29. Pundits began urging Vancouverites to see themselves "in a global context," and called for "flexible land use controls" to house the population of an "emerging international city." Goldberg, Michael A., and H. Craig Davis. (1988) "Global Cities and Public Policy: The Case of Vancouver, British Columbia." *UBC Planning Papers,* 17, 15, 17.

30. On megaprojects in Vancouver and elsewhere, see Olds, Kris. (2001) *Globalization and Urban Change: Capital, Culture, and Pacific Rim Mega-Projects.* Oxford: Oxford University Press.

31. Smith, Heather Anne. (2000) *Where Worlds Collide: Social Polarization at the Community Level in Vancouver's Gastown/Downtown Eastside.* Ph.D. diss., Department of Geography, University of British Columbia.

32. In 2002, commercial properties in the core of the Downtown Eastside declined 5% in value, while the gentrifying Gastown district, in the northwestern corner of the neighborhood, saw above average increases. Bula, Frances. (2002) "Real Estate Market Has Exceptional Year." *Vancouver Sun,* January 17 2002, B1.

33. Bula, Frances. (1997) "Real Estate Boom Looms for Hastings Street." *Vancouver Sun,* March 5, 1997, A10.

34. Sarti, Robert. (1997) "City Seeks to End Loss of Low-Cost Housing." *Vancouver Sun,* April 4, B4. The Downtown Eastside contained just over 5,000 SRO units in 2000—80% of the city's remaining stock. This has declined from 5,600 units in 1994 ("Downtown Eastside Community Monitoring Report 2000." City of Vancouver, 9.)

35. Alex Yuen, real estate agent, quoted in Bula, "Real estate boom," A10.

36. Sarti, "City Seeks to End Loss of Low-Cost Housing," B4.

37. Osborn, "raise shit," quotes at 285, 288, 284.

38. Quoted in Geisler, Charles C. (1995) "Land and Poverty in the United States: Insights and Oversights." *Land Economics,* 71 (1): 16–34 at 17.

39. Geisler, "Land and Poverty in the United States," 18.

40. Delaney, David. (1997) *Geographies of Judgment: Legal Reasoning and the Geopolitics of Race, 1836–1948.* Austin: University of Texas Press; Smart, Carol. (1989) *Feminism and the Power of Law.* New York: Routledge.

41. Ellis, Reuben J. (1993) "The American Frontier and the Contemporary Real Estate Advertising Magazine." *Journal of Popular Culture,* 27, 3, 119–133.

42. Darian-Smith, Eve. (1999) *Bridging Divides: The Channel Tunnel and English Legal Identity in the New Europe.* Berkeley: University of California Press.

43. Mitchell, Don. (1997) "The Annihilation of Space by Law: The Roots and Implications of Anti-Homeless Laws in the United States." *Antipode,* 29: 303–335.

44. Rose, *Property and Persuasion;* Hollowell, Peter, ed. (1982) *Property and Social Relations.* London: Heinemann; Singer, *Entitlement;* Singer, Joseph, and J. M. Beerman. (1993) "The Social Origins of Property." *Canadian Journal of Law and Jurisprudence.* 6, 2, 217–248;

Boulding, Kenneth E. (1991) "Reflections on Property, Liberty and Polity." *Journal of Social Behavior and Personality,* 6, 6, 1–16.

45. Hallowell, A. Irving. (1942–43) "The Nature and Function of Property as a Social Institution." *Journal of Legal and Political Sociology,* 1: 115–138 at 133.

46. Anon, (n.d.) "Woodward's Window Project: Bringing Woodward's Back to Life . . . and Back to the Community." Flyer. Copy with author.

47. Interview with author, Downtown Eastside activist, 18 June 1996.

48. Fama proposed to spend $50 million on the construction of the units, ranging in price from $160,000 to $190,000 each, plus two floors of retail space. Sarti, Robert. (1995) "Stab in Heart or New Heart for Skid Road?" *Vancouver Sun,* April 7, B3. Other estimates put the total costs at $60 million ($20m. purchase cost, $40m. construction costs).

49. Put another way, Aghtai may have thought he was buying a speculative shell, but for local activists it was still "Woodward's," even though the store had long gone. A community manifesto in 1997 argued that "private developers will not be allowed to buy and sell this community like a monopoly game . . . The community has agreed that Woodward's will be a cornerstone to our future, not someone else's." Quoted in Sommers, The Place of the Poor, 267. Nearly ten years after the store's closure, it continues to be identified as "Woodward's." Such is its iconic status that some who have opposed turning Woodward's over to social housing, have argued that it needs to be physically destroyed in order to make other uses possible. Bryce Rositch, in Anon. (2002) "What Should We Do with Woodward's?" *Vancouver Sun,* September 28, B4, B5.

50. Half of the residential space was to be developed by Fama as market housing, with the provincial government building 210 units of nonprofit co-op housing in the remainder. "Woodward's to Be Flagship of Partnership to Create Downtown Affordable Housing." Province of British Columbia press release, February 15, 1996. Copy with author.

51. Marg Green, quoted in Bula, Frances. (1997) "Eastside Groups Vow to Ensure Woodward's Has Social Housing." *Vancouver Sun,* April 7, B5.

52. Interview with author, Downtown Eastside activist, 18 June 1996.

53. Struthers, Andrew. (2002) "On the Street Where They Live." *Vancouver Sun,* October 12, D3, D4. A huge 'W' (which once revolved) is built over the old store.

54. Reddy, Steven, and Keir Nicoll. (2002) "Housing activisits occupy Downtown Eastside building." *The Peak,* September 23, 7.

55. *http://vancouver.indymedia.org/features/Squat/* (Accessed April 23, 2003)

56. Collins, Jerry. (1997) "Given the Bum's Rush by Bureaucrats." *British Columbia Report,* April 21, 8, 4, 16.

57. Mulgrew, Ian. (2001) "Low-key Lee Set to Run against McPhail." *Vancouver Sun,* Jan 12, b4.

58. A frequent accusation is that local community groups oppose new developments not because of an ethical objection to displacement but due to a fear that gentrification will upset the local status quo: "this elite's main goal is to maintain poverty and a perceived state of crisis so they continue to justify their existence—and state funding—as front line troops in the war against poverty." Collins, Jerry. (1995) "Save Our Slum." *British Columbia Report,* August 7, 12–16 at 14. It is interesting to speculate on whether this is simply a cynical accusation, or whether it reflects a fundamental failure to make sense of opposition to "obvious improvements." Perhaps the only rationale for possible opposition, given a market-oriented mindset, is to assume that community groups are entrepreneurial actors.

59. The Vancouver Port Corporation is an autonomous federal Crown corporation. It is required to operate entirely from its own resources without public subsidy. This has meant that it has been forced to raise revenues in order to finance operating expenses and any capital expansion projects. This ambiguous position as a quasiprivate public agency, operating on federal land (claimed by local First Nations), became an issue for many local activists, as will be shown.

60. Interview with author, 8 May 1996.

61. VLC was heavily financed by trade-union pension funds. This generated some local tensions, given the historic connections between some Downtown Eastside community organizations and the union movement. VLC initially began by developing rental housing, but quickly moved to larger, more entrepreneurial projects. It was then fronted by Jack Poole. In the 1970s and 1980s he ran a development company, Daon, which played a leading role in inner-city

gentrification in Vancouver (Ley, *The New Middle Class.*) Poole is now Chair and CEO of the organization that lead the successful Vancouver-Whistler 2010 Winter Olympics bid.

62. City of Vancouver (1994) *City of Vancouver Casino Review: A Discussion Paper* at 23.
63. J. Meyers, letter to editor, *Vancouver Sun* 14 July 1994, at 14.
64. Interview with author, May 8, 1996.
65. Anon. (1984) *Carnegie Crescent,* July, 6.
66. CRAB activists linked their occupation to a similar mass squat in the 1970s at the entrance to Stanley Park, designed to stop a massive luxury hotel and commercial project on Port land. This ultimately became Devonian Park. Another motivation for the CRAB movement was the unequal allocation of green space between the east and west side.
67. Conn, Heather. (1986) "Trashing the People's Park." *City Magazine,* 8, 2, 4–5. The story of CRAB Park has never been properly documented. Until his untimely death in the 1980s, Doug Konrad was working on such a detailed study.
68. Walzer, Michael. (1986) "Pleasures and Costs of Urbanity." *Dissent,* Fall, 470–475.
69. Bharb Gudmundson quoted in Sarti, Robert. (1994) "Waterfront Casino Plan Decried at Downtown Residents." *Vancouver Sun,* 25 April, a2.
70. Quoted in Dunphy, M. (1994) "Vancouver's Big Gamble." *The Georgia Straight,* March 25–April 1, 7–8, at 8, my emphasis. It was not just the potential for exclusion, but also a concern at access that proved important. Due to an intervening rail line, there has long been conflict over the lack of access to the park, particularly for wheel-chair users. The CRAB acronym became "Create a Real *Accessible* Beach," in response. Hostility has been directed at the City and Gastown "yuppies" that are accused of conniving to deny access to the site by some activists. The park remains, as one put it, "a very bittersweet thing because its there but you can't get at it, you know. Its just always a reminder of how the neighborhood gets screwed and continues to be screwed." Interview with author, Downtown Eastside activist 4, 23 March 1996. This has prompted marches and blockades.
71. Lydersen, Kari. (2001) "Dept. of Space and Land Reclamation," *Punk Planet,* 46, Nov./Dec., 112–113 at 112.
72. See manifesto at *http://www.spacehijackers.co.uk/html/writing/dslr.html* (Accessed June 4, 2002.)
73. Smith, Neil. (1996) *The New Urban Frontier: Gentrification and the Revanchist City.* New York: Routledge, 3–29, 218–222, quotes at 5, 3, 220.
74. Under section 289.1 of the Vancouver Charter, "the real property comprised in every street, park, or public square in the city shall be absolutely vested in fee-simple in the city."
75. Anon. (1994) "Cope Commissioner Opposes Casino Plan." *Courier,* 12 June, 2.
76. Interview with author, May 8, 1996. Another response to such claims is to frame them as "NIMBY-ism." The effect is to present opposition as small-minded, parochial, and exclusionary. See, referencing Woodward's, Campbell, Charles. (2002) " 'Not In My Back Yard' The Universal Cry," *Vancouver Sun,* November 7, a21.
77. Rose, *Property and Persuasion.*
78. Rose points to the example of adverse possession as a case in which ownership rights can be actually given up to another if the owner fails to "enact" title (by removing the encroacher, for example). Property as a social institution is also predicated on enactments, she notes, such as the story telling of theorists such as Locke.
79. Narrative is minimally defined by Ewick and Silbey as having three elements: a) a selective appropriation of past events and characters, b) a temporal ordering of those events, and c) an "emplotment" that relates these events. Ewick, Patricia, and Susan Silbey. (1995) "Subversive Stories and Hegemonic Tales: Toward a Sociology of Narrative." *Law and Society Review,* 29, 2, 197–226, at 200.
80. White, James Boyd. (1985) *Heracles' Bow: Essays on the Rhetoric and Poetics of the Law.* Madison: University of Wisconsin Press, 169.
81. Ewick and Silbey, *Subversive Stories,* 213.
82. Delgado, Richard. (1989) "Storytelling for Oppositionists and Others: A Plea for Narrative." *Michigan Law Review,* 87, 2411–2441.
83. Milner, Neal. (1993) "Ownership Rights and Rites of Ownership." *Law and Social Inquiry,* 18, 227–253 at 251.
84. Heasley, Lynne. (1998) *Many Paths in the Woods: An Ecological Narrative of Property in the Kickapoo Valley.* Presented at Who owns America II, University of Wisconsin-Madison.

85. Note that, until 1989, hotel residents were not protected by the Residential Tenancy Act (which governs evictions, rent increases, and so on) but were regarded as "guests," rather than tenants. As a result, they could be evicted at any time, for any reason. Guests' goods could be seized by the owner (legally, the "innkeeper").

86. "If we see the kind of evictions we saw at Expo, it will mean people will have no place to go and there will be more deaths." Jeff Sommers, DES activist, in relation to Seaport, quoted in Lee, Jeff. (1994) "Dislocation of Poor Downtown Residents Feared." *Vancouver Sun,* 23 April, a5.

87. "Expo was certainly the cardinal event in the Downtown Eastside in the last eighty years. I would say nothing else has touched it like that, the Depression and nothing else has been as catastrophic." (Interview with author, community leader, 27 June 1996. Expo has again been invoked in concerns over the Vancouver-Whistler Winter Olympics bid.

88. Expo also saw an attempt to mobilize the state to limit private property rights, as the Downtown Eastside Residents Association lobbied for a rent freeze in area hotels during the Expo period, and the granting of full tenancy rights for hotel residents. Overcoming considerable political resistance, the city supported DERA's plan, but proved unsuccessful when petitioning the provincial government for enabling legislation. See Hassan, Shlomo, and David Ley. (1994) *Neighbourhood Organizations and The Welfare State,* Toronto, University of Toronto Press, 199–200.

89. The reference to the figure of Olaf Solheim, and other retired resource workers, also speaks to a conscious attempt to contest negative representations of the residents of the area from outside, discussed in the following chapter.

90. Anon. (1994) *Carnegie Newsletter,* 1–2.

91. During the Expo evictions of 1986, one neoliberal pundit, an advisor to the provincial government, opined that "displaced rooming house tenants" would "save everyone a lot of trouble if they were all put on buses to the Kootenays [a region 300 miles from Vancouver]." Quoted in Olds, Kris. (1998) "Canada: Hallmark Events, Evictions, and Housing Rights." In Azuela, Antonio, Emilio Duhau, and Enrique Ortiz, eds. *Evictions and the Right to Housing: Experience from Canada, Chile, the Dominican Republic, South Africa, and South Korea.* Ottawa: IDRC (no pages). Online at http://www.idrc.ca/books/focus/861/chapt1.html. A report for a local foundation, interested in the possibilities for providing nonprofit housing for area residents, noted that this could be developed "more efficiently in areas with lower land costs." Real Estate Foundation. (1999) *Vancouver's Downtown Eastside: Gentrification and Developing Housing for Low-Income Persons.* Vancouver, 4.

92. Hassan and Ley, *Neighbourhood Organizations,* 202.

93. Both comments come from an interview with the author (Downtown Eastside activist, 23 March 1996).

94. Murphy, Howard. (1993) "Colonialism, History, and the Construction of Place: The Politics of Landscape in Northern Australia." In Bender, Barbara, ed. *Landscape: Politics and Perspectives.* Providence, R.I.: Berg Publishers, 205–243 at 205.

95. Carl Sauer, quoted in Mitchell, Don. (1996) *The Lie of the Land: Migrant Workers in the Californian Landscape.* Minneapolis: University of Minnesota Press. The argument here is indebted to Mitchell.

96. Mitchell, *The Lie of the Land:* "one cannot understand a landscape independent of how it has been represented. . . . But neither can one understand a landscape independent of its material form on the ground (and thus independent of how it was made)." (8) On landscape as visual ideology, see Cosgrove, Denis (1985) "Prospect, Perspective, and the Evolution of the Landscape Idea." *Transactions, Institute of British Geographers, N.S.,* 10, 45–62.

97. Rasmussen offers another take on the recursive links between the material and representational landscapes of property, in a fascinating analysis of the significance of the nomadic tent to the Tuareg of northern Niger. Spatial representations and practices relating to the tent seem inseparable from a web of shifting power relations and social identities, and are particularly important in terms of prevailing gender roles and relations. As a space, the tent cannot be understood absent an analysis of property relations; yet those property relations are inseparable from the material spatial practices and spatial representations that relate to the tent. Indeed, to separate the two is to engage in a culturally specific epistemological enframing. Rasmussen, Susan. (1996) "The Tent as Cultural Symbol and Field Site: Social and Symbolic Space, 'Topos,' and Authority in a Tuareg Community." *Anthropological Quarterly,* 69, 1, 14–26.

98. Mitchell, *Lie of the Land,* at 32, 30.

99. Bender, Barbara. (1993) "Landscape—Meaning and Action." In Bender, Barbara., ed. *Landscape: Politics and Perspectives.* Providence, R.I.: Berg Publishers, 1–17 at 2. See also Olwig, Kenneth. (1996) "Recovering the Substantive Nature of Landscape." *Annals of the Association of American Geographers,* 86, 4, 630–653.

100. Peluso, Nancy. (1996) "Fruit Trees and Family Trees in an Anthropegenic Forest: Ethics of Access, Property Zones, and Environmental Change in Indonesia." *Comparative Studies in Society and History,* 38, 3, 510–548 at 543.

101. Seed, *Ceremonies of Possession,* at 25.

102. Cosgrove, Denis. (1984) *Social Formation and Symbolic Landscape.* London: Croom Helm. The phrase was first coined by John Berger (1972) *Ways of Seeing.* London: Penguin.

103. Rose, *Property and Persuasion,* 267, 269.

104. Harley, John B. (1988) "Maps, Knowledge, and Power." In Cosgrove, Denis, and Steven Daniels, eds. *The Iconography of Landscape: Essays on the Symbolic Representation, Design, and Use of Past Environments.* Cambridge: Cambridge University Press, 277–312.

105. Note that I am not saying that such maps objectively achieve such a separation between space and the sovereign eye. Cartesian maps are material in many ways. However, the appearance of detachment is critical.

106. Olwig, "Recovering the Substantive Nature of Landscape."

107. Mitchell, *Colonising Egypt.*

108. Brigham, John, and Diana R. Gordon. (1996) "Law in Politics: Struggles over Property and Public Space on New York's Lower East Side." *Law and Social Inquiry,* 21, 2, 265–283, at 277–278, my emphasis.

109. An interesting extension of this argument states that the local community has some claim over the private hotels of the area, given the fact that hotel residents have "bought" the hotels many times over with their rents.

110. Interview with author, Downtown Eastside activist, 18 June 1996. Given that many residents occupy small and often disagreeable hotel rooms, the availability of spaces like Woodward's takes on an added significance. A local community center has been described as the community's "living room" in similar fashion.

111. Crawford, Margaret. (1999) "Blurring the Boundaries: Public Space and Private Life." In Chase, John, Margaret Crawford, and John Kaliski, eds. *Everyday Urbanism.* New York: Monacelli Press, 22–35 at 28. As we shall see in the following chapter, other interests have also used representations of the material landscape to articulate a sense of loss; however, this claim is now used to argue for private ownership as the means to recover decaying buildings from decaying bodies.

112. For a discussion of the enduring significance of such rights in the British context, see Parker, Gavin. (2002) *Citizenships, Contingency and the Countryside: Rights, Culture, Land and the Environment.* London: Routledge. Rose, citing U.S. cases, also notes that "a long period of public use was and still is said to deprive a private owner of the right to exclude the public from a travelled way." Rose, *Property and Persuasion,* 112.

113. Vogt, Roy. (1999) *Whose property?,* 115–116.

114. Lynd, Staughton. (1987) "The Genesis of the Idea of a Community Right to Industrial Property," *Journal of American History,* 74, 3, 926–958, at 927.

115. Singer, Joseph W. (1988) "The Reliance Interest in Property." *Stanford Law Review,* 40, 3, 611–751, at 622.

116. Radin, Margaret. (1993) *Reinterpreting Property.* Chicago: University of Chicago Press, at 81.

117. Radin, *Reinterpreting Property,* 47–48.

118. Anon. (1982) *Carnegie Crescent,* Nov. 1982, 11.

119. CRAB (1983) "There Is One Vision for a Waterfront Park: Over 100 People Attend Beach Party." CRAB press release, Sept. 23. Copy with author.

120. Interview with author, CRAB activist, 18 April 1996.

121. Sarti, Robert. (1984) "CRAB People Invade Waterfront." *Vancouver Sun,* Aug. 20, A15. Not only was Expo beginning to loom large, given the threat to the housing stock, but Expo organizers had proposed a number of pavilions for the Central Waterfront. BC Place is a large sports stadium, developed close to the neighborhood, that was opposed by many local activists. cf. Anon. (1983) "B.C. Dis-Place." *Carnegie Crescent,* Vol III, No 4, August, 1.

122. Meisel, Sam. (1985) "CRAB Makes WAVES." *Carnegie Crescent* April, 4.

123. Anon. (1984) "Jim Green, Speaking for Vancouver Waterfront Coalition: Eastsiders Told to 'Keep on Crabbing.' " *For The Record,* 8, Jan–June.

124. Anon. (1984) "CRAB Meeting Renews Call for Park." *For The Record,* 8, Jan–June.

125. Interview with author, CRAB activist, 18 April 1996.

126. Some of these are of considerable antiquity, but are still acknowledged by local organizers. For example, the Powell Street Grounds (now Oppenheimer Park) was a rallying point for demonstrations and labor marches in the early twentieth century, leading to several battles with the police. A series of demonstrations by unemployed men during the Depression (many of whom lived in squatter encampments in the Downtown Eastside) prompted the city's mayor to read the Riot Act in Victory Square, on the eastern border of the neighborhood, in April 1935. A group of unemployed men occupied the Carnegie Library at Hastings and Main the following month. Many of these sites, such as the Carnegie Library (now a community center and site for local organizing) continue to be locally symbolic landmarks, "charged with a collective memory of conflict." Hassan and Ley, *Neighbourhood Organizations,* 175.

127. Another DERA co-op, Tellier Tower, commemorates Gerry Tellier, a long-term resident and one of the four leaders of the 1935 On-to-Ottawa trek of the Relief Camp Workers.

128. The local commons is not just confined to material spaces. Longstanding collective organizations, such as Co-Op Radio, located in the Downtown Eastside, maintain a virtual commons: see Kidd, Dorothy. (1998) *Talking the Walk: The Communication Commons amidst the Media Enclosures.* Ph.D. diss., Simon Fraser University, School of Communications.

129. Interview with author, Downtown Eastside community leader 27 June 1996.

130. Shayler, John. (1995) "Woodward's: Give up or buy in?" *Carnegie Newsletter,* 15 April, 5. My emphasis.

131. Locke, Second Treatise, section 27.

132. Peluso, "Fruit Trees and Family Trees in an Anthropegenic Forest," 525.

133. Corr, *No Trespassing!* at 58.

134. Radin, *Reinterpreting Property,* 112.

135. Although the courts have confined the scope of public trust law somewhat, Sax argues that public trust can be reasonably and productively expanded to a broader set of questions that relate to "situations in which diffuse public interests need protection against tightly organized groups with clear and immediate goals," including environmental and poverty related controversies. Sax, Joseph L. (1970) "The Public Trust Doctrine in Natural Resource Law: Effective Judicial Intervention." *Michigan Law Review,* 68, 471–566, at 556–557. On Canada, see von Tigerstrom, Barbara. (1998) "The Public Trust Doctrine in Canada." *Journal of Environmental Law and Practice,* 7, 379–401.

136. Rose, *Property and Persuasion,* 121–122.

137. Rose, *Property and Persuasion,* 110. A propos CRAB Park, the public trust doctrine is well developed in relation to legal decisions ensuring and even expanding public access to beaches and waterfront on the principle that the public has always had customary rights to such spaces, even if this compromises the rights of private landowners. The persistence of this right can be seen in the continuing controversies around beach access in Malibu, California. See, for example, LaJeunesse, William. (2002) "Beach Battle Pits Stars against Public." *http://www.foxnews.com/story/0,2933,58065,00.html.* For a more general discussion, see Rose, *Property and Persuasion,* 105–162.

138. Interview with author, 18 April 1996, my emphasis.

139. Laclau and Mouffe, *Hegemony and Socialist Strategy.*

140. Ibid.

141. Crenshaw, Kimberle W. (1988) "Race, Reform, and Retrenchment: Transformation and Legitimation in Anti-Discrimination Law." *Harvard Law Review,* 101, 7, 1331–1387, at 1382. On the political geographies of rights, see Blomley, Nicholas, and Geraldine Pratt. (2001) "Canada and the Political Geographies of Rights." *The Canadian Geographer,* 45, 1, 151–166.

142. City of Vancouver. (1994b) *Central Waterfront Port Lands: Policy Statement.* Planning Department, Vancouver and Vancouver Port Corporation.

143. City of Vancouver, *Central Waterfront Port Lands,* 15.

144. Many maps also localize the site, excluding the adjacent neigborhood. As is often the case, the salient issues as far as the planning authorities are concerned relate to the site itself, with sec-

ondary attention given to the immediate surrounds. Air photos were also used on occasion: one of these, included in a brochure from the developers, is taken from the southeast. Although this may be coincidental, the effect is to exclude the Downtown Eastside and to position the site in relation to downtown and the tourist landscape of Stanley Park and the waterfront.

145. Lefebvre, Henri. (1991) *The Production of Space.* Cambridge: Blackwell.
146. Lefebvre, *The Production of Space,* at 38, 33.
147. Mitchell, *Colonizing Egypt,* 79.
148. Pinder, David. (1996) "Subverting Cartography: The Situationists and Maps of the City." *Environment and Planning, A,* 28, 405–427 at 407.
149. In an interview, a representative of Vancouver Port Corporation (VPC) upbraided me for using the former term, noting that "around here, we don't use that word." Interestingly, city officials tended to switch between the two terms, depending on the audience. For one discussion of the politics of spatial naming, see Myers, Garth. (1996) "Naming and Placing the Other: Power and the Urban Landscape in Zanzibar." *Tijdschrift voor Economische en Sociale Geografie,* 87, 3, 237–246.
150. One point of contention has been the tendency to identify areas—such as Gastown—as separate neighborhoods, rather then subsuming them within the Downtown Eastside, as area activists insist. Ultimately the Downtown Eastside appears as a "leftover." For a more general treatment of the politics of mapping in this context, and their relation to property, see Blomley, Nicholas, and Sommers, Jeff. (1999) "Mapping Urban Space: Governmentality and Cartographic Struggles in Inner-City Vancouver." In Smandych, R. ed. *Governable Places: Readings in Governmentality and Crime Control.* Smandych, R., ed. Aldershot: Dartmouth Publishing, 261–286. I revisit this point in the next chapter.
151. Forbes, Ann A. (1995) "Heirs to the Land: Mapping the Future of the Makalu-Barun." *Cultural Survival Quarterly,* Winter, 69–71, at 70.
152. "What's happening is a systematic attempt to define the Downtown Eastside out of existence, to chop it up into disconnected sections and crowd it out by other 'neighbourhoods' that are dominated by business interests and developers and upscale new settlers. If that were to happen, the people of the Downtown Eastside would lose their unified voice and their power to resist the changes that are so harmful to them. The residents are the people who actually live here, long term. And our neighborhood is not just a bunch of lines drawn on a map by planners or developers." Doinel, A. (1995) "The Incredible Shrinking Neighbourhood," *Carnegie Newsletter,* March 1, 2–3.
153. Anon. (1995) "Can You Find the Downtown Eastside on These Maps???" *Newsletter of the Carnegie Community Action Project,* November, 1, 2.
154. *Vancouver Sun* (1994) "Crab Park's Views in Doubt if Waterfront Casino Built." 8 August, A3.
155. Anon. (n.d.) "Seeing is Believing." Copy with author.
156. *Vancouver Sun* (1994) "Crab Park's Views in Doubt if Waterfront Casino Built." 8 August, A3.
157. Anon. (1994) *Picture This: Drawings Created by Downtown Eastside Residents.* Copy with author (original emphasis).
158. For an interesting example of such a layering, see Greg Curnoe's journal/collage that traces the "occupancy of . . . one small plot of land hundreds of years back into aboriginal times when land . . . was not plotted according to the laws of geometry." Curnoe, Greg. (1995) *Deeds/Abstracts: The History of a London Lot.* London Ont: Brick Books, 198. I revisit the politics of spatial layering in the final chapter.
159. Anon. (1994) *Picture This.* CRAB activists originally aimed for this entire waterfront to be park land.
160. Anon. (1994) *Picture This.*
161. Lefebvre's recognition that the distinction between perceived, conceived, and lived space is not absolute but entails a dialectic mingling is useful here. Lefebvre, *The Production of Space,* 40.

Chapter 3

1. Singer, "Property and Social Relations," 3–20, at 13. See also Ryan, Alan. (1984) *Property and Political Theory.* Oxford: Basil Blackwell.
2. Sayer Andrew, and Michael Storper. (1997) "Ethics Unbound: For a Normative Turn in Social Theory." *Society and Space,* 15, 1, 1–17 at 8.

3.   Clark, Gordon. (1986) "Making Moral Landscapes: John Rawls' Original Position." *Political Geography Quarterly,* Supplement to 5, 147–162. Proctor, James D. (1998) "Ethics in Geography: Giving Moral Form to the Geographical Imagination." *Area,* 30, 1, 8–18. Smith, David M. (2000) *Moral Geographies: Ethics in a World of Difference.* Edinburgh: Edinburgh University Press.

4.   Sayer and Storper, "Ethics Unbound," 10.

5.   Smith, David M. (1998) "How Far Should We Care? On the Spatial Scope of Beneficence." *Progress in Human Geography,* 22, 15–38.

6.   Sayer and Storper, "Ethics Unbound," 10.

7.   Collins, Damian, and Nicholas K. Blomley. (2003) "Private Needs and Public Space: Politics, Poverty, and Anti-panhandling Bylaws in Canadian Cities." In Law Commission of Canada eds. *New Perspectives on the Public-Private Divide.* Vancouver: University of British Columbia Press.

8.   Cresswell, Tim. (1996). *In Place/Out of Place: Geography, Ideology, and Transgression.* Minneapolis: University of Minnesota Press.

9.   Although Meacham argues that these towns, and subsequent Garden Cities relied for inspiration on the villages of a pre-industrial English squirearchy. Meacham, Standish. (1999) *Regaining Paradise: Englishness and the Early Garden City Movement.* New Haven, Conn.: Yale University Press.

10. Driver, Felix. (1988) "Moral Geographies: Social Science and the Urban Environment in Mid-Nineteenth-Century England." *Transactions of the Institute of British Geographers,* 13, 275–287.

11. Quoted in Sommers, The place of the poor, 63.

12. Perin, Constance. (1977) *Everything in its Place: Social Order and Land Use in America.* Princeton, N.J.: Princeton, 3, 4.

13. Cosgrove, Denis. (1989) "Power and Place in Venetian Territories." In Agnew, John, and James S. Duncan, eds. *The Power of Place: Bringing Together Geographical and Sociological Imagination.* London: Unwin Hyman, 104–123, at 104.

14. Burk, Adrienne. (2003) "Private Griefs, Public Places." *Political Geography* 22, 3, 317–333.

15. Mitchell, "The Annihilation of Space by Law," 316.

16. Proctor, James D. (1998) "Ethics in Geography: Giving Moral Form to the Geographical Imagination." *Area,* 30, 1, 8–18 at 13.

17. Smith, *Moral Geographies,* 17.

18. Collins, Jerry. (1995) "Save Our Slum." *British Columbia Report,* August 7, 12–16 at 1.

19. Cited in Deutsche Rosalyn and C. G. Ryan. (1984) "The Fine Art of Gentrification." *October,* 31, 91–111. For antigentrification examples in the legal literature, see Marcuse, Peter. (1985) "To Control Gentrification: Anti-Displacement Zoning and Planning for Stable Residential Districts." *Review of Law and Social Change,* 13, 931–953; Kolodney, Lawrence K. (1991) "Eviction Free Zones: The Economics of Legal Bricolage in the Fight against Displacement." *Fordham Urban Law Journal,* 18, 507–543; McGee, Henry W. (1992) "Afro-American Resistance to Gentrification and the Demise of Integrationist Ideology in the United States." *Land Use and Environment Law Review,* 23, 215–234; Dubin, Jon C. (1993) "From Junkyards to Gentrification: Explicating a Right to Protective Zoning in Low-Income Communities of Color." *Minnesota Law Review,* 77, 739–801.

20. See for example Robinson, Tony. (1995) "Gentrification and Grassroots Resistance in San Francisco's Tenderloin." *Urban Affairs Review,* 30, 4, 483–513.

21. Hartman, Chester, Dennis Keating, and Richard LeGates. (1982) *Displacement: How to Fight it.* Legal Services Anti-Displacement Project, at 4.

22. Hartman, et al., *Displacement,* 205, 5.

23. Caulfield, Jon. (1989) "Gentrification and Desire." *Canadian Review of Sociology and Anthropology.* 26(4), 617–632 at 627.

24. Quoted in Stoll, Michael. (2001) "Fear, Promise on 6th Street," *San Francisco Examiner.* Smith cites several examples of progentrification arguments in New York. Rosalyn Deutsche also notes the manner in which dominant ideologies are implicated in gentrification. See Deustche, Rosalyn. (1986) "Krzysztof Wodiczko's Homeless Projection and the Site of Urban 'Revitalisation.' " *October,* 38, 63–98. See also the extended discussion reproduced in Barry, Joseph, and John Devevlany. (1987) *Yuppies Invade my House at Dinnertime.* Hoboken, N.J.: Big River Publishing.

25. Smith, Neil. (1996) *The New Urban Frontier: Gentrification and the Revanchist City.* London: Routledge.

26. Reid, Laura, and Neil Smith. (1994) "John Wayne meets Donald Trump: The Lower East Side as Wild Wild West." In Kearns, Gerry, and Chris Philo, eds. *Selling Places: The City as Cultural Capital, Past and Present.* Oxford: Pergamon Press, 193–208 at 195.
27. Smith, *The New Urban Frontier.* See also Rosaldo, Renato. (1996) "Foreword." *Stanford Law Review,* 48, 1036–1045 at 1037.
28. There are few examples of the uses of the frontier metaphor in Vancouver, however, presumably reflecting the differing historical context of Canadian colonization. Loo argues that the British Columbia frontier was not Turnerian, but imperial and metropolitan. Loo, Tina. (1994) *Making Law, Order, and Authority in British Columbia, 1821–1871.* Toronto: University of Toronto Press. However, it is ironic to note that many of the businesses in the area played an historic role in the opening up of the province's "resource frontier." Woodward's, for example, got its start as an outfitter for the Yukon Goldrush. Now, ironically, it is the Downtown Eastside that has become a capitalist frontier in its own right.
29. Birmingham & Wood. (1969) *Restoration Report: A Case for Renewed Life in the Old City.* Vancouver, B.C.
30. This is despite some strong connections between Gastown property owners and the ruling civic party, in power until 2002.
31. Rose, *Property as Persuasion,* 38.
32. Anon. (1995) "101 Reasons . . . to Support this Application." *Gastown: Gastown Business Improvement Area Newsletter,* June, 4.
33. Ibid., 3
34. Ibid., 4
35. Quoted in Deutsche, Rosalyn. (1996) *Evictions: Art and Spatial Politics.* Cambridge: MIT Press, 13.
36. Bolen, Dennis. (1996) "Urban Evolution Eventually Will Drop Its Blanket over Downtown's Decay." *Vancouver Sun,* December 4, A7.
37. Jaconetty, Thomas A. (1994) " 'Highest and best use' revisited." *Assessment Journal,* 1 (3) 36–39 at 36.
38. Derbes, Max J. (1981) "Highest and best use—what is it?" In American Institute of Real Estate Appraisers, eds. *Readings in Highest and Best Use.* Chicago: American Institute of Real Estate Appraisers, 3–15.
39. Brenner and Theodore. (2002) "Cities and the geographies of 'actually existing neoliberalism,' " 371.
40. Park, Robert Ezra. (1932; 1952) "Succession, an Ecological Concept." In *Human Communities: The City and Human Ecology, Volume II: The Collected Papers of Robert Ezra Park.* Glencoe, Ill.: The Free Press, 223–232 at 225.
41. von Thünen, quoted in Clark, Eric. (1987) *The Rent Gap and Urban Change: Case Studies in Malmo 1860–1985.* Lund: Lund University Press at 30.
42. Lefcoe reminds us that the land use deemed "best" has not always been that which yielded the highest rents. However, at the very least, an expectation or presumption, against which land uses that do not produce the highest economic return are positioned as departures, remains. Lefcoe, George. (1975) "The Highest and Best Use of the Land: The Long Way Home." In Lenz, Elinor, and Alice Lebel, eds. *Land and the Pursuit of Happiness: A Bicentennial Anthology.* Los Angeles: Western Humanities Center, UCLA Extension.
43. Hurd, Richard M. (1903; 1924) *Principles of City Land Values.* New York: The Record and Guide, at v, 48, 80.
44. Rose, *Property as Persuasion,* 26.
45. Blackstone, William. (1765; 1838) *Commentaries on the Laws of England.* Second volume. New York: W. E. Dean, at 3, 8, 15 (original emphasis). Dilley argues for the need to recognize "economic" accounts, such as those of Locke and Blackstone, as discursive, ideological and deeply metaphorical. Dilley, Roy, ed. (1992) *Contesting Markets: Analyses of Ideology, Discourse, and Practice.* Edinburgh: Edinburgh University Press.
46. Locke, John. (1690; 1980) *Second Treatise of Government.* Indianapolis: Hackett Publishing Co. Inc., at § 51, 32.
47. Cronon, William. (1992) "A Place for Stories: Nature, History, and Narrative." *The Journal of American History,* 78, 4, 1347–1376 at 1350; Rose, *Property and Persuasion.*
48. Ashcraft, Richard. (1987) *Locke's Two Treatises of Government.* London: Allen and Unwin, 135.
49. Locke, *Two Treatises,* at § 34, 32, 35, 38.
50. Ashcraft, *Locke's Two Treatises of Government,* 136.

51. cf. Smith, *The New Urban Frontier;* Wilson, David. (1996) "Metaphors, Growth Coalition Discourses, and Black Poverty in a U.S. City." *Antipode,* 28, 1, 72–96.

52. Sassen, Saskia. (1996) "Analytic Borderlands: Race, Gender, and Representation in the New City." In King, Anthony D., ed. *Re-Presenting the City: Ethnicity, Capital, and Culture in the Twenty-First-Century Metropolis.* New York: New York University Press, 192.

53. Ward, R. (1997) "Victory Square." *The Georgia Straight,* 31, 1540, June 26–July 3, 15, 17–19 at 15.

54. Bolen, "Urban Evolution," A7.

55. Jonathan Baker, quoted in Collins, "Save Our Slum." "Many residents would love to live in the downtown core—why should this be such a legitimate goal for the down and out when it is unattainable for others? Focusing most of our shelter and social housing on the Downtown Eastside creates a huge distortion in the social and economic make up of the region," Reid, Angus. (2002) "Downtown Eastside a Regional Problem." *Vancouver Sun,* November 2, A 21.

56. Keller, Jeff. (1992) "The Most Dangerous Game." *Equity.* March, 52–53; 55–58 at 57–58.

57. Aird, Elizabeth. (1995) "To Have Haves and Have-nots Ideal Outcome of Woodward's Site Dispute." *Vancouver Sun,* May 9, B1.

58. Bula, Frances. (1995) "Yuppies in the 'Hood.'" *Vancouver Sun,* June 24, A1, A2, at A1, my emphasis.

59. Cole, Ian, and Barry Goodchild. (2001) "Social Mix and the 'Balanced Community' in British Housing Policy—A Tale of Two Epochs." *GeoJournal,* 51, 351–360, at 352.

60. Gell, P. Lyttleton. Undated pamphlet "The Municipal Responsibilities of the 'Well-to-Do.'" Quoted in Meacham, *Regaining Paradise,* 9. Meacham also notes the ways in which English urban reformers presumed a cultural paternalism, wherein the poor were expected to accept the tutelage of the middle class.

61. Cole and Goodchild, "Social Mix," 355.

62. Ibid, 357.

63. Ibid, 356.

64. Quoted in Stoll, Michael. (2001) "Fear, Promise on 6th Street," *San Francisco Examiner.*

65. Associated most famously with Wilson. Wilson, W. J. (1987) *The Truly Disadvantaged, the Inner City, the Underclass and Public Policy.* Chicago: University of Chicago Press. One consequence of this, other than the policy goal of social mix, is that of the "deconcentration" of the poor, a strategy which has justified the demolition of public housing projects in U.S. inner cities. Crump, Jeff. (2002) "Deconcentration by Demolition: Public Housing, Poverty, and Urban Policy." *Society and Space,* 20, 581–596.

66. Anon. (2002) "What Should We Do with Woodward's?" *Vancouver Sun,* September 28, 2002, B4, B5.

67. Quoted in Sarti, Robert. (1995) "Lowest Income Area Caught in Condo Vise." *Vancouver Sun,* Feb 14, B12.

68. Ng, Kai-Ling. (1995) "City Approves Woodward's Plans." *Gastown Tribune,* August, 4, 14.

69. Quoted in Berry, Christopher J. (1980) "Property and Possession: Two Replies to Locke—Hume and Hegel." *Nomos* 22 Pennock, J. Roland, and John W. Chapman, eds. New York: New York University Press, 89–100 at 79.

70. Goetz, Edward G., and Mara Sidney. (1994) "Revenge of the Property Owners: Community Development and the Politics of Property." *Journal of Urban Affairs,* 16, 4, 319–334; Krueckeberg, Donald A. (1998) "Who Rents America? Owners, Tenants, and Taxes." Paper presented at Who Owns America II, Madison, Wisconsin.

71. Quoted in "Save Our Slum" at 14. Her comments perhaps reflect both a pragmatic realization of the class privileges of gentrifiers, as well as an almost alchemical faith in the power of money. The irony in all this is that many first-wave gentrifiers are not likely to be the rich, but at the bottom of the real estate food chain, given the relative affordability of new condos and lofts in the area compared to housing elsewhere.

72. Smith, "New Globalism, New Urbanism," 452–472, 445.

73. City of Vancouver. (1998) *City of Vancouver: Housing Plan for the Downtown Eastside, Chinatown, Gastown, Strathcona,* July (draft), 12.

74. Walzer, "Pleasures and Costs of Urbanity," 470–475.

75. Ross, Neil. (1995) "Welcome to My Neighbourhood." *Globe and Mail,* January 9, A18, my emphasis. There is an extensive body of writing that characterizes the Downtown Eastside in negative terms, relying upon a "skid row" terminology of welfare abuse, poverty, madness,

aboriginality, sex, and drugs. See for example: Collins, "Save Our Slum"; Shaw, G. (1983) "Skid Road: The Flop Side and the Flip Side." *Vancouver Sun,* April 16; McMartin, Pete. (1996) "In a Beseiged Neighborhood, DERA Becomes a Prize to Fight Over." *Vancouver Sun,* Sept 23, B1; Deverell, W. (1993) "Back Alleys: Welfare Wednesday." *The Vancouver Review,* Winter, 26; Ross, N. (1995) "Welcome to My Neighbourhood." *Globe and Mail,* January 9, A18.

76. Bolen, "Urban Evolution," A7.

77. Developer, Interview with author, 16 May 1996.

78. Interview, Gastown activist, 14 May 1996.

79. Park, Robert. (1925; 1967) "The Mind of the Hobo: Reflections upon the Relation between Mentality and Locomotion." In Park, Robert E., Ernest W. Burgess, and Roderick D. McKenzie, eds. *The City.* Chicago: The University of Chicago Press, 156–160.

80. Shamir, Ronen. (2001) "Suspended in Space: Bedouins under the Law of Israel." In Blomley, Nicholas, David Delaney, and Richard T. Ford, eds. *The Legal Geographies Reader,* Oxford: Blackwell, 134–142, at 142.

81. The legal significance of mobility was made evident in a recent hearing before the rentals-man concerning the proposed eviction of tenants from the Dominion Hotel, whose owner sought to convert a long-term residential hotel into short-stay tourist accommodation. Identifying the tenants as "guests," the landlord aimed to evict them at short notice. These eviction notices were deemed illegal, with the rentalsman finding that the tenants were, in fact, "residents," and thus entitled to at least two months notice before eviction. Many of the tenants, it should be noted, had lived in the hotel long-term—one for thirty years. As one commented, "This is my home, not some one-night stand" (quoted in Sarti, Robert. (1997) "Gastown Hotel Tenants Wait for Ruling on Eviction." *Vancouver Sun,* May 31, A17; see also Bula, Frances. (1997) "Bid to Evict Hotel Tenants Rules Illegal." *Vancouver Sun,* June 6, B1).

82. Interview with author, Gastown activist, 16 May 1996; my emphasis. One source refers to area residents as "social service clients who frequent the area." Anonymous, 1996, "We're the block busters!!" *Newsletter of the Carnegie Community Action Project,* November 15, 3.

83. "Just because a bunch of Indians wandered up and down the Rocky Mountain trench for a few hundred years, doesn't mean they own it" (attributed to Allan Williams, Social Credit Attorney-General, 1975) cited in Sterritt, Neil J. (1989) "Unflinching resistance to an im-placable invader." In *Drumbeat: Anger and renewal in Indian country.* Boyce, Richardson, ed. Toronto: Summerhill Press, 167–294 at 292. Indians in seventeenth-century New Eng-land were said to have no right to their traditional lands, as they do not have any "settled places . . . nor any ground as they challenge for their owne possession, but change their habitation from place to place." Francis Higginson, quoted in Tully, James. (1993) *An Ap-proach to Political Philosophy: Locke in Contexts.* Cambridge: Cambridge University Press, at 150. I revisit these points in chapter 4.

84. Comaroff, John. (1995) "The Discourse of Rights in Colonial South Africa: Subjectivity, Sovereignty, Modernity." In Sarat, Austin, and Thomas R. Kearns, eds. *Identities, Politics, and Rights.* Ann Arbor: University of Michigan Press, 193–236.

85. Merivale, Herman. (1841; 1967) *Lectures on Colonization and Colonies.* New York: Augustus M. Kelley, at 394.

86. Green, Marg (n.d.) *The Downtown Eastside: A Time for Mediation or a Time to Take a Stand.* Copy with author.

87. Hassan, Shlomo, and David Ley. (1994) *Neighbourhood Organizations and the Welfare State.* Toronto: University of Toronto Press, 195.

88. City of Vancouver Archives, Planning Dept, Series 69. My thanks to Jeff Sommers for this reference.

89. Ryan, Simon. (1996) *The Cartographic Eye: How Explorers Saw Australia.* Cambridge: Cam-bridge University Press, 125.

90. Davis, John E. (1991) *Contested Ground: Collective Action and the Urban Neighborhood.* Ithaca, N.Y.: Cornell University Press, at 245.

91. Interview with author, Downtown Eastside community leader, 27 June 1996.

92. Interview with author, Downtown Eastside Residents Association, 2 July 1996.

93. Doinel, A. (1995) "The Incredible Shrinking Neighborhood," *Carnegie Newsletter,* March 1, 2–3.

94. See Sommers, Jeff. (1998) "Mapping Men: The Intersecting Politics of Space and Masculin-ity in Vancouver, 1962–1986," *Urban Geography* 19, 287–310 for a discussion of masculinity in the Downtown Eastside.

95. Hassan and Ley, *Neighbourhood Organizations*, 185.
96. *Concord Pacific Place: The Ultimate Waterfront Community; Living! Vancouver's new waterfront lifestyle*, 1, 2, 3. (Concord Pacific promotional materials: Copies with author)
97. Interview with author, Downtown Eastside community leader, 27 June 1996.
98. Tom Laviolette, letter to editor, *Vancouver Sun*, December 11, 1996, A18.
99. Interview with author, Downtown Eastside community leader, 27 June 1996.
100. "Woodward's Window Project: Bringing Woodward's Back to Life . . . and Back to the Community." Undated flyer, copy with author.
101. Interview with author, Downtown Eastside activist 1, 18 June 1996.
102. Cohen, Morris R. (1927) "Property and Sovereignty." *Cornell Law Quarterly*, 13, 8–30 at 12, 13.
103. This hit home: For example, the developer who proposed the building of micro suites noted above (in return for the right to develop market housing) found himself vilified by activists, who juxtaposed a photo of his luxurious house with his proposed units.
104. Interview with author, Downtown Eastside activist 1, 18 June 1996.
105. Interview with author, Downtown Eastside activist 2, 16 March 1996 (my emphasis).
106. Woodward's Window Project, "Bringing Woodward's Back to Life." Undated flyer, copy with author.
107. Aird, Elizabeth. (1995) "To Have Haves and Have-nots Ideal Outcome of Woodward's Site Dispute." *Vancouver Sun*, May 9 1995, B1.
108. McCoy, Michael. (1995) "A Dispatch from the 'Gentrification' Wars." *Vancouver Sun*, May 19, A 19.
109. Smith, "New Globalism," 445.
110. Cole and Goodchild, "Social Mix"; Dansereau, Francine, Annick Germain, and Catherine Éveillard. (1997) "Social Mix: Old Utopias, Contemporary Experience, and Challenges." *Canadian Journal of Urban Research*, 6, 1, 1–23; Gans, Herbert. (1961) "Planning and Social Life." *Journal of the American Association of Planners*, May, 134–141; Ostendorf, Wim, Sako Musterd, and Sjoerd de Vos. (2001) "Social Mix and the Neighbourhood Effect. Policy Ambitions and Empirical Evidence." *Housing Studies*, 16, 3, 371–380.
111. Cole and Goodchild, "Social Mix," 357–358.
112. *"Paris Place: The Best Things in Life Are Here."* Real estate promotional material: International Village, Vancouver, Canada. Copy with author.
113. Urban Design and Development Consultants. (1992) "A Discussion Paper of Issues and Topics Affecting the Viability and Growth of Gastown: Suggestions Leading to a Community Plan for Gastown." Mimeograph, 2, 6.
114. Gastown Historical Area Planning Committee. (1996) "Minutes of 25 September, 1996." (emphases added) Copy with author.
115. Curran, Winifred. (2002) *Evicting Memory: Displacing Work and Home in a Gentrifying Neighborhood*. Presented at Upward Neighbourhood Trajectories: Gentrification in a New Century. University of Glasgow.
116. Interview with author, Downtown Eastside activist 1, 18 June 1996. For one academic treatment of the issues of meaning, identity, and urban space in the context of redevelopment, see Brion, Dennis J. (1992) "The Meaning of the City: Urban Redevelopment and the Loss of Community." *Indiana Law Review*, 685–740.
117. Compare with the photo essay in Solnit, Rebecca, and Susan Schwartzenberg. (2000) *Hollow City: The Siege of San Francisco and the Crisis of American Urbanism*. London: Verso, 149–152, documenting the conversion of various long-established stores to Starbucks coffee bars.
118. Interview with author, Downtown Eastside activist 3, 23 March 1996. Compare with the creation of a "new landscape" in Moline, Illinois that inscribes the mythologized history of local capital, obscuring working-class histories in the process. Crump, Jeff. (1999) "What Cannot Be Seen Will Not Be Heard: The Production of Landscape in Moline, Illinois." *Ecumeme*, 6, 3, 295–317.
119. *Carnegie Newsletter*, Nov 1, 1995.
120. Bula, Frances. (2002) "Mayoral Hopeful Opens Campaign." *Vancouver Sun*, June 19, B3.
121. Osborn, "raise shit," 288.
122. cf. Pratt, Mary Louise. (1992) *Imperial Eyes: Travel Writing and Transculturation*. New York: Routledge.
123. I am grateful for Gerry Pratt's suggestion that I acknowledge this politics: Unfortunately I do not have the space to do it justice, particularly in relation to Chinatown, which has its

own complicated story. See Anderson, Kay. (1987) "The Idea of Chinatown: The Power of Place and Institutional Practice in the Making of a Racial Category." *Annals of the Association of American Geographers,* 77, 4: 580–598. There are interesting reworkings of social mix, for example, and spatial difference, in the claims of the Community Alliance. It claims that there are too many social services already in the Downtown Eastside, so new services should not be located here, but elsewhere in order to prevent an unhealthy concentration of the poor. Policing tactics are criticized: forms of public disorder (such as open drug use) are said to be tolerated in the area, yet not elsewhere. The law, it is argued, must be applied equally. For one uneven, though interesting review of the recent politics of drugs and space in the area, see the recent documentary produced by Vancouver filmmaker Nettie Wild, *Fix: The Story of an Addicted City,* 2002, Canada Wild Productions. On the complicated ways in which "community" can become a contradictory construction, see Blomley, Nicholas, and Jeff Sommers. (1999) "Mapping Urban Space: Governmentality and Cartographic Struggles in Inner-City Vancouver." In *Governable Places: Readings in Governmentality and Crime Control.* Smandych, R., ed. Aldershot: Dartmouth Publishing, 261–286.

124. See, for example, Wood, Denis. (1992) "How Maps Work." *Cartographica,* 29, 3&4, 66–74.
125. Osborn, "raise shit," 280, 281.

Chapter 4

1. *http://www.pacificislandtravel.com/north_america/canada/about_destin/victoria.html* (accessed October 29, 2002)
2. He was likely describing Whidbey Island, not the site of Victoria. James Douglas, chief factor in charge of Fort Victoria, and the second governor of the Colony of Vancouver Island was very enthusiastic about the site of Victoria. I am indebted to Cole Harris for this, and many other points in this chapter.
3. *http://www.pacificislandtravel.com/north_america/canada/about_destin/victoria.html* (accessed October 29, 2002)
4. Freedman, Joel, and John Lutz. (2000) "Victoria's Secrets." *The Ring.* Victoria: University of Victoria. September 22. (online at *http://communications.uvic.ca/Ring/00sept22/viewpoint2.html;* accessed October 29, 2002)
5. *http://web.uvic.ca/~hist66/walktour/tour/bastion.html* (accessed October 29, 2002).
6. Quoted in Fisher, Robin. (1977) *Contact and Conflict: Indian-European Relations in British Columbia, 1774–1890.* Vancouver: University of British Columbia Press, 114.
7. *http://web.uvic.ca/~hist66/walktour/tour/songhees.html* (accessed October 29, 2002). Initially, the colonial authorities signed treaties with native people on southern Vancouver Island. However, after 1864, native title was "distinctly denied," given the prevalent view that "Indians had been and remained primitive savages who were incapable of concepts of land title and who most certainly should not be perceived as land owners," Tennant, Paul. (1990) *Aboriginal Peoples and Politics.* Vancouver: University of British Columbia Press, 39–40. The Lekwammen were actually moved on at least two other occasions from one reserve site to another.
8. Tennant, *Aboriginal Peoples,* 40–41.
9. Said, Edward. (1993) *Culture and Imperialism.* New York: Alfred Knopf, 7.
10. Hume, Stephen. (2001) "Legislature Is on Our Lands: B.C. natives," *Vancouver Sun,* A1, A8. Note also that the lawsuit coincided with growing controversy over the new provincial government's insistence to hold a referendum on aboriginal land claims. At time of writing, this suit is still unresolved.
11. Gregory, Derek. (2000) "Post-colonialism." In Johnston, Ronald J., Derek Gregory, Geraldine Pratt, and Michael Watts, eds. *The Dictionary of Human Geography,* Oxford: Blackwell, 612–615, 612.
12. Important exceptions include, for example, Jacobs, *Edge of Empire;* Driver, Felix, and David Gilbert, eds. (1999) *Imperial Cities: Landscape, Display, and Identity.* Manchester: Manchester University Press; Yeoh, Brenda. (2001) "Postcolonial Cities," *Progress in Human Geography,* 25, 3, 456–468; Hamer, David. (1990) *New Towns in the New World.* New York: Columbia University Press.
13. Anderson, Kay. (2000) "Thinking 'Postnationally': Dialogue across Multicultural, Indigenous, and Settler Spaces," *Annals of the Association of American Geographers,* 90 (2) 381–391

at 381. This silence, it has been noted, has been particularly striking in the United States; while slavery has come to dominate the national imagination, scholars have marginalized the foundational importance of colonial dispossession.

14. Gonzalez, Mario, and Elizabeth Cook-Lynn. (1998) *The Politics of Hallowed Ground: Wounded Knee and the Struggle for Indian Sovereignty*. Urbana: University of Illinois Press.
15. Jacobs, *Edge of Empire*, 105.
16. I have chosen to focus on Canada, Australasia, and the United States given their similarities (for example, a common law tradition and some shared ideological understandings of property). This is at the exclusion of other settler states, such as Israel or Indonesia.
17. Pratt, Mary Louise. (1992) *Imperial Eyes; Travel Writing and Transculturation*. London: Routledge.
18. Although see Bryan for the dangers of using categories such as "property" and "possession" when describing aboriginal claims. In so doing, we are in danger of redescribing a native reality that may be ontologically different, and thus engaging in a "dialogical excursion that is neither invited nor welcomed by Aboriginal peoples." Not only do we force people into categories that may be inappropriate, but we also do so using a language of property that comes freighted with a colonial and "civilizing" logic, as I discuss below. Bryan, "Property as Ontology," at 5.
19. Comaroff, John L. (2001) "Colonialism, Culture, and the Law: A Foreword." *Law and Social Inquiry*, 26, 2, 305–314 at 309.
20. For a succinct global summary, see Erica-Irene A. Daes (1999) *Human Rights of Indigenous Peoples:* United Nations Commission on Human Rights (*http://www.unhchr.ch/Huridocda/ Huridoca.nsf/TestFrame/154d71ebbbdc126a802567c4003502bf?Opendocument;* accessed November 5, 2002). North American overviews include Deloria, Vine, and Clifford M. Lytle. (1983) *American Indians, American Justice*. Austin: University of Texas Press; and Berger, Thomas R. (1991) *A Long and Terrible Shadow*. Vancouver: Douglas and McIntyre. On the role of legal violence, see Blomley, Nicholas. (2003) "Law, Property, and the Geography of Violence: The Frontier, the Survey, and the Grid." *Annals of the Association of American Geographers*, 93, 1, 121–141.
21. Hamer, *New Towns*.
22. McCann, Larry, and Peter Smith. (1991) "Canada becomes Urban: Cities and Urbanization in Historical Perspective." In Bunting, Trudi E., and Pierre Filion, eds. *Canadian Cities in Transition*. Don Mills, Ont.: Oxford University Press, 69–99.
23. Harris, Cole. (1997) *The Resettlement of British Columbia: Essays on Colonialism and Geographic Change*. Vancouver: University of British Columbia Press.
24. Hamer, *New Towns*, 215.
25. Jacobs, Jane M. (1997) "Resisting Reconciliation: The Secret Geographies of (Post) Colonial Australia." In Pile, Steve, and Michael Keith, eds. *Geographies of Resistance*. London: Routledge, 202–218.
26. Johnson, Louise. (1994) "Occupying the Suburban Frontier: Accommodating Difference on Melbourne's Urban Fringe." In Blunt, Alison, and Gillian Rose, eds. *Writing Women and Space: Colonial and Postcolonial Geographies*. New York: Guilford Press, 141–168, at 146.
27. McDonald, Robert A. J. (1979) "City-Building in the Canadian West: A Case Study of Economic Growth in Early Vancouver, 1886–1913." *B.C. Studies*, 43, 3–28.
28. McGregor, Donald A. (1911) "The Marvel of Vancouver." *British Columbia Magazine*, June, 457–472 at 469.
29. J A Hobson, quoted in Woodcock, George. (1990) *British Columbia, A History of the Province*. Vancouver: Douglas & McIntyre, 159.
30. Johnson, "Occupying the Suburban Frontier," at 146.
31. Barnett, Homer G. (1955) *The Coast Salish of British Columbia*. Eugene: University of Oregon Press, at 30.
32. Miranda, Louis, and Philip Joe. "How the Squamish Remember George Vancouver." Fisher, Robin, and Hugh Johnston. (1993) *From Maps to Metaphors: The Pacific World of George Vancouver*. Vancouver: University of British Columbia Press, 3–5 at 5.
33. Royal Commission on Aboriginal Peoples (1998) *Report of the Royal Commission on Aboriginal Peoples: Restructuring the Relationship*, Volume 2, part 2. Ottawa: Canada Communication Group; Bryan, "Property as Ontology," 3–31; Brody, Hugh. (2000) *The Other Side of Eden: Hunters, Farmers, and the Shaping of the World*. Vancouver: Douglas and McIntyre;

Turner, Nancy J., and James T. Jones. (2000) *Occupying the Land: Traditional Patterns of Land and Resource Ownership among First Peoples of British Columbia.* Presented at IACSP, Bloomington, Indiana. (*http://www.indiana.edu/~iascp/iascp2000.htm*, accessed October 29, 2001). Although indigenous relations to land have an undeniable specificity, I wonder whether the divide between aboriginal and nonnative forms of land tenure are greater in theory than in fact. For example, with their general emphasis on myth and story-telling as a basis for claims to land, as well as the centrality of non-alienable and collective tenures, caught up in local landscapes, indigenous understandings of land tenure clearly depart from the ownership model. Yet I am left wondering about the degree to which they differ from the "community claim" within the Downtown Eastside, as well as pre modern systems of land ownership within the West. We might also recognize the mythologies that underpin Western law. cf. Fitzpatrick, Peter. (1992) *The Mythology of Modern Law.* New York: Routledge.

34. Barnett, "The Coast Salish."
35. Ibid., 253.
36. Ibid., 255.
37. *http://www.squamish.net/about/assert2.htm#selfdetermine* (accessed January 7, 2003)
38. Williams, Jr., Robert A. (1990) *The American Indian in Western Legal Thought.* Oxford: Oxford University Press, 6. Although this did not preclude legal abuse and selectivity. See, for example, Luna, Guadalupe T. (1998) "Chicana/Chicano Land Tenure in the Agrarian Domain: On the Edge of a 'Naked Knife,' " *Michigan Journal of Race and Law,* 4, 39–144.
39. Patton, Paul. (2000) "The Translation of Indigenous Land into Property: The Mere Analogy of English Jurisprudence . . ." *parallax,* 6, 1, 25–38 at 27.
40. Kedar, "The Legal Transformation of Ethnic Geography," at 928.
41. Gregory argues that dispossession was realized through a set of spatial strategies, noting in particular the role of "naming," "othering," and "spatializing." Gregory, Derek. (1994) *Geographical Imaginations.* Oxford: Blackwell, 168–174.
42. Comaroff, John L. (2001) "Colonialism, Culture, and the Law: A Foreword." *Law and Social Inquiry,* 26, 2, 305–314 at 309.
43. Edney, Mathew G. (1993) "The Patronage of Science and the Creation of Imperial Space: The British Mapping of India, 1799–1843." *Cartographica,* 30: 61–67 at 62.
44. Kain, R.J.P., and E. Baigent. (1992) *The Cadastral Map in the Service of the State: A History of Property Mapping.* Chicago: University of Chicago Press, at 329. See Blomley, Nicholas. (2003) "Law, Property, and the Geography of Violence: The Frontier, the Survey, and the Grid." *Annals of the Association of American Geographers,* 93, 1, 121–141.
45. Brealey, Ken. (1998) "Travels from Port Ellice: Peter O'Reilly and the Indian Reserve System in British Columbia." *B. C. Studies,* 115/116: 181–236.
46. Johnson, "Occupying the Suburban Frontier," at 155.
47. Although in British law, the Crown acquired title in 1846 when sovereign jurisdiction was assigned to Britain (my thanks to Cole Harris for this point).
48. Harris, Cole. (1993) "The Lower Mainland, 1820–81." In Wynn, Graeme, and Tim Oke, *Vancouver and Its Region.* Vancouver: University of British Columbia Press, 38–68, at 67.
49. Statistics Canada (2003) *Aboriginal Peoples of Canada: A Demographic Profile.* Statistics Canada, p. 10. 49% of the aboriginal population is deemed urban, up from 47% in 1996.
50. Burt, Larry W. (1986) "Roots of the Native American Urban Experience: Relocation Policy in the 1950s." *The American Indian Quarterly,* 10 (Spring), 85–99.
51. Ablon, Joan. (1964) "Relocated American Indians in the San Francisco Bay Area: Social Interaction and Indian Identity." *Human Organization,* 23, Winter, 296–304 at 303.
52. Jacobs, *Edge of Empire,* 105.
53. Johnson, "Occupying the Suburban Frontier," at 144.
54. Culhane, Dara. (1998) *At the Pleasure of the Crown: Anthropology, Law, and First Nations.* Burnaby, B.C.: Talonbooks, 31. See also Furniss, Elizabeth. (1997–98) "Pioneers, Progress, and the Myth of the Frontier: The Landscape of Public History in Rural British Columbia." *BC Studies,* 115/116, 7–44.
55. Healy, Chris. (1997) *From the Ruins of Colonialism: History as Social Memory.* Cambridge: Cambridge University Press, 5.
56. Taylor, Affrica. (2000) " 'The Sun Always Shines in Perth': A Postcolonial Geography of Identity, Memory, and Place." *Australian Geographical Studies,* 38, 1, 27–35 at 28.
57. Fitzpatrick, *The Mythology of Modern Law,* at 77.

58. Locke, *Second Treatise of Government.* § 124.
59. Hobbes, Thomas. (1651; 1988). *Leviathan.* London: Penguin, 186.
60. Fitzpatrick, *The Mythology of Modern Law,* at 65.
61. Locke, *Second Treatise,* § 49, original emphasis.
62. Although, of course, we must be cautious about treating colonial discourses as unitary.
63. Fitzpatrick, *The Mythology of Modern Law,* 81.
64. Ibid., 65.
65. Fitzpatrick, *The Mythology of Modern Law;* Nunn, Kenneth B. (1997) "Law as a Eurocentric Enterprise," *Law and Inequality,* 15, 2, 323–371.
66. See Tully, James. (1993) *An Approach to Political Philosophy: Locke in Contexts.* Cambridge: Cambridge University Press, at 140–141.
67. Genesis 1:28.
68. John Cotton, quoted in Tully, *An Approach to Political Philosophy,* at 150, 151. See Tully (137–176) for the argument that Locke's conceptions, in particular, provided a vital underpinning for colonial dispossession.
69. Turner, Frederick J. (1892; 1961) *Frontier and Section: Selected Essays of Frederick J. Turner.* Prentice-Hall, Englewood Cliffs, 43.
70. The masculinism of the Lockean project needs to be underscored. As Carolyn Merchant notes, a "recovery plot" undergirds narratives of "improvement": the Fall, following the expulsion from the Garden of Eden, requires the "reclamation of land, and recovery of property." However, at least one version of Genesis legitimates this recovery through masculine domination over both nature and Eve; "While fallen Adam becomes the inventor of the tools and technologies that will restore the garden, fallen Eve becomes the Nature that must be tamed into submission." Merchant, Carolyn. (1996) *Earthcare: Women and the Environment.* New York: Routledge, 28, 32. Eve/Nature, in the recovery plot, appears in three gendered forms: as virginal, and full of potentiality; as disorderly and chaotic, requiring improvement; and as fertile and ripened.
71. Cronon, William. (1992) "A Place for Stories: Nature, History, and Narrative." *The Journal of American History,* 78, 4: 1347–1376, at 1352. Hamer speculates that Turner's concept of the frontier as an inexorable force may have been influenced by his experiences in his home town of Portage, Wisconsin. Hamer, *New Towns,* 220.
72. Shamir, Ronen. (2001) "Suspended in Space: Bedouins under the Law of Israel." In Blomley, Nicholas, David Delaney, and Richard T. Ford, eds. *The Legal Geographies Reader,* Oxford: Blackwell, 135–142 at 138. See also Kedar, "The Legal Transformation of Ethnic Geography."
73. Mathews, J. B. (n.d.) "Before the Whitemans Came." Draft of a pamphlet (noted as "suitable for anniversary of Vancouver's arrival") VCA: Add MSS 54 506-A-2 File 1, p. 1, 2. One history of Vancouver describes its precontact landscape with "its forests, its bears, its wolves, its deep and its Indians." Morley, Alan. (1961) *From Milltown to Metropolis,* Vancouver: Mitchell Press, 15.
74. McInnes, C. (2000) "Gardom Angers Native Leaders," *Vancouver Sun,* March 2, A1, A2.
75. Anticonquest has been defined as "the strategies of representation whereby European bourgeois subjects seek to secure their innocence in the same moment as they assert European hegemony": Pratt, *Imperial Eyes,* 7. For an example, see Luna, "Chicana/Chicano Land Tenure," 39–144.
76. Macionis, John J., and Vincent N. Parillo. (1998) *Cities and Urban Life.* Upper Saddle River, N.J.: Prentice Hall, 61; Nicol, Eric. (1970) *Vancouver,* Doubleday, Toronto 1998.
77. Although at one stage, mention is made of fort settlements "involved in the pacification of the native Indians" that became the nuclei for later towns and cities. Johnston, Ronald J. (1982) *The American Urban System.* Harlow: Longman, 67.
78. Nicol, *Vancouver,* 26. One important exception is Harris, Cole. (1992) "The Lower Mainland, 1820–81." In Wynn, Graeme, and Tim Oke, eds. *Vancouver and Its Region.* Vancouver: UBC Press, 38–68.
79. Chivallon, Christine. (2001) "Bristol and the Eruption of Memory: Making the Slave-Trading Past Visible." *Social and Cultural Geography,* 2, 3, 347–363, at 349.
80. Reekie, Isabel M. (1968) *Red Paddles.* Vancouver: Mitchell Press, 82, 83.
81. Roinc, Chris. (1996) The Squamish Aboriginal Economy, 1860–1940. Master's thesis, Department of History, Simon Fraser University, 15.
82. Anon. (1984) "Indians Vow to Halt Aquarium 'Dozers.' " *The Province,* November 21, 5.

83. Mather, Susan. (1998) *One of Many Homes: Stories of Dispossession from "Stanley Park,"* Master's thesis, Department of History, Simon Fraser University.

84. Seed, Patricia. (1995) *Ceremonies of Possession in Europe's Conquest of the New World, 1492–1640.* Cambridge: Cambridge University Press, 19, 25.

85. Anderson, Kay. (2000) "Savagery and Urbanity: Struggles over Aboriginal Housing, Redfern, 1970–73." In Read, Peter, ed. *Settlement: A History of Aboriginal Housing.* Canberra: Aboriginal Studies Press, 130–144. There are potential complications to my claim: for example, one important strain of thought (particularly in North America) codes the city as the antithesis of civilization, rather than its apotheosis (my thanks to Cole Harris for this reminder). For those reasons, native people may also be deemed "out of place" within rural settings. While true, such anti-urban strains have often also been suspicious of material progress and other markers of "improvement." To the extent that growth-oriented discourse has come to dominance, the view of cities as nonnative spaces may also be more prevalent.

86. Hamer, *New Towns*.

87. Hamer, *New Towns,* at 208, 210, 211.

88. John Graves Simcoe, quoted in Isin, Engin. (1992) *Cities without Citizens.* Montreal: Black Rose Books, 122.

89. Hamer, *New Towns,* 213.

90. Bentham, Jeremy. (1843; 1978) "Security and Equality of Property." In Macpherson, Crawford Brough, ed. *Property: Mainstream and Critical Positions.* Toronto: University of Toronto Press, at 56, my emphasis. W. H. New explores the ways in which Canadian "pioneer" spaces were similarly bounded. "On the other side of these conceptual edges were presumed to lie the territories of anarchy—by which in practice were meant wilderness, forest, moral corruption, Indians, Catholics, and French" (80). New, W. H. (1997) *Land Sliding: Imagining Space, Presence, and Power in Canadian Writing.* Toronto: University of Toronto Press.

91. Hamer, *New Towns,* 216, 217, 218–19.

92. Fisher, *Contact and Conflict,* 114. A 1911 amendment to Canada's Indian Act eliminated the need for band council approval for reserve sales. Section 46 gave municipalities the right to expropriate parts of reserves to build roads, railways, or other public facilities subject to the approval of the federal government. And section 49a gave government the right to relocate any reserve situated near a town of 8,000 or more residents without having to obtain the prior approval of the reserve residents. Ray, Arthur. (1996) *I Have Lived Here Since the World Began: An Illustrated History of Canada's Native People.* Canada: Lester Pub., 260. My thanks to Paige Raibmon for this information. It is interesting to speculate on the degree to which the desire for native removal was driven by market concerns or racial anxieties or, put another way, the specific ways in which the two combined.

93. Jacobs, *Edge of Empire,* 108. Samantha Wells also documents the strategies of banishment, containment, separation, and relocation used against aboriginal peoples in and around Darwin, Australia. Wells, Samantha. (2000) "Labour, Control, and Protection: The Kahlin Aboriginal Compound, Darwin, 1911–38." In Read, Peter, ed. *Settlement: A History of Aboriginal Housing.* Canberra: Aboriginal Studies Press, 64–74.

94. Hamer, *New Towns,* 212–213.

95. Hamer, *New Towns,* 214.

96. Hood, R. A. (1929) *By Shore and Trail in Stanley Park.* Toronto: McLelland and Stewart, 36.

97. The Haida and Kwakiutl were apparently deemed more worthy of memorialization than local natives as they were said to be braver and more intelligent. Although a "fading memory," Vancouver "will always have a link with the days when this proud race was in its glory." Golder, Stephen. (1925) "Indian Village in Stanley Park." *Vancouver Province,* April 12, 1 (Magazine section). Interestingly, there are unspecified reports that the parks board modified its support for this project due to objections from the Squamish band council. Krangle, Karenn. (1984) "Indians Say Pool Site is Old Village." *Vancouver Sun,* March 23, B8.

98. Goodfellow, Rev. John C. (192-) *The Totem Poles in Stanley Park.* Vancouver: AHC, 13, 26.

99. Raley, G. H. (1945) *A Monograph of the Totem Poles in Stanley Park, Vancouver, British Columbia.* Vancouver: Lumberman Printing, 5.

100. An historical geography of urban totem poles needs to be written. Other poles were acquired to mark dates of colonial significance, such as the fifty-year anniversary of Vancouver's foundation or the arrival of George Vancouver in 1792. Gunn, S. W. A. (1965) *A*

Complete Guide to the Totem Poles in Stanley Park, Vancouver, B.C. Vancouver: W.E.G. Mc-Donald. Francis notes the ways in which totem poles came to be increasingly appropriated by nonnatives as a symbol of their own in the service of tourist dollars or national identity. Francis, Daniel. (1992) *The imaginary Indian.* Vancouver: Pulp Press, 182–189. Although totem poles are commonly placed in corporate or state sites across Vancouver, they have also become used to advance native claims to cultural survival and urban presence. For example, in 1985 a totem pole was erected at the new Urban Native Education Centre in Vancouver. The Centre's administrator saw it as a reminder "that there is a visible and strong presence of native people here in the province. We are not relics." Nathan, H. (1985) "Totem Pole at Gate Symbolizing New Life at City Native Centre." *Vancouver Sun,* June 27, B4. For a contemporary analysis of "ethnic tourism," the city and native people, see D'Arcus, Bruce. (2000) "The 'Eager Gaze of the Tourist' Meets 'Our Grandfather's Guns': Producing and Contesting the Land of Enchantment in Gallup, New Mexico." *Society and Space,* 18, 693–714. As Yeoh asks: "What constitutes 'history' in multi-ethnic postcolonial nations where the perspective of hindsight is continually destabilized; what becomes valorized and mapped as 'heritage' in official imaginative geographies . . . are difficult questions." Yeoh, *Postcolonial Cities,* 461.

101. Chivallon, "Bristol and the Eruption of Memory." See also Brear, Holly Beachey. (1995) *Inherit the Alamo: Myth and Ritual at an American Shrine.* Austin: University of Texas Press.
102. Nelson, Jennifer. (2001) *The operation of whiteness and forgetting in Africville: a geography of racism.* Ph.D. diss., Department of Sociology and Equity Studies in Education, University of Toronto, 247–248.
103. Macdonald, Bruce. (1992) *Vancouver: A Visual History.* Vancouver: Talon Books.
104. City of Vancouver Archives Add MSS 54, V. 13.
105. Corporation of the City of Vancouver, *Annual Report* - year ended 31 December 1908, City of Vancouver Archives, Microfilm PS (1) 1908, 1.
106. Hamilton also found time to paint watercolors of the town site. Housed in the Vancouver Archives, they are an important reminder of the "visual ideologies" that inform both the science of mapmaking and the art of landscape painting. See Cosgrove, Denis. (1985) "Prospect, Perspective, and the Evolution of the Landscape Idea." *Transactions, Institute of British Geographers, N.S.,* 10, 45–62.
107. Orlove, Benjamin. (1993). "The Ethnography of Maps: The Cultural and Social Contexts of Cartographic Representation in Peru." *Cartographica,* 30, 1, 29–45 (describing state maps as telling a story, with a narrative type that assumes that future acts are preordained).
108. Hamer, *New Towns,* 178. See also Paul Carter's discussion of the urban grid as an ordering device. Carter, Paul. (1988) *The Road to Botany Bay.* New York: Knopf, 202–229.
109. Address to Hamilton bestowing freedom of the city upon him in 1938. Hamilton L. A., Major Mathews Collection, Vancouver City Archives, Add MSS 54, 504-D-3, file 44.
110. The plaque is at the intersection of Hastings and Hamilton Street, now the boundary of the Downtown Eastside. In the following chapter, I consider a rather different monument within the neighborhood that can usefully be juxtaposed with Hamilton's plaque.
111. Similar mappings perhaps continue: Dunn and Leeson, for example, note the ways in which the massive development of London's Docklands used the terms "New City" and "Virgin Site" to conceptually remap the area. Imagining it as a "a blank canvas upon which we can paint the future," this remapping obliterated existing geographies of use and occupation. Dunn, Peter, and Loraine Leeson. (1993) "The Art of Change in Docklands." In Bird, Jon, et al., eds. *Mapping the Future.* London: Blackwell, 136–149 at 138.
112. Sennett, Richard. (1990) *Conscience of the Eye: The Design and Social Life of Cities from the Middle Ages to the Present.* New York: Knopf, 48, 53. Compare with Sack's discussion of the "empty lot" as an example of the emptying of space through territorialization. Sack, Robert D. (1986) *Human Territoriality: Its Theory and History.* Cambridge: Cambridge University Press.
113. Reekie, *Red Paddles,* 19.
114. Lacy, Suzanne. (1995) *Mapping the Terrain: New Genre Public Art.* Seattle: Bay Press, at 234.
115. *http://www.heapofbirds.com/hachivi_edgar_heap_of_birds.htm* accessed November 10, 2002.
116. The installation was part of series of twelve similar signs, entitled "Native Hosts," that acknowledges other First Nations. The placement of these signs was also significant: for example, some were placed near a monument to King George VII. While this may "recall the empire that changed life so irrevocably for the people's named in the signs," as one observer

notes, it could also signal the importance of the Royal Proclamation of 1763 to native claims to land and sovereignty. Oleksijczuk, Denise. (1991) "Nature in History: A Context for Landscape Art." In Vancouver Art Gallery ed. *Lost Illusions: Recent landscape art.* Vancouver: Vancouver Art Gallery, 5–24, 20.

117. *Mabo v. Queensland* [No. 2] 175 C.R. 1; *Delgamuukw v. British Columbia* (1997) 3 S.C.R. 1010.

118. My thanks to Wendy Gibbons for her research on this, as well as informants such as Maureen Tehan and Jane M. Jacobs.

119. Peters, Evelyn. (1996) " 'Urban' and 'Aboriginal': An Impossible Contradiction." In Caulfield, Jon, and Linda Peake, eds. *City Lives and City Forms: Critical Research and Canadian Urbanism.* Toronto: University of Toronto Press, 47–62.

120. Anderson, Kay, and Jane M. Jacobs. (1997) "From Urban Aborigines to Aboriginality and the City: One Path through the History of Australian Cultural Geography." *Australian Geographical Studies.* 35, 1, 12–22, at 19.

121. Blomley, Nicholas. (1996) " 'Shut the province down': First Nations' Blockades in British Columbia, 1984–1995," *B.C. Studies.* 111, Autumn, 5–35, 18.

122. Sandler, Jeremy. (2002) "Aboriginal Group Complains about Bid for 2010 Olympics," *Vancouver Sun,* June 27, B4.

123. *www.squamish.net*

124. Zaharoff, William J. (1978) *Success in Struggle: The Squamish People and Kitsilano Indian Reserve No. 6.,* Master's thesis, Department of History, Carleton University. The Squamish fought a lengthy legal challenge (begun in 1977), arguing that the federal government breached its fiduciary duty in failing to protect their interests, claiming that the Squamish band members on the reserve were forced to sell under threat of eviction, and seeking the return of the lands. Hall, Neal. (1998) "Native Indians Seek Return of Land Near Vancouver's Centre." *Vancouver Sun,* Feb 2, B1. This was finally settled out of court.

125. Compare with Sparke's discussion of "contrapuntal cartographies." Sparke, Mathew. (1998) "A Map that Roared and an Original Atlas: Canada, Cartography, and the Narration of Nation." *Annals of the Association of American Geographers,* 88, 3, 463–495, at 467.

126. Jacobs, Jane M. (1997) "Resisting Reconciliation: The Secret Geographies of (Post) Colonial Australia." In Pile, Steve, and Michael Keith, eds. *Geographies of Resistance.* London: Routledge, 202–218, at 213.

127. Jacobs, "Resisting Reconciliation," 216–217, 217.

128. See Jacob's discussion of the Aboriginal occupation of the Old Swan brewery in Perth, for example. Jacobs, *Edge of Empire.*

129. Smith, Paul Chaat, and Robert Allen Warrior. (1996) *Like a Hurricane: The Indian Movement from Alcatraz to Wounded Knee.* New York: The New Press, 89.

130. Fortunate Eagle, Adam. (2002) *Heart of the Rock: The Indian Invasion of Alcatraz.* Norman: University of Oklahoma Press.

131. Fortunate Eagle, Adam. (1994) "Urban Indians and the Occupation of Alcatraz Island." *American Indian Culture and Research Journal,* 18, 4 33–58, at 38.

132. Fortunate Eagle, *Heart of the Rock,* 207. The island was also said to be of symbolic importance—according to oral histories, it was known as the rock with the rainbow inside or "Diamond Island." The diamond would heal and restore balance to native people. (*http://www.nativepeoples.com/np_web%20exclusives/alcatraz_documentary/alcatraz_documentary,* accessed October 30, 2002)

133. Jacobs, "Resisting Reconciliation," 216–217, my emphasis.

134. Squamish Nation. (2001) *Xay Temixw Land Use Plan: For the Forests and Wilderness of the Squamish Nation Traditional Territory.* Land and Resources Committee, Squamish Nation, 7, my emphasis.

135. Anon. (1984) "Indians Vow to Halt Aquarium 'Dozers.' " *The Province,* November 21, page 5.

136. Fortunate Eagle, "Urban Indians," 38.

137. Fortunate Eagle, *Heart of the Rock,* 207, 208.

138. Anderson and Jacobs, "From Urban Aborigines to Aboriginality and the City," 19.

139. Taylor, "The sun always shines in Perth," 31.

140. Wendy Grant, quoted in Braham, Daphne. (1994) "Land Claims Drawing Attention of Business." *Vancouver Sun,* Sept. 10, c1, c2. Advertisements in early Vancouver newspapers often showed a bulls-eye centred on the downtown, selling the speculative potential of the area.

141. Anderson, Kay J. (1993) "Place Narratives and the Origins of Inner Sydney's Aboriginal Set-tlement, 1972–73." *Journal of Historical Geography,* 19, 3, 314–335 at 325. Anderson has also pointed to the ways in which indigenous settlements like Redfern also unsettle the "divided self" characteristic of the modern city, in which the bestial is always latent within the civi-lized self. Anderson, "Savagery and Urbanity," 130–144.

142. Anderson, "Place Narratives," 331.

143. Quoted in Robinson, Scott. (1994) "The Aboriginal Embassy: An Account of the Protests of 1972." *Aboriginal History,* 18, 1, 49–63, at 50.

144. Fickling, David (2002) "Raising the Sovereignty Stakes." *Guardian,* August 19 (*http:// www.guardian.co.uk/elsewhere/journalist/story/0,7792,77055,00.html* (accessed October 29, 2002). See also Dow, Coral. (2000) *Aboriginal Tent Embassy: Tent or Eyesore?* (*http:// www.aph.gov.au/library/pubs/chron/1999–2000/2000chr03.htm* accessed October 29, 2002)

145. Ibid., no page numbers.

146. This sparked outrage from one Senator who described it as a "collection of ramshackle and illegal buildings" (in Dow, *Aboriginal Tent Embassy*). As one poet responded: "Senator MacDonald says/it looks ramshackle/Well Senator, it is a tent,/it's asking white Australia/to pay the bloody rent" (Anon, no date, Dow, *Aboriginal Tent Embassy http://www. geocities.com.ubinz/JT/poem/AboriginalTentEmbassy.html:* accessed October 29, 2002)

147. Robinson, "The Aboriginal Embassy," 51. The site is claimed by two local tribes, the Ngu-nawal and Ngunnawal.

148. Cowan, Greg. (n.d.) *Nomadic Resistance. http://gregory.cowan.com/nomad/4.htm* accessed June 4, 2002.

149. Quoted in Huggan, Graham. (1991) "Maps, Dreams, and the Presentation of Ethnographic Narrative: High Brody's 'Maps and Dreams' and Bruce Chatwin's 'The Songlines.' " *Ariel* 22, 1, 57–69 at 62.

150. Hui, Stephen. (2002) "Aboriginal Students Dispute UniverCity Plans." *The Peak,* Nov. 4, 3, 10.

151. Lautens, Trevor. (1995) "Not an Inch to the Indians." *Vancouver Sun,* April 4 A13.

152. Yaffe, Barbara. (2000) "Aboriginal Claim on Private Land Opens New Legal Chapter." *Van-couver Sun,* Jan. 18, A19. The reference to oral evidence relates to the *Delgamuukw* decision. The centrality of the ownership model is such that dominant interests seem relieved when native people conform to it. For example, a glowing article described a Squamish joint ven-ture to build a $75 million mall on eighteen hectares of aboriginal land. It was pointed out that the Squamish also own forty hectares of land leased to a shopping center. The Vancou-ver–based Native Investment and Trade Association identified "enormous opportunities . . . for private developers to develop aboriginal-controlled property." The absence of munici-pal zoning laws, and the availability of undeveloped land allows reserve lands "to be de-veloped creatively in the highest and best use, as dictated by the market and the wishes of the partners." Chow, Wyng. (2002) "Natives partners in huge mall project." *Vancouver Sun,* F1, F2.

153. Bell, Stewart. (1995) "Staking Claim." *Vancouver Sun,* April 1 A1.

154. Nedelsky, Jennifer. (1990) "Law, Boundaries, and the Bounded Self." *Representations,* 30: 162–189.

155. Howitt, Richie. (2001) "Frontiers, Borders, Edges: Liminal Challenges to the Hegemony of Exclusion." *Australian Geographical Studies,* 39, 2, 233–245, at 234, 237.

156. Bell, Stewart. (1995) "Staking claim." *Vancouver Sun,* April 1, A1.

157. Bell, Stewart. (1995) "Our Home and Native Land?" *Vancouver Sun,* April 1, B1, B2. Why these are deemed "mini-states" is left unexplored. A politician from North Vancouver framed his response to native claims within a similar rubric: "Spokesmen for our native people say that 'first nations' own this province 'lock, stock and barrel.' Simply put: three percent of B.C.'s population owns all of the land and natural resources in B.C. The rest of us—97 percent—are squatters. They say we have squatters' rights and little else." Letter from Jack Davis, MLA, North Vancouver-Seymour, *Terrace Standard,* August 8, 1990.

158. Gelder and Jacobs, *Uncanny Australia,* at xiv.

159. Ibid., 23, 138.

160. Bhahba, Homi K. (1990a) "Introduction: Narrating the Nation." In Bhahba, Homi K., ed. *Nation and Narration.* London and New York: Routledge, 1–7 at 3.

161. Peters, Evelyn. (1998) "Subversive Spaces: First Nations Women and the City." *Society and Space,* 16, 665–685 at 680.

162. Howitt, Richie. (2001) "Frontiers, Borders, Edges: Liminal Challenges to the Hegemony of Exclusion." *Australian Geographical Studies*, 39, 2, 233–245.

Chapter 5

1. Hayden, Dolores. (1997) *The Power of Place: Urban Landscapes as Public History.* Cambridge: MIT Press at 93. Compare with Deutsche's discussion of the "homeless projection" in *Evictions.*
2. Blomley, Nicholas. (2003) "Law, Property and the Geography of Violence: The Frontier, the Survey, and the Grid," *Annals of the Association of American Geographers*, 93, 1, 131–152; Sarat, Austin, and Thomas R. Kearns, eds. (1992) *Law's Violence.* Michigan: University of Michigan Press.
3. Young, James. (2000) *At Memory's Edge.* New Haven: Yale University Press; Burk, Adrienne. (2003) "Private Griefs, Public Places." *Political Geography*, 22, 3, 317–333.
4. Couldry, Nick. (1995) "Speaking up in a Public Space: The Strange Case of Rachel Whitehead's *House,*" *New Formations*, 25: 96–113 at 96.
5. Akin to the Situationist credo of "detournement." Pinder, David. (1996) "Subverting Cartography: The Situationists and Maps of the City." *Environment and Planning, A,* 28: 405–427.
6. A striking comparison is with Wanda Hurren's "map-poems" that, according to Catherine Nash "re-embody the abstract spaces of the map" (274) without annulling the latter. Hurran, Wanda. (1998) "Living with/in the Lines: Poetical Possibilities for World Writing." *Gender, Place, and Culture.* 5, 3: 301–304; Nash, Catherine. (1999) "Wanda Hurren's World Writing." *Gender, Place, and Culture.* 6, 3: 273–274.
7. Hill-Tout, Charles. (1978) *The Squamish and the Lillooet.* Vol. 2 of *The Salish People: The Local Contribution of Charles Hill-Tout,* edited by Ralph Maud. Vancouver: Talonbooks, 20.
8. Francis, Daniel. (1992) *The Imaginary Indian: The Image of the Indian in Canadian Culture.* Vancouver: Arsenal Pulp Press.
9. Walking, more generally, figures centrally in many recent artistic countermaps—for example, the work of Richard Long and Hamish Fulton. Curnow, Wynstan. (1999) "Mapping and the Expanded Field of Contemporary Art." In Cosgrove, Denis, ed. *Mappings.* London: Reaktion Books.
10. Hayden, *The Power of Place.*
11. Radin, Margaret. (1986) "Residential Rent Control." *Philosophy and Public Affairs*, 15, 4.
12. Cohen, "Property and Sovereignty." Compare with Deutsche's discussion of the work of Hans Haacke in New York. Deutsche, *Evictions.*
13. Agarwal, Bina. (1994) "Gender and Command over Property: A Critical Gap in Economic Analysis and Policy in South Asia." *World Development*, 22, 10: 1455–1478.
14. Pateman, Carole. (1988) *The Sexual Contract.* Oxford: Polity Press.
15. Rose, *Property and Persuasion*, 233–234.
16. Merchant, *Earthcare.*
17. Brace, Laura. (1999) *Husbanding the Earth and Hedging out the Poor.* Paper presented at Land and Freedom Conference, University of Newcastle, New South Wales, July, at 3–4.
18. Kolodny, Annette. (1975) *The Lay of the Land.* Chapel Hill: University of North Carolina Press; Parker, Patricia. (1987) *Literary Fat Ladies: Rhetoric, Gender, Property.* London: Methuen.
19. Bottomley, Anne. (1996) Figures in a Landscape: Feminist Perspectives on Law, Land, and Landscape. In Bottomley, Anne, ed. *Feminist Perspectives on the Foundational Subjects of Law.* London: Cavendish Publishing Limited at 123.
20. Rose, Gillian. (1996) *Feminism and Geography.* Minneapolis: University of Minnesota Press at 110.
21. Bottomley, "Figures," 124.
22. Latour, Bruno. (1986) "Visualization and Cognition: Thinking with Eyes and Hands." *Knowledge and Society: Studies in the Sociology of Culture Past and Present*, 6, 1–40 at 21. David Turnbull notes that maps are nonindexical, that is they are not dependent for their truth on their context; "in Western society knowledge gains its power through denying, or rendering transparent, the inherent indexicality of all statements or knowledge claims. In the Western tradition the way to imbue a claim with authority is to attempt to eradicate all signs of its local, contingent, social, and individual production." Turnbull, David. (1989) *Maps Are Territories: Science Is an Atlas.* Chicago: University of Chicago Press, 42.

23. "Public art is artwork that depends on its context; it is an amalgamation of events—the physical appearance of a site, it's history, the socioeconomic dimensions of the community, and the artist's intervention." James Clark, quoted in Hayden, *The Power of Place,* 68.
24. Compare with William Least Heat-Moon's "deep map" of the American prairire. Heat-Moon, William Least. (1991) *Prairyerth (a Deep Map).* Boston: Houghton Mifflin.
25. Smith, Neil. (1993) "Homeless/Global: Scaling Places." In Bird, et al., eds. *Mapping the Futures: Local Cultures, Global Change.* London: Routledge.
26. Holdsworth, Deryck W. (1986) "Cottages and Castles for Vancouver Home-seekers." *B C Studies,* 69–70, 11–32.
27. Mitchell, Katharyne. (1993) "Multiculturalism, or the United Colours of Capitalism?" *Antipode,* 25, 4, 263–294, and (1996) "Visions of Vancouver: Ideology, Democracy and the Future of Urban Development." *Urban Geography,* 17, 6, 478–501.
28. Fitzpatrick, *The Mythology of Modern Law.*
29. Anderson, Kay. (1987) "The Idea of Chinatown: The Power of Place and Institutional Practice in the Making of a Racial Category." *Annals of the Association of American Geographers,* 77, 4: 580–598. The supplication lists several residents who are categorized simply as undifferentiated "ethnics," such as "Orientals," "Chinese," and "Greeks," and—most generically of all—"Foreigners." A city directory for 1923 lists almost the entire three hundred block of Cordova as "Orientals." This may have been class differentiated; the directory for 1916 lists some named Europeans and Japanese, as well as "foreigners," "Japanese," etc; perhaps the named Japanese were owners, rather than renters, or were employed in respectable jobs?
30. Especially when we remember the racist conflation of people of Japanese and Chinese ancestry into the category "Oriental."
31. Anderson, "The Idea of Chinatown," 31.
32. The men went first. The only Japanese-Canadians listed in the three hundred block in 1942 were women.
33. Other new genre public art is also concerned with urban dispossession, racialization, and social memory. For example, the "projections" of Jewish artist Shimon Attie, with their focus on the Holocaust, are designed to transform "the sites of history into the sites of memory"; his aim is to "peel back the wallpaper of today and reveal the history buried underneath" (Young, *At Memory's Edge,* 70). "[W]ithout a deliberate act of remembrance, buildings, streets, or ruins remain little more than inert pieces of the cityscape." (62) On gentrification and its dispossessions, the work of Rachel Whitehead is similarly striking (Couldry, "Speaking up in Public Space," 96–113.)
34. Kogawa, Joy. (1994) *Obasan.* New York, Anchor Books; see also Miki, Roy, and Cassandra Kobayashi. (1991) *Justice in Our Time: The Japanese Canadian Redress Settlement.* Vancouver: Talonbooks.
35. Kobayashi, Audrey. (1992) *Memories of Our Past: A Brief History and Walking Tour of Powell Street.* Vancouver: NRC Publishing, at 24.
36. Ibid., 24.
37. Sennett, *The Conscience of the Eye.*
38. While this is largely echoed in the academic literature, see Bondi, Liz. (1999) "Gender, Class, and Gentrification: Enriching the Debate," *Environment and Planning D: Society and Space,* 17 261–282.
39. Goldberg, David Theo. (1993) *Racist Culture.* Oxford: Blackwell.
40. Gelder and Jacobs, *Uncanny Australia,* quotes at 26.
41. An important exception is Jane Jacobs discussion of gentrification in London's Spitalfields. See Jacobs, *Edge of Empire.*
42. Smith, *The New Urban Frontier,* at xiv, xv.
43. An intriguing and complicated echo of this avoidance also seems to occur in at least one other setting where aboriginality appears undeniable. Wendy Shaw illustrates the ways in which dominant depictions of gentrification and redevelopment in the aboriginal settlement of Redfern, Sydney, (discussed in chapter 4) relied upon imagery drawn from Harlem, New York, in a bizarre defusal and displacement of the aboriginal presence. Shaw, Wendy S. (2000) "Ways of Whiteness: Harlemising Sydney's Aboriginal Redfern." *Australian Geographical Studies,* 38 3, 291–305.
44. Sommers, "Mapping Men," 287–310.

45. Razack, Sherene. (2000) "Gendered Racial Violence and Spatialized Justice: The Murder of Pamela George." *Canadian Journal of Law and Society,* 15 (2): 91–130, at 97.
46. Peters, "Subversive Spaces," 665–685.
47. Sanchez, Lisa. (1998) "Boundaries of Legitimacy: Sex, Violence, Citizenship, and Community in a Local Sexual Economy." *Law and Social Inquiry,* 22 (3): 543–580 at 551, 577.
48. Ibid., 575, 547.
49. Peters, "Subversive Spaces"; Razack, "Gendered Racial Violence."
50. Lowman, John. (2000) "Violence and the Outlaw Status of (Street) Prostitutes in Canada." *Violence against Women,* 6, 9, 987–1011.
51. For a recent exploration of the link between spatial representation, art and Vancouver's "missing women," see Oleksijczuk, Denise Blake. (2002) "Haunted Spaces." In Shier, Reid, ed. *Stan Douglas: Every Building on 100 West Hastings,* Vancouver: Arsenal Pulp Press/ Contemporary Art Gallery, 96–117.
52. Razack, "Gendered Racial Violence," 129, 93.
53. Rose, "The Several Futures of Property," 143.
54. "[T]hat there can be no such thing as production, nor, consequently, society, where property does not exist in any form, is a tautology. . . . But it becomes ridiculous when from that one jumps at once to a definite form, e.g. private property." Marx, quoted in Waldron, Jeremy. (1988) *The Right to Private Property.* Oxford: Clarendon Press, 38.
55. Macpherson, Crawford Brough. (1987) *The Rise and Fall of Economic Justice and Other Essays.* Oxford: Oxford University Press, at 77.
56. Singer, Joseph. (2000) "Property and Social Relations: From Title to Entitlement." In Geisler, Charles, and Gail Daneker, eds. *Property and Values: Alternatives to Public and Private Ownership.* Washington: Island Press.
57. I am indebted to Don Mitchell for this point.
58. Salsich, Peter W. (2000) "Toward a Property Ethic of Stewardship: A Religious Perspective." In Geisler, Charles, and Gail Daneker, eds. *Property and Values: Alternatives to Public and Private Ownership.* Washington, D.C.: Island Press, 41–62.
59. Bowles, Samuel, and Herbert Gintis. (1987) *Democracy and Capitalism: Property, Community, and the Contradictions of Modern Social Thought.* New York: Basic Books. See also Williams, Patricia. (1991) The Alchemy of Race and Rights, 164–5 and Robertson, M. (1997) "Reconceiving Private Property."
60. The prevalent claim that the commons has been enclosed does not strike me as a very productive place from which to begin, politically speaking. If we recognize that public space can be appropriated more informally, or that propertied claims to space are enacted, and dependent on social production, and that, as argued here, private space can be rendered public, and that "public" spaces can be claimed for a local "counterpublic," different possibilities emerge.
61. Lefebvre, Henri. (1996) *Writings on Cities.* Oxford: Blackwell, 173–174.

Bibliography

Ablon, Joan. (1964) "Relocated American Indians in the San Francisco Bay Area: Social Interaction and Indian Identity." *Human Organization*, 23, Winter, 296–304.

Abramson, Allen, and Theodossopoulos, Dimitrios, eds. (2000) *Land, Law and Environment: Mythical Land, Legal Boundaries.* London: Pluto Press.

Abromowitz, David M. (2000) "An Essay on Community Land Trusts: Toward Permanently Affordable Housing." In Geisler, Charles, and Gail Daneker, eds. *Property and Values: Alternatives to Public and Private Ownership.* Washington D.C.: Island Press, 213–231.

Agarwal, Bina. (1994) "Gender and Command over Property: A Critical Gap in Economic Analysis and Policy in South Asia." *World Development*, 22, 10, 1455–1478.

Anderson, Kay. (1987) "The Idea of Chinatown: The Power of Place and Institutional Practice in the Making of a Racial Category." *Annals of the Association of American Geographers*, 77, 4, 580–598.

———. (1991) *Vancouver's Chinatown: Racial Discourse in Canada, 1885–1980.* Montreal: McGill-Queen's University Press.

———. (1993) "Place Narratives and the Origins of Inner Sydney's Aboriginal Settlement, 1972–73." *Journal of Historical Geography*, 19, 3, 314–335.

———. (2000) "Savagery and Urbanity: Struggles over Aboriginal Housing, Redfern, 1970–73." In Read, Peter, ed. *Settlement: A History of Aboriginal Housing.* Canberra: Aboriginal Studies Press, 130–144.

———. (2000) "Thinking 'Postnationally': Dialogue across Multicultural, Indigenous, and Settler Spaces." *Annals of the Association of American Geographers*, 90, 2, 381–391.

Anderson, Kay, and Jane M. Jacobs. (1997) "From Urban Aborigines to Aboriginality and the City: One Path through the History of Australian Cultural Geography." *Australian Geographical Studies.* 35, 1, 12–22.

Ardrey, Robert. (1966) *The Territorial Imperative.* New York: Atheneum.

Ashcraft, Richard. (1987) *Locke's Two Treatises of Government.* London: Allen and Unwin.

Azuela, Antonio. (1987) "Low-Income Settlements and the Law in Mexico City." *International Journal of Urban and Regional Research*, 11, 4, 522–542.

Badcock, Blair. (2002) *Making sense of cities.* New York: Arnold.

Bakan, Joel. (1997) *Just Words: Constitutional Rights and Social Wrongs.* Toronto: University of Toronto Press.

Banner, Stuart. (1999) "Two Properties, One Land: Law and Space in Nineteenth-century New Zealand." *Law and Social Inquiry*, 24, 4, 807–852.

Barman, Jean, and Cole Harris. (1997/98) "Editorial." *B.C. Studies*, 115/116, 4.

189

Barnett, Homer G. (1955) *The Coast Salish of British Columbia*. Eugene: University of Oregon Press.

Barry, Joseph, and John Derevlany. (1987) *Yuppies Invade My House at Dinnertime: A Tale of Brunch, Bombs, and Gentrification in an American City*. Hoboken: Big River Publishing.

Bender, Barbara. (1993) "Landscape—Meaning and Action." In Bender, Barbara, ed. *Landscape: Politics and Perspectives*. Providence R.I.: Berg Publishers, 1–17.

Bentham, Jeremy. (1843; 1978) "Security and Equality of Property." In Macpherson, C. B., ed. *Property: Mainstream and Critical Positions*. Toronto: University of Toronto Press.

Berger, John. (1972) *Ways of Seeing*. London: Penguin.

Berger, Thomas R. (1991) *A Long and Terrible Shadow*. Vancouver: Douglas and McIntyre.

Berry, Christopher J. (1980) "Property and Possession: Two Replies to Locke—Hume and Hegel." In Pennock, J. Roland, and John W. Chapman, eds. *Nomos* 22 New York: New York University Press, 89–100.

Bethell, Tom. (1998) *The Noblest Triumph: Property and Prosperity through the Ages*. New York: St. Martin's Press.

Bhahba, Homi K. (1990) "Introduction: Narrating the Nation." In Bhabha, Homi K., ed. *Nation and Narration*. New York: Routledge.

Blackstone, William. (1765; 1838). *Commentaries on the Laws of England*. 2nd vol. New York: W. E. Dean.

Blomley, Nicholas. (1994) *Law, Space and the Geographies of Power*. New York: Guilford.

———. (1996) " 'Shut the province down': First Nations Blockades in British Columbia, 1984–1995." *B.C. Studies*. 111, Autumn, 5–35.

———. (2003) "From 'What?' to 'So what?': Law and Geography in Retrospect." In Holder, Jane, and Carolyn Harrison, eds. *Law and Geography: Current Legal Issues*. Vol. 5, Oxford: Oxford University Press, 17–34.

———. (2003) "Law, Property and the Geography of Violence: The Frontier, The Survey, and the Grid." *Annals of the Association of American Geographers*, 93, 1, 121–141.

———. "Un-real Estate: Proprietary Space and Public Gardening." Unpublished paper.

———. (forthcoming) "Law and Geography: Lessons from Beatrix Potter." *The Canadian Geographer*.

Blomley, Nicholas, and Joel C. Bakan. (1992) "Spacing Out: Towards a Critical Geography of Law." *Osgoode Hall Law Journal*, 30, 3, 661–690.

Blomley, Nicholas, and Jeff Sommers. (1999) "Mapping Urban Space: Governmentality and Cartographic Struggles in Inner-city Vancouver." In Smandych, R., ed. *Governable Places: Readings in Governmentality and Crime Control*. Aldershot: Dartmouth Publishing, 261–286.

Blomley, Nicholas, and Geraldine Pratt. (2001) "Canada and the Political Geographies of Rights." *The Canadian Geographer*. 45, 1, 151–166.

Blomley, Nicholas, David Delaney, and Richard T. Ford, eds. (2001) *The Legal Geographies Reader: Law, Power and Space*. Oxford: Blackwell.

Bondi, Liz. (1999) "Gender, Class and Gentrification: Enriching the Debate." *Environment and Planning D: Society and Space*, 17, 261–282.

Borrows, John. (1997) "Living between Water and Rocks: First Nations, Environmental Planning, and Democracy." *University of Toronto Law Journal*, 47, 417–468.

———. (2002) *Recovering Canada: The Resurgence of Indigenous Law*. Toronto: University of Toronto Press.

Bottomley, Anne. (1996) "Figures in a Landscape: Feminist Perspectives on Law, Land, and Landscape." In Bottomley, Anne, ed. *Feminist Perspectives on the Foundational Subjects of Law*. London: Cavendish Publishing Limited.

Boulding, Kenneth E. (1991) Reflections on Property, Liberty, and Polity. *Journal of Social Behavior and Personality*, 6, 6, 1–16.

Bowles, Samuel, and Herbert Gintis. (1987) *Democracy and Capitalism: Property, Community and the Contradictions of Social Thought*. New York: Basic Books.

Brace, Laura. (1999) "Husbanding the Earth and Hedging out the Poor." Paper presented at Land and Freedom Conference, University of Newcastle, New South Wales.

Brealey, Ken. (1998) "Travels from Port Ellice: Peter O'Reilly and the Indian Reserve System in British Columbia." *B. C. Studies*, 115/116, 181–236.

Brear, Holly Beachey. (1995) *Inherit the Alamo: Myth and Ritual at an American Shrine*. Austin: University of Texas Press.

Brenner, Neil, and Nik Theodore. (2002) "Cities and the Geographies of 'Actually Existing Neoliberalism.' " *Antipode*, 34, 3, 349–379.

Brigham John, and Diana R. Gordon. (1996) "Law in Politics: Struggles over Property and Public Space on New York's Lower East Side." *Law and Social Inquiry*, 21, 2, 265–283.

Brion, Dennis J. (1992) "The Meaning of the City: Urban Redevelopment and the Loss of Community." *Indiana Law Review*, 685–740.

Brody, Hugh. (2000) *The Other Side of Eden: Hunters, Farmers, and the Shaping of the World.* Vancouver: Douglas and McIntyre.

Bromley, Daniel W. (1991) *Environment and Economy: Property Rights and Public Policy.* Oxford: Blackwell.

———. (1998) "Rousseau's Revenge: The Demise of the Freehold Estate." In Jacobs, Harvey M., ed. *Who Owns America? Social Conflict over Property Rights.* Madison: University of Wisconsin Press, 19–28.

Bryan, Bradley. (2000) "Property as Ontology: On Aboriginal and English Understandings of Ownership." *Canadian Journal of Law and Jurisprudence*, 13, 1, January, 3–31.

Burk, Adrienne. (2003) "Private Griefs, Public Places." *Political Geography*, 22, 3, 317–333.

Burt, Larry W. (1986) "Roots of the Native American Urban Experience: Relocation Policy in the 1950s." *The American Indian Quarterly*, 10, Spring, 85–99.

Carter, Paul. (1988) *The Road to Botany Bay.* New York: Knopf.

Caulfield, Jon. (1989) "Gentrification and Desire." *Canadian Review of Sociology and Anthropology*, 26, 4, 617–632.

Chivallon, Christine. (2001) "Bristol and the Eruption of Memory: Making the Slave-Trading Past Visible." *Social and Cultural Geography*, 2, 3, 347–363.

Choko, Marc, and Richard Harris. (1990) "The Local Culture of Property: A Comparative History of Housing Tenure in Montreal and Toronto." *Annals of the Association of American Geographers*, 80, 1, 73–95.

Clark, Eric. (1987) *The Rent Gap and Urban Change: Case Studies in Malmo, 1860–1985.* Lund: Lund University Press.

Clark, Gordon. (1986) "Making Moral Landscapes: John Rawls' Original Position." *Political Geography Quarterly*, Supplement to 5, 147–162.

Clark, Gordon L. (1985) *Judges and the Cities: Interpreting Local Autonomy.* Chicago: Chicago University Press.

Cockburn, Julio Calderon. (2002) "The Mystery of Credit." *Land Lines*, 14, 2, 5–8.

Cohen, David, and Allen C. Hutchinson. (1990) "Of Persons and Property: The Politics of Legal Taxonomy." *Dalhousie Law Journal*, 13, 1, 20–54.

Cohen, Morris R. (1927) "Property and Sovereignty." *Cornell Law Quarterly*, 13, 8–30.

Cole, Ian, and Barry Goodchild. (2001) "Social Mix and the 'Balanced Community' in British Housing Policy—A Tale of Two Epochs." *GeoJournal*, 51, 351–360.

Collins, D., and Nicholas Blomley. (2003) "Private Needs and Public Space: Politics, Poverty, and Anti-panhandling By-laws in Canadian Cities." In Law Commission of Canada, eds. *New Perspectives on the Public-Private Divide.* Vancouver: University of British Columbia Press.

Comaroff, John L. (1995) "The Discourse of Rights in Colonial South Africa: Subjectivity, Sovereignty, Modernity." In Sarat, Austin, and Thomas R. Kearns, eds. *Identities, Politics, and Rights.* Michigan: University of Michigan Press, 193–236.

———. (2001) "Colonialism, Culture, and the Law: A Foreword." *Law and Social Inquiry*, 26, 2, 305–314.

Conn, Heather. (1986) "Trashing the People's Park." *City Magazine*, 8, 2, 4–5.

Corr, Anders. (1999) *No Trespassing! Squatting, Rent Strikes, and Land Struggles Worldwide.* Cambridge, Mass.: South End Press.

Cosgrove, Denis. (1984) *Social Formation and Symbolic Landscape.* London: Croom Helm.

———. (1985) "Prospect, Perspective, and the Evolution of the Landscape Idea." *Transactions, Institute of British Geographers*, N.S., 10, 45–62.

———. (1989) "Power and Place in Venetian Territories." In Agnew, John, and James S. Duncan, eds. *The Power of Place: Bringing Together Geographical and Sociological Imagination.* London: Unwin Hyman, 104–123.

Couldry, Nick. (1995) "Speaking up in a Public Space: The Strange Case of Rachel Whitehead's House." *New Formations*, 25, 96–113.

Cowan, Gregory. (2002) *Nomadology in Architecture: Ephemerality, Movement and Collaboration.* Ph.D. Dissertation, University of Adelaide (online at *http://www.gregory.cowan.com/nomad/*).

Crawford, Margaret. (1999) "Blurring the Boundaries: Public Space and Private Life." In Chase, John, Margaret Crawford, and John Kaliski, eds. *Everyday Urbanism.* New York: Monacelli Press, 22–35.

Crenshaw, Kimberle W. (1988) "Race, Reform and Retrenchment: Transformation and Legitimation in Anti-discrimination Law." *Harvard Law Review,* 101, 7, 1331–1387.

Cresswell, Tim. (1996) *In Place/Out of Place: Geography, Ideology, and Transgression.* Minneapolis: University of Minnesota Press.

Cronon, William. (1992) "A Place for Stories: Nature, History, and Narrative." *The Journal of American History,* 78, 4, 1347–1376.

Crump, Jeff. (1999) "What Cannot Be Seen Will Not Be Heard: The Production of Landscape in Moline, Illinois." *Ecumeme,* 6, 3, 295–317.

———. (2002) "Deconcentration by Demolition: Public Housing, Poverty, and Urban Policy." *Society and Space,* 20, 581–596.

Cuff, Dana. (1998) "Community Property: Enter the Architect or, The Politics of Form." In Bell, Michael, and Sze Tsung Leong, eds. *Slow Space.* New York: Monacelli Press, 120–140.

Culhane, Dara. (1998) *The Pleasure of the Crown: Anthropology, Law, and First Nations.* Burnaby, B.C.: Talonbooks.

Curnoe, Greg. (1995) *Deeds/Abstracts: The History of a London Lot.* London Ont.: Brick Books.

Curnow, Wynstan. (1999) "Mapping and the Expanded Field of Contemporary Art." In Cosgrove, Denis, ed. *Mappings.* London: Reaktion Books.

Curran, Winifred. (2002) *Evicting Memory: Displacing Work and Home in a Gentrifying Neighborhood.* Presented at Upward Neighbourhood Trajectories: Gentrification in a New Century. University of Glasgow.

D'Arcus, Bruce. (2000) "The 'eager gaze of the tourist' meets 'our grandfather's guns': Producing and Contesting the Land of Enchantment in Gallup, New Mexico." *Society and Space,* 18, 693–714.

Daes, Erica-Irene A. (1999) *Human Rights of Indigenous Peoples:* United Nations Commission on Human Rights (E/cn.4/sub.z/1999/13).

Dansereau, Francine, Annick Germain, and Catherine Éveillard. (1997) "Social Mix: Old Utopias, Contemporary Experience and Challenges." *Canadian Journal of Urban Research,* 6, 1, 1–23.

Darian-Smith, Eve. (1999) *Bridging Divides: The Channel Tunnel and English Legal Identity in the New Europe.* Berkeley: University of California Press.

Davis, John Emmeus. (1991) *Contested Ground: Collective Action and the Urban Neighborhood.* Ithaca: Cornell University Press.

———. (2000) "Homemaking: The Pragmatic Politics of Third Sector Housing." In Geisler, Charles, and Gail Daneker, eds. *Property and Values: Alternatives to Public and Private Ownership.* Washington D.C.: Island Press, 233–258.

Delaney, David. (1997) *Geographies of Judgment: Legal Reasoning and the Geopolitics of Race, 1836–1948.* Austin: University of Texas Press.

Delgado, Richard. (1989) "Storytelling for Oppositionists and Others: A Plea for Narrative." *Michigan Law Review,* 87, 2411–2441.

Deloria, Vine, and Clifford M. Lytle. (1983) *American Indians, American Justice.* Austin: University of Texas Press.

Derbes, Max J. (1981) "Highest and Best Use—What Is It?" In American Institute of Real Estate Appraisers, ed. *Readings in Highest and Best Use.* Chicago: American Institute of Real Estate Appraisers, 3–15.

Deustche, Rosalyn. (1986) "Krzysztof Wodiczko's Homeless Projection and the Site of Urban 'Revitalisation.' " *October,* 38, 63–98.

———. (1996) *Evictions: Art and Spatial Politics.* Cambridge: MIT Press.

Deutsche, Rosalyn, and C. G. Ryan. (1984) "The Fine Art of Gentrification." *October,* 31, 91–111.

Dilley, Roy, ed. (1992) *Contesting Markets: Analyses of Ideology, Discourse, and Practice.* Edinburgh: Edinburgh University Press.

Dimas, Pete R. (1999) *Progress and a Mexican American Community's Struggle for Existence: Phoenix's Golden Gate Barrio.* New York: Peter Lang.

Donahue, Charles. (1980) "The Future of the Concept of Property Predicted from its Past." In Pennock, J. Roland, and John W. Chapman, eds. *Nomos* 22 New York: New York University Press, 28–68.

———. (1998) "Property Law." *The New Encyclopaedia Britannica.* vol. 26, 15th ed., 180–205.

Driver, Felix. (1988) "Moral Geographies: Social Science and the Urban Environment in Mid-Nineteenth-Century England." *Transactions of the Institute of British Geographers*, 13, 275–287.

Driver, Felix, and David Gilbert, eds. (1999) *Imperial Cities: Landscape, Display, and Identity.* Manchester: Manchester University Press.

Dubin, Jon C. (1993) "From Junkyards to Gentrification: Explicating a Right to Protective Zoning in Low-income Communities of Color." *Minnesota Law Review,* 77, 739–801.

Dunn, Peter, and Loraine Leeson. (1993) "The Art of Change in Docklands." In Bird, Jon, et al., eds. *Mapping the Futures: Local Cultures, Global Change.* London: Blackwell.

Edney, Mathew G. (1993) "The Patronage of Science and the Creation of Imperial Space: The British Mapping of India, 1799–1843." *Cartographica*, 30, 61–67.

Ellis, Reuben J. (1993) "The American Frontier and the Contemporary Real Estate Advertising Magazine." *Journal of Popular Culture,* 27, 3, 119–133.

Ely, James W. (1998) *The Guardian of Every Other Right.* Oxford: Oxford University Press.

Ewick, Patricia, and Susan Silbey. (1995) "Subversive Stories and Hegemonic Tales: Toward a Sociology of Narrative." *Law and Society Review,* 29, 2, 197–226.

Exodus Collective (1998) "Exodus: Movement of Jah People." In Wolff, Richard, et al., eds. *Possible Urban Worlds: Urban Strategies at the End of the Twentieth Century.* Basel: Birkhäuser Verlag.

Featherstone, Dave. (1998) "The 'Pure Genius' Land Occupation: Reimagining the Inhuman City." In Wolff, Richard, et al., eds. *Possible Urban Worlds: Urban Strategies at the End of the Twentieth Century.* Basel: Birkhäuser Verlag.

Feldman, Thomas D., and Andrew E. G. Jonas. (2000) "Sage Scrub Revolution? Property Rights, Political Fragmentation, and Conservation Planning in Southern California under the Federal Endangered Species Act." *Annals of the Association of American Geographers,* 90 (2), 256–292.

Felstine, William L. F., Richard Abel, and Austin Sarat. (1980–81) "The Emergence and Transformation of Disputes: Naming, Blaming, Claiming." *Law and Society Review,* 15, 3–4, 631–654.

Fernandes, Edesio. (2001) "Regularising Informal Settlements in Brazil: Legislation, Security of Land Tenure and City Management." Law and Geography colloquium, University College London.

Fernandes, Edesio, and Ann Varley, eds. (1998) *Illegal Cities: Law and Urban Change in Developing Countries.* London: Zed Books.

Fisher, Robin. (1977) *Contact and Conflict: Indian-European Relations in British Columbia, 1774–1890.* Vancouver: University of British Columbia Press.

Fitzpatrick, Peter. (1992). *The Mythology of Modern Law.* New York: Routledge.

Forbes, Ann A. (1995) "Heirs to the Land: Mapping the Future of the Makalu-Barun." *Cultural Survival Quarterly,* Winter, 69–71.

Fortunate Eagle, Adam. (1994) "Urban Indians and the Occupation of Alcatraz Island." *American Indian Culture and Research Journal,* 18, 4, 33–58.

———. (2002) *Heart of the Rock; the Indian Invasion of Alcatraz.* Norman: University of Oklahoma Press.

Francis, Daniel. (1992) *The Imaginary Indian.* Vancouver: Pulp Press.

Fraser, Nancy. (1990) "Rethinking the Public Sphere: A Contribution to Actually Existing Democracy." *Social Text,* 25/26, 56–79.

Furniss, Elizabeth. (1997–98) "Pioneers, Progress and the Myth of the Frontier: The Landscape of Public History in Rural British Columbia." *B.C. Studies,* 115/116, 7–44.

Gad, Gunter, and Malcolm Mathew. (2000) "Central and Suburban Downtowns." In Bunting, Trudi, and Pierre Filion, eds. *Canadian Cities in Transition: The Twenty-First Century.* Don Mills, Ont.: Oxford University Press, 248–273.

Gans, Herbert. (1961) "Planning and Social Life." *Journal of the American Association of Planners,* May, 134–141.

Geisler, Charles. (1995) "Land and Poverty in the United States: Insights and Oversights." *Land Economics,* 71, 1, 16–34.

———. (2000) "Property Pluralism." In Geisler, Charles, and Gail Daneker, eds. *Property and Values: Alternatives to Public and Private Ownership.* Washington D.C.: Island Press, 65–86.

Gelder, Ken, and Jane M. Jacobs. (1998) *Uncanny Australia: Sacredness and Identity in a Postcolonial Nation.* Victoria: Melbourne University Press.

Gibson, Kristina. (2002) " '11,000 Vacant Lots, Why Take Our Garden Plots?' Community Garden Preservation Strategies in New York City's Gentrified Lower East Side." Paper presented at Rights to the City conference, Rome.

Gibson-Graham J. K. (1996) The End of Capitalism (as We Knew It): A Feminist Critique of Political Economy. Oxford: Blackwell.

Goetz, Edward G., and Mara Sidney. (1994) "Revenge of the Property Owners: Community Development and the Politics of Property." Journal of Urban Affairs, 16, 4, 319–333.

Goldberg, David Theo. (1993) Racist Culture. Oxford: Blackwell.

Goldberg, Michael A., and H. Craig Davis. (1988) "Global Cities and Public Policy: The Case of Vancouver, British Columbia." U.B.C. Planning Papers, 17.

Gonzalez, Mario, and Elizabeth Cook-Lynn. (1998) The Politics of Hallowed Ground: Wounded Knee and the Struggle for Indian Sovereignty. Urbana: University of Illinois Press.

Goodfellow, Reverend John C. (192-) The Totem Poles in Stanley Park, Vancouver AHS.

Gregory, Derek. (1994) Geographical Imaginations. Oxford: Blackwell.

———. (2000) "Post-Colonialism." In Johnston, Ronald J., Derek Gregory, Geraldine Pratt, and Michael Watts, eds. The Dictionary of Human Geography. Oxford: Blackwell, 612–615.

Grell, Britta, Jens Sambale, and Dominik Veith. (1998) "Inner!City!Action!—Crowd Control, Interdictory Space, and the Fight for Socio-Spatial Justice." In Richard Wolff, et al., eds. Possible Urban Worlds: Urban Strategies at the End of the Twentieth Century. Basel: Birkhäuser Verlag.

Grey, Thomas. (1980) "The Disintegration of Property." In Pennock, J. Roland, and John W. Chapman, eds. Nomos, 22, 69–85.

Grunebaum, James O. (1987) Private Ownership. New York: Routledge and Kegan Paul.

Gunn, S. W. A. (1965) A Complete Guide to the Totem Poles in Stanley Park, Vancouver, B.C., Vancouver: W. E. G. McDonald.

Hale, Robert L. (1923) "Coercion and Distribution in a Supposedly Noncoercive State." Political Science Quarterly, 38, 470–494.

Hallowell, A. Irving. (1942–43) "The Nature and Function of Property as a Social Institution." Journal of Legal and Political Sociology, 1, 115–138.

Hamer, David. (1990) New Towns in the New World. New York: Columbia University Press.

Hamilton, Jonette Watson. (2002) "Theories of Categorization: A Case Study of Cheques." Canadian Journal of Law and Society, 17, 1, 115–138.

Hann, C. M. (1998) Property Relations: Renewing the Anthropological Tradition. New York: Cambridge University Press.

Harley, John B. (1988) "Maps, Knowledge, and Power." In Cosgrove, Denis, and Steven Daniels, eds. The Iconography of Landscape: Essays on the Symbolic Representation, Design, and Use of Past Environments. Cambridge: Cambridge University Press, 277–312.

Harris, Cole. (1992) "The Lower Mainland, 1820–81." In Wynn, Graeme, and Timothy Oke, eds. Vancouver and Its Region. Vancouver: U.B.C. Press, 38–68.

———. (1997) The Resettlement of British Columbia: Essays on Colonialism and Geographic Change. Vancouver: University of British Columbia Press.

Harris, J. W. (1995) "Private and Non-Private Property: What is the Difference?" Law Quarterly Review, 111, 421–444.

Hartman, Chester, Dennis Keating, and Richard LeGates. (1982) Displacement: How to Fight It. Berkeley, Calif.: National Housing Law Project.

Harvey, David. (1985) The Urbanization of Capital. Oxford: Blackwell.

———. (1989) "From Managerialism to Entrepreneuralism: The Transformation in Urban Governance in Late Capitalism." Geografiska Annaler, Vol. 71, B(1) 3–17.

Hassan, Shlomo, and David Ley. (1994) Neighbourhood Organizations and the Welfare State. Toronto: University of Toronto Press.

Hayden, Dolores. (1997) The Power of Place: Urban Landscapes as Public History. Cambridge, Mass.: MIT Press.

Healy, Chris. (1997) From the Ruins of Colonialism: History as Social Memory. Cambridge: Cambridge University Press.

Heasley, Lynne. (1998) Many Paths in the Woods: An Ecological Narrative of Property in the Kickapoo Valley. Presented at Who Owns America II conference, University of Wisconsin-Madison.

Heat-Moon, William Least. (1991) Prairyerth (A Deep Map). Boston: Houghton Mifflin.

Heller, Michael A. (1999) "The Boundaries of Private Property." Yale Law Journal, 108, 1163–1223.

Hening, Glenn (n.d.) "The stain on the soul of surfing," *http://www.surflink.com/features/stain 4.html.* (September 30, 2002).

Hill-Tout, Charles. (1978) *The Squamish and the Lillooet.* vol. 2 of *The Salish People: The Local Contribution of Charles Hill-Tout,* edited by Ralph Maud. Vancouver: Talonbooks.

Hindle, Steve. (1999) "Hierarchy and Community in the Elizabethan Parish: The Swallowfield Articles of 1596," *Historical Journal* 42, 3, October, 835–851.

Hobbes, Thomas. (1651; 1988) *Leviathan.* London: Penguin.

Hoebel, E. Adamson. (1966) *Anthropology: The Study of Man.* New York: McGraw-Hill.

Hohfeld, Wesley Newcomb. (1919) *Some Fundamental Legal Conceptions as Applied in Judicial Reasoning.* New Haven, Conn.: Yale University Press.

Holdsworth, Deryck W. (1986) "Cottages and Castles for Vancouver Home-Seekers." *B. C. Studies,* 69–70, 11–32.

Hollowell, Peter G., ed. (1982) *Property and Social Relations.* London: Heinemann.

Hood, R. A. (1929) *By Shore and Trail in Stanley Park.* Toronto: McLelland and Stewart.

Howitt, Richie. (2001) "Frontiers, Borders, Edges: Liminal Challenges to the Hegemony of Exclusion." *Australian Geographical Studies,* 39, 2, 233–245.

Huggan, Graham. (1991) "Maps, Dreams and the Presentation of Ethnographic Narrative: High Brody's 'Maps and Dreams' and Bruce Chatwin's 'The Songlines'." *Ariel* 22, 1, 57–69.

Hurd, Richard M. (1903; 1924) *Principles of City Land Values.* New York: The Record and Guide.

Hurran, Wanda. (1998) "Living with/in the Lines: Poetical Possibilities for World Writing." *Gender, Place, and Culture,* 5, 3, 301–304.

Hutchinson, Allan C. (1991) "Crits and Crickets: A Deconstructive Spin (or Was It Googly?)" In Devlin, R. F., ed. *Canadian Perspectives on Legal Theory.* Toronto: Emond-Montgomery.

Ingerson, Alice E. (1997) "Urban Land as Common Property." *Land Lines,* 9, 2, 1–3.

Isin, Engin. (1992) *Cities without Citizens.* Montreal: Black Rose Books.

Jacobs, Harvey, ed. (1998) *Who Owns America? Social Conflict over Property Rights.* Madison: University of Wisconsin Press.

Jacobs, Jane. (1961) *The Death and Life of Great American Cities.* New York: Vintage.

———. (1996) *Edge of Empire: Postcolonialism and the City.* London: Routledge.

———. (1997) "Resisting Reconciliation: The Secret Geographies of (Post) Colonial Australia." In Pile, Steve, and Michael Keith, eds. *Geographies of Resistance.* London: Routledge, 202–218.

Jaconetty, Thomas A. (1994) " 'Highest and Best Use' Revisited." *Assessment Journal,* 1 (3) 36–39.

Johnson, Louise. (1994) "Occupying the Suburban Frontier: Accommodating Difference on Melbourne's Urban Fringe." In Blunt, Alison, and Gillian Rose, eds. *Writing Women and Space: Colonial and Postcolonial Geographies.* New York: Guilford Press, 141–168.

Johnston, Ronald J. (1982) *The American Urban System.* Harlow: Longman.

Kain, R. J. P., and E. Baigent. (1992) *The Cadastral Map in the Service of the State: A History of Property Mapping.* Chicago: University of Chicago Press.

Kayden, Jerold S. (2000) *Privately Owned Public Space: The New York City Experience.* New York, John Wiley and Sons.

Kearns, Gerry, and Chris Philo, eds. (1993) *Selling Places: The City as Cultural Capital, Past and Present.* New York: Pergamon.

Kedar, Alexandre. (2001) "The Legal Transformation of Ethnic Geography: Israeli Law and the Palestinian Landholder, 1948–1967." *New York University Journal of International Law and Politics,* 33, 4, 923–1000.

Keil, Roger. (2002) " 'Common sense' Neoliberalism: Progressive Conservative Urbanism in Toronto, Canada." *Antipode,* 34, 3, 578–601.

Kidd, Dorothy. (1998) *Talking the Walk: The Communication Commons amidst the Media Enclosures.* Ph.D. diss. Simon Fraser University, School of Communications.

Kirby, Andrew. (2002) "From Berlin Wall to Garden Wall: Boundary Formation around the Home." Paper presented at the Meetings of the Association of American Geographers, Los Angeles.

Kobayashi, Audrey. (1992) *Memories of Our Past: A Brief History and Walking Tour of Powell Street.* Vancouver: NRC Publishing.

Kofman, Elenore. (1998) "Whose City? Gender, Class, and Immigration in Globalizing European Cities." In Fincher, Ruth, and Jane M. Jacobs, eds. *Cities of Difference.* New York: Guilford.

Kogawa, Joy. (1994) *Obasan.* New York: Anchor Books.

Kolodney, Lawrence K. (1991) "Eviction Free Zones: The Economics of Legal Bricolage in the Fight against Displacement." *Fordham Urban Law Journal,* 18, 507–543.

Kolodny, Annette. (1975) *The Lay of the Land.* Chapel Hill: University of North Carolina Press.

Krueckeberg, Donald A. (1995) "The Difficult Character of Property: To Whom Do Things Belong?" *Journal of the American Planning Association,* 61, 3, 301–309 at 301.

———. (1998) "Who Rents America? Owners, Tenants, and Taxes." Paper presented at Who Owns America II conference, Madison, Wisconsin.

Laclau, Ernesto, and Chantal Mouffe. (1985) *Hegemony and Socialist Strategy: Toward a Radical Democratic Politics.* London: Verso.

Lacy, Suzanne. (1995) *Mapping the Terrain: New Genre Public Art.* Seattle: Bay Press.

Latour, Bruno. (1986) "Visualization and Cognition: Thinking with Eyes and Hands." *Knowledge and Society: Studies in the Sociology of Culture Past and Present,* 6, 1–40.

Lee, Roger. (2000) "Shelter from the Storm? Geographies of Regard in the Worlds of Horticultural Consumption and Production." *Geoforum* 31, 137–157.

———. (2002) "Nice Maps, Shame about the Theory? Thinking Geographically about the Economic." *Progress in Human Geography,* 26, 3, 333–355.

Lefcoe, George. (1975) "The Highest and Best Use of the Land: The Long Way Home." In Lenz, Elinor, and Alice Lebel, eds. *Land and the Pursuit of Happiness: A Bicentennial Anthology.* Los Angeles: Western Humanities Center, UCLA Extension.

Lefebvre, Henri. (1976) "Reflections on the Politics of Space." *Antipode,* 8, 30–37.

———. (1991) *The Production of Space.* Oxford: Blackwell.

Ley, David. (1996) *The New Middle Class and the Remaking of the Central City.* Don Mills, Ont.: Oxford University Press.

Linn, Karl. (1999) "Reclaiming the Sacred Commons." *New Village Journal,* 1. Accessed online at *http://www.newvillage.net/Journal/Issue1/1sacredcommon.html.* September 30, 2002.

Locke, John. (1690; 1980) *Second Treatise of Government.* Indianapolis: Hackett Publishing Co. Inc.

Loo, Tina. (1994) *Making Law, Order, and Authority in British Columbia, 1821–1871.* Toronto: University of Toronto Press.

Lowman, John. (2000). "Violence and the Outlaw Status of (Street) Prostitution in Canada." *Violence Against Women,* 6, 9, 987–1011.

Luna, Guadalupe T. (1998) "Chicana/Chicano Land Tenure in the Agrarian Domain: On the Edge of a 'Naked Knife,' " *Michigan Journal of Race and Law,* 4, 39–144.

Lydersen, Kari. (2001) "Dept. of Space and Land Reclamation," *Punk Planet,* 46, Nov./Dec., 112–113.

Lynd, Staughton. (1987) "The Genesis of the Idea of a Community Right to Industrial Property in Youngstown and Pittsburgh, 1977–1987," *Journal of American History,* 74, 3, 926–958.

Macdonald, Bruce. (1992) *Vancouver: A Visual History.* Vancouver: Talon Books.

Macionis, John J., and Vincent N. Parillo. (1998) *Cities and Urban Life.* Upper Saddle River, N.J.: Prentice Hall.

Macklem, Patrick. (1990) "Property, Status, and Workplace Organizing." *University of Toronto Law Journal,* 40, 74–108.

Macpherson, Crawford Brough. (1978) "The Meaning of Property." In Macpherson, Crawford Brough, ed. *Property: Mainstream and Critical Positions.* Toronto: University of Toronto Press: 1–14.

———. (1987) *The Rise and Fall of Economic Justice and Other Essays.* Oxford: Oxford University Press.

Malouf, David. (1993) *Remembering Babylon.* New York: Pantheon.

Marchak, M. Patricia. (1998) "Who Owns Natural Resources in the United States and Canada?" *Working Paper no. 20,* Land Tenure Center, North American Program, University of Wisconsin, Madison.

Marcuse, Peter. (1985) "To Control Gentrification: Anti-displacement Zoning and Planning for Stable Residential Districts." *Review of Law and Social Change.* 13, 931–953.

Marx, Karl. (1975) "On the Jewish Question." In Colletti, L. ed. *Early Writings.* Harmondsworth, Penguin.

———. (1867; 1976) *Capital: A Critique of Political Economy.* Volume I. Harmondsworth: Penguin Books.

Marx, Karl, and Friedrich Engels. (1975) *Collected Works.* Vol. 5. New York: International Publishers.

Mather, Susan. (1998) *One of Many Homes: Stories of Dispossession from 'Stanley Park.'* Master's thesis, Department of History, Simon Fraser University.

McCann, Larry, and Peter Smith. (1991) "Canada Becomes Urban: Cities and Urbanization in Historical Perspective." In Bunting, Trudi E., and Pierre Filion, eds. *Canadian Cities in Transition.* Don Mills, Ont.: Oxford University Press, 69–99.

McClain, Linda. (1995) "Inviolability and Privacy: The Castle, the Sanctuary, and the Body." *Yale Journal of Law and the Humanities,* 7, 2, 195–242.

McDonald, Robert A. J. (1979) "City-Building in the Canadian West: A Case Study of Economic Growth in Early Vancouver, 1886–1913." *B.C. Studies,* 43, 3–28.

McGee, Henry W. (1992) "Afro-American Resistance to Gentrification and the Demise of Integrationist Ideology in the United States." *Land Use and Environment Law Review,* 23, 215–234.

McGregor, Donald A. (1911) "The Marvel of Vancouver." *British Columbia Magazine,* June, 457–472.

Meacham, Standish. (1999) *Regaining Paradise: Englishness and the Early Garden City Movement.* New Haven, Conn.: Yale University Press.

Merchant, Carolyn. (1996) *Earthcare: Women and the Environment.* New York: Routledge.

Merivale, Herman. (1841; 1967) *Lectures on Colonization and Colonies.* New York: Augustus M. Kelley.

Miki, Roy, and Cassandra Kobayashi. (1991) *Justice in Our Time: The Japanese Canadian Redress Settlement.* Vancouver: Talonbooks.

Milner, Neal. (1993) "Ownership Rights and Rites of Ownership." *Law and Social Inquiry,* 18, 227–253.

Minda, Garry. (1995) *Postmodern Legal Movements.* New York: New York University Press.

Miranda, Louis, and Philip Joe. (1993) "How the Squamish Remember George Vancouver." In Fisher, Robin, and Hugh Johnston, eds. *From Maps to Metaphors: The Pacific World of George Vancouver.* Vancouver: University of British Columbia Press, 3–5.

Mitchell, Don. (1995) "The End of Public Space? People's Park, Definitions of the Public, and Democracy." *Annals of the Association of American Geographers,* 85, 1, 108–133.

———. (1996) *The Lie of the Land: Migrant Workers in the Californian Landscape.* Minneapolis: University of Minnesota Press.

———. (1997) "The Annihilation of Space by Law: The Roots and Implications of Anti-Homeless Laws in the United States." *Antipode,* 29: 303–335.

———. (2003) *The Right to the City: Social Justice and the Fight for Public Space.* New York: Guilford Press.

Mitchell, Katharyne. (1993) "Multiculturalism, or the United Colours of Capitalism?" *Antipode,* 25, 4, 263–294.

———. (1996) "Visions of Vancouver: Ideology, Democracy, and the Future of Urban Development." *Urban Geography,* 17, 6, 478–501.

Mitchell, Timothy. (1991) *Colonising Egypt.* Berkeley: University of California Press.

Mollenkopf, John. (1981) "Community and Accumulation." In Dear, Michael, and Allen J. Scott, eds. *Urbanization and Urban Planning in Capitalist Societies.* London: Methuen, 319–337.

Morley, Alan. (1961) *From Milltown to Metropolis.* Vancouver: Mitchell Press.

Morris, Jan. (1990) *City to City.* Toronto: Macfarlane Walter & Ross.

Murdie, Robert A., and Carlos C. Tiexeira. (2000) "The City as Social Space." In Bunting, Trudi, and Pierre Filion, eds. *Canadian Cities in Transition: The Twenty-First Century.* Don Mills, Ont.: Oxford University Press.

Murphy, Howard. (1993) "Colonialism, History, and the Construction of Place: The Politics of Landscape in Northern Australia." In Bender, Barbara, ed. *Landscape: Politics and Perspectives.* Providence, R.I.: Berg Publishers, 205–243.

Myers, Garth. (1996) "Naming and Placing the Other: Power and the Urban Landscape in Zanzibar." *Tijdschrift voor Economische en Sociale Geografie,* 87, 3, 237–246.

Nash, Catherine. (1999) "Wanda Hurren's World Writing." *Gender, Place, and Culture,* 6, 3, 273–274.

Nedelsky, Jennifer. (1990) *Private Property and the Limits of American Constitutionalism.* Chicago: University of Chicago Press.

———. (1990) "Law, Boundaries, and the Bounded Self." *Representations,* 30, 162–189.

Nelson, Jennifer. (2001) *The Operation of Whiteness and Forgetting in Africville: A Geography of Racism.* Ph.D. diss., Department of Sociology and Equity Studies in Education, University of Toronto.

Neuwirth, Robert. (2002) "Squatters' rites." *City Limits Monthly*, Sept/Oct. Online at *www.citylimits.org* (accessed Aug. 22, 2002).

Newman, Oscar. (1972) *Defensible Space: Crime Prevention through Environmental Design*. New York: Macmillan.

Nicol, Eric. (1970) *Vancouver*. Toronto: Doubleday.

Nunn, Kenneth B. (1997) "Law as a Eurocentric Enterprise," *Law and Inequality*. 15, 2, 323–371.

Olds, Kris. (1998) "Canada: Hallmark Events, Evictions, and Housing Rights." In Azuela, Antonio, Emilio Duhau, and Enrique Ortiz, eds. *Evictions and the Right to Housing: Experience from Canada, Chile, the Dominican Republic, South Africa, and South Korea*. Ottawa: International Development Research Centre.

———. (2001) *Globalization and Urban Change: Capital, Culture, and Pacific Rim Mega-Projects*. Oxford: Oxford University Press.

Oleksijczuk, Denise. (1991) "Nature in History: A Context for Landscape Art." In Vancouver Art Gallery, ed. *Lost Illusions: Recent Landscape Art*. Vancouver: Vancouver Art Gallery, 5–24.

Oleksijczuk, Denise Blake. (2002) "Haunted Spaces." In Shier, Reid, ed. *Stan Douglas: Every Building on 100 West Hastings*. Vancouver: Arsenal Pulp Press/Contemporary Art Gallery, 96–117.

Olwig, Kenneth. (1996) "Recovering the Substantive Nature of Landscape." *Annals of the Association of American Geographers*, 86, 4, 630–653.

Orlove, Benjamin. (1993) "The Ethnography of Maps: The Cultural and Social Contexts of Cartographic Representation in Peru." *Cartographica*, 30, 1, 29–45.

Osborn, Bud. (1998) "raise shit—a downtown eastside poem of resistance." *Society and Space*, 16, 3, 280–288.

Ostendorf, Wim, Sako Musterd, and Sjoerd de Vos. (2001) "Social Mix and the Neighbourhood Effect. Policy Ambitions and Empirical Evidence." *Housing Studies*, 16, 3, 371–380.

Ostrom, Elinor. (1990) *Governing the Commons: The Evolution of Institutions for Collective Action*. Cambridge: Cambridge University Press.

Park, Robert. (1925; 1967) "The Mind of the Hobo: Reflections upon the Relation between Mentality and Locomotion." In Park, Robert E., Ernest W. Burgess, and Roderick D. McKenzie, eds. *The City*. Chicago: University of Chicago Press, 156–160.

———. (1932; 1952) "Succession, an Ecological Concept." In *Human Communities: The City and Human Ecology, Volume II; The Collected Papers of Robert Ezra Park*. Glencoe, Ill.: The Free Press, 223–232.

Parker, Gavin. (2002) *Citizenships, Contingency and the Countryside: Rights, Culture, Land, and the Environment*. London: Routledge.

Parker, Patricia. (1987) *Literary Fat Ladies: Rhetoric, Gender, Property*. London: Methuen.

Pateman, Carole. (1988) *The Sexual Contract*. Oxford: Polity Press.

Patton, Paul. (2000) "The Translation of Indigenous Land into Property: The Mere Analogy of English Jurisprudence . . ." *parallax*, 6, 1, 25–38.

Peck, Jamie. (2001) "Neoliberalizing States: Thin Policies/Hard Outcomes." *Progress in Human Geography*, 25, 3, 445–455.

Peller, Gary. (1985) "The Metaphysics of American Law." *California Law Review*, 73, 1152–1290.

Peluso, Nancy. (1996) "Fruit Trees and Family Trees in an Anthropegenic Forest: Ethics of Access, Property Zones and Environmental Change in Indonesia." *Comparative Studies in Society and History*, 38, 3, 510–548.

Pennington, Mark. (2002) *Liberating the Land: The Case for Private Land-Use Planning*. London: Institute of Economic Affairs.

Perin, Constance. (1977) *Everything in Its Place: Social Order and Land Use in America*. Princeton, N.J.: Princeton University Press.

Peters, Evelyn. (1996) " 'Urban' and 'Aboriginal': An Impossible Contradiction." In Caulfield, Jon, and Linda Peake, eds. *City Lives and City Forms: Critical Research and Canadian Urbanism*. Toronto: University of Toronto Press.

———. (1998) "Subversive Spaces: First Nations Women and the City." *Society and Space*, 16, 665–685.

Pinder, David. (1996) "Subverting Cartography: The Situationists and Maps of the City." *Environment and Planning*, A, 28, 405–427.

Pipes, Richard. (1999) *Property and Freedom*. New York, Vintage Books.

Pratt, Geraldine. (1989) "Incorporation Theory and the Reproduction of Community Fabric." In Wolch, Jennifer, and Michael Dear, eds. *The Power of Geography: How Territory Shapes Social Life.* Boston: Unwin Hyman: 291–315.

Pratt, Mary Louise. (1992) *Imperial Eyes: Travel Writing and Transculturation.* Routledge: New York.

Proctor, James D. (1998) "Ethics in Geography: Giving Moral Form to the Geographical Imagination." *Area,* 30, 1, 8–18.

Radin, Margaret. (1986) "Residential Rent Control." *Philosophy and Public Affairs,* 15, 4, 350–380.

———. (1993) *Reinterpreting Property.* Chicago: University of Chicago Press.

Raley, G. H. (1945) *A Monograph of the Totem-Poles in Stanley Park, Vancouver, British Columbia.* Vancouver: Lumberman Printing.

Rasmussen, Susan. (1996) "The Tent as Cultural Symbol and Field Site: Social and Symbolic Space, 'Topos,' and Authority in a Tuareg Community." *Anthropological Quarterly,* 69, 1, 14–26.

Ray, Arthur J. (1996) *I Have Lived Here Since the World Began: An Illustrated History of Canada's Native People.* Canada: Lester Publishing.

Razack, Sherene. (2000) "Gendered Racial Violence and Spatialized Justice: The Murder of Pamela George." *Canadian Journal of Law and Society,* 15 (2): 91–130.

Razzaz, Omar M. (1993) "Examining Property Rights and Investment in Informal Settlements: The Case of Jordan." *Land Economics,* 69, 4, 341–355.

Reekie, Isabel M. (1968) *Red Paddles.* Vancouver: Mitchell Press.

Reid, Laura, and Neil Smith. (1994) "John Wayne Meets Donald Trump: The Lower East Side as Wild Wild West." In Kearns, Gerry, and Chris Philo, eds. *Selling Places: The City as Cultural Capital, Past and Present.* Oxford: Pergamon Press, 193–208.

Robertson, Michael. (1995) "Property and Ideology." *Canadian Journal of Law and Jurisprudence,* 8, No. 2, 275–296.

———. (1997) "Reconceiving Private Property." *Journal of Law and Society,* 24, 4, 465–485.

Robinson, Tony. (1995) "Gentrification and Grassroots Resistance in San Francisco's Tenderloin." *Urban Affairs Review,* 30, 4, 483–513.

Robinson, Scott. (1994) "The Aboriginal Embassy: An Account of the Protests of 1972." *Aboriginal History,* 18, 1, 49–63.

Roine, Chris. (1996) *The Squamish Aboriginal Economy, 1860–1940.* Master's thesis, Department of History, Simon Fraser University.

Rosaldo, Renato. (1996) "Foreword." *Stanford Law Review,* 48, 1036–1045.

Rose, Carol. (1994) *Property and Persuasion: Essays on the History, Theory and Rhetoric of Ownership.* Boulder, Colo.: Westview Press.

———. (1998) "The Several Futures of Property: Of Cyperspace and Folk Tales, Emission Trades and Ecosystems." *Minnesota Law Review,* 83, 129, 129–182.

Rose, Gillian. (1996) *Feminism and Geography.* Minneapolis: University of Minnesota Press.

Rose, Mitch. (2002) "The Seductions of Resistance: Power, Politics, and a Performative Style of Systems." *Environment and Planning, D, Society and Space,* 20, 383–400.

Ross, Warren, and J. Brian Phillips. (1995) *The Government vs. Freedom: In Defense of Property Rights.* http://pw1.netcom.com/~wsross/property/propert1.html

Roweis, Shoukry T., and Allen J. Scott. (1981) "The Urban Land Question." In Dear, Michael, and Allen J. Scott, eds. *Urbanization and Urban Planning in Capitalist Society.* London: Methuen, 123–158.

Royal Commission on Aboriginal Peoples. (1998) *Report of the Royal Commission on Aboriginal Peoples: Restructuring the Relationship,* Vol. 2, part 2. Ottawa: Canada Communication Group.

Ryan, Alan. (1984) *Property and Political Theory.* Oxford: Basil Blackwell.

Ryan, Simon. (1996) *The Cartographic Eye: How Explorers Saw Australia.* Cambridge: Cambridge University Press.

Sack, Robert D. (1986) *Human Territoriality: Its Theory and History.* Cambridge: Cambridge University Press.

Said, Edward. (1993) *Culture and Imperialism.* New York: Alfred A. Knopf.

Salsich, Peter W. (2000) "Toward a Property Ethic of Stewardship: A Religious Perspective." In Geisler, Charles, and Gail Daneker, eds. *Property and Values: Alternatives to Public and Private Ownership.* Washington D.C.: Island Press, 41–62.

Sanchez, Lisa. (1998) "Boundaries of Legitimacy: Sex, Violence, Citizenship, and Community in a Local Sexual Economy." *Law and Social Inquiry,* 22, 3, 543–580.

Sarat, Austin, and Thomas R. Kearns, eds. (1992) *Law's Violence.* Ann Arbor, Mich.: University of Michigan Press.

Sassen, Saskia. (1996) "Analytic Borderlands: Race, Gender and Representation in the New City" in King, Anthony D. ed. *Re-presenting the City: Ethnicity, Capital and Culture in the Twenty-First-Century Metropolis.* New York: New York University Press.

———. (2000) "The Global City: Strategic Site/New Frontier." In Isin, Engin, ed. *Democracy, Citizenship, and the Global City.* New York: Routledge, 48–61.

Sax, Joseph L. (1970) "The Public Trust Doctrine in Natural Resource Law: Effective Judicial Intervention." *Michigan Law Review,* 68, 471–566.

———. (1984) "Do Communities Have Rights? The National Parks as a Laboratory of New Ideas." *University of Pittsburgh Law Review,* 45, 499–511.

———. (2001) *Playing Darts with a Rembrandt: Public and Private Rights in Cultural Treasures.* Ann Arbor, Mich.: University of Michigan Press.

Sayer, Andrew, and Michael Storper. (1997) "Ethics Unbound: For a Normative Turn in Social Theory." *Society and Space,* 15, 1, 1–17.

Schmelzkopf, Karen. (1995) "Urban Community Gardens as a Contested Space." *Geographical Review,* 85, 3, 364–379.

Scott, James. (1998) *Seeing like a State: How Certain Schemes to Improve the Human Condition Have Failed.* New Haven, Conn.: Yale University Press.

Seed, Patricia. (1995) *Ceremonies of Possession in Europe's Conquest of the New World, 1492–1640.* Cambridge: Cambridge University Press.

Sennett, Richard. (1990) *Conscience of the Eye: The Design and Social Life of Cities from the Middle Ages to the Present.* New York: Knopf.

Shamir, Ronen. (2001) "Suspended in Space: Bedouins under the Law of Israel." In Blomley, Nicholas, David Delaney, and Richard T. Ford, eds. *The Legal Geographies Reader.* Oxford: Blackwell, 134–142.

Shaw, Wendy S. (2000) "Ways of Whiteness: Harlemising Sydney's Aboriginal Redfern." *Australian Geographical Studies,* 38 3, 291–305.

Singer, Joseph W. (1988) "The Reliance Interest in Property." *Stanford Law Review,* 40, 3, 611–751.

———. (1996) "No Right to Exclude: Public and Private Accommodations and Private Property." *Northwestern University Law Review,* 90, 4, 1283–1497.

———. (2000) "Property and Social Relations: From Title to Entitlement." In Geisler, Charles, and Gail Daneker, eds. *Property and Values: Alternatives to Public and Private Ownership.* Washington D.C.: Island Press, 3–20.

———. (2000) *Entitlement: The Paradoxes of Property.* New Haven, Conn.: Yale University Press.

Singer, Joseph, and J. M. Beerman. (1993) "The Social Origins of Property." *Canadian Journal of Law and Jurisprudence.* 6, 2, 217–248.

Smart, Carol. (1989) *Feminism and the Power of Law.* New York: Routledge.

Smith, David M. (2000) *Moral Geographies: Ethics in a World of Difference.* Edinburgh: Edinburgh University Press.

———. (1998) "How Far Should We Care? On the Spatial Scope of Beneficence." *Progress in Human Geography,* 22, 15–38.

Smith, Heather Anne. (2000) *Where Worlds Collide: Social Polarization at the Community Level in Vancouver's Gastown/Downtown Eastside.* Ph.D. diss., Department of Geography, University of British Columbia.

Smith, Neil. (1993) "Homeless/Global: Scaling Places." In Bird, Jon, et al., eds. *Mapping the Futures: Local Cultures, Global Change.* London: Routledge.

———. (1996) *The New Urban Frontier: Gentrification and the Revanchist City.* New York: Routledge.

———. (1997) "Social Justice and American Urbanism: The Revanchist City." In Merrifield, Andy, and Erik Swyngedouw, eds. *The Urbanization of Injustice.* New York: New York University Press, 117–136.

———. (2002) "New Globalism, New Urbanism: Gentrification as Global Urban Strategy." *Antipode,* 34, 3, 452–472.

Smith, Neil, and Jeff Derksen. (2002) "Urban Regeneration: Gentrification as Global Urban Strategy." In Shier, Reid, ed. *Stan Douglas: Every Building on 100 West Hastings Street.* Vancouver: Contemporary Art Gallery/Arsenal Pulp Press, 62–95.

Smith, Paul Chaat, and Robert Allen Warrior. (1996) *Like a Hurricane: The Indian Movement from Alcatraz to Wounded Knee.* New York: The New Press.

Solnit, Rebecca, and Susan Schwartzenberg. (2000) *Hollow City: The Siege of San Francisco and the Crisis of American Urbanism.* London: Verso.

Sommers, Jeffrey. (1998) "Mapping Men: The Intersecting Politics of Space and Masculinity in Vancouver, 1962–1986." *Urban Geography,* 19, 287–310.

———. (2001) The Place of the Poor: Poverty, Space, and the Politics of Representation in Downtown Vancouver, 1950–1997. Ph.D. diss., Department of Geography, Simon Fraser University.

Soto, Hernando de. (2000) *The Mystery of Capital: Why Capitalism Triumphs in the West and Fails Everywhere Else.* New York: Basic Books.

Sparke, Mathew. (1998) "A Map That Roared and an Original Atlas: Canada, Cartography, and the Narration of Nation." *Annals of the Association of American Geographers,* 88, 3, 463–495.

Squamish Nation. (2001) *Xay Temixw Land Use Plan: For the Forests and Wilderness of the Squamish Nation Traditional Territory.* Land and Resources Committee, Squamish Nation.

Steinberg, Theodore. (1995) *Slide Mountain or the Folly of Owning Nature.* Berkeley: University of California Press.

Taylor, Affrica. (2000) " 'The Sun Always Shines in Perth': A Post-colonial Geography of Identity, Memory, and Place." *Australian Geographical Studies,* 38, 1, 27–35.

Tennant, Paul. (1990) *Aboriginal Peoples and Politics.* Vancouver: University of British Columbia Press.

Thompson, Edward P. (1975) *Whigs and Hunters: The Origins of the Black Acts.* London: Allen Lane.

Tigerstrom, Barbara von. (1998) "The Public Trust Doctrine in Canada." *Journal of Environmental Law and Practice,* 7, 379–401.

Tully, James. (1993) *An Approach to Political Philosophy: Locke in Contexts.* Cambridge: Cambridge University Press.

Turnbull, David. (1989) *Maps are Territories: Science Is an Atlas.* Chicago: University of Chicago Press.

Turner, Frederick J. (1892; 1961) *Frontier and Section: Selected Essays of Frederick J. Turner.* Englewood Cliffs, N.J.: Prentice-Hall.

Turner, Nancy J., and James T. Jones. (2000) *Occupying the Land: Traditional Patterns of Land and Resource Ownership among First Peoples of British Columbia.* Presented at IACSP, Bloomington, Indiana. *http://www.indiana.edu/~iascp/iascp2000.htm*

Underkuffler, Laura S. (1990) "On Property: An Essay." *Yale Law Journal,* 100, 1, 127–148.

Unger, Roberto. (1983) "The Critical Legal Studies Movement." *Harvard Law Review,* 96, 3, 320–432.

Varley, Ann. (2002) "Private or Public: Debating the Meaning of Tenure Legalization." *International Journal of Urban and Regional Research,* 26, 3, 449–461.

Vogt, Roy. (1999) *Whose property? The Deepening Conflict between Private Property and Democracy in Canada.* Toronto: University of Toronto Press.

Waldron, Jeremy. (1988) *The Right to Private Property.* Oxford: Clarendon Press.

———. (1990) "Homelessness and the Issue of Freedom." *U.C.L.A. Law Review,* 39, 295–324.

Walzer, Michael. (1983) *Spheres of Justice: A Defense of Pluralism and Equality.* New York: Basic Books.

———. (1984) "Liberalism and the Art of Separation." *Political Theory,* 12, 3, 315–330.

———. (1986) "Pleasures and Costs of Urbanity." *Dissent,* Fall, 470–475.

Wells, Samantha. (2000) "Labour, Control, and Protection: The Kahlin Aboriginal Compound, Darwin, 1911–38." In Read, Peter, ed. *Settlement: A History of Aboriginal Housing.* Canberra: Aboriginal Studies Press, 64–74.

White, James Boyd. (1985) *Heracles' Bow: Essays on the Rhetoric and Poetics of the Law.* Madison: University of Wisconsin Press.

Williams, Patricia. (1991) *The Alchemy of Race and Rights.* Cambridge, Mass.: Harvard University Press.

Williams, Robert A. Jr. (1990) *The American Indian in Western Legal Thought.* Oxford: Oxford University Press.

Wilson, David. (1996) "Metaphors, Growth Coalition Discourses, and Black Poverty in a U.S. City." *Antipode,* 28, 1, 72–96.

Wilson, James Q., and George L. Kelling. (1982) "Broken Windows." *Atlantic Monthly,* 249, 3, 29–38.

Wilson, William J. (1987) *The Truly Disadvantaged, the Inner City, the Underclass and Public Policy.* Chicago: University of Chicago Press.

Wood, Denis. (1992) "How Maps Work." *Cartographica,* 29, 3/4, 66–74.

Woodcock, George. (1990) *British Columbia, A History of the Province*. Vancouver: Douglas & McIntyre.

Wyly, Elvin, and Hammel, Daniel. (2002) "Neoliberal Housing Policy and the Gentrification of the American Urban System." Paper presented at Upward Neighbourhood Trajectories: Gentrification in a New Century. University of Glasgow. Online at *http://www.gla.ac.uk/departments/urbanstudies/gentpaps/gentpap.html*

Yeoh, Brenda. (2001) "Postcolonial Cities," *Progress in Human Geography,* 25, 3, 456–468.

Young, Iris Marion. (1990) *Justice and the Politics of Difference*. Princeton, N.J.: Princeton University Press.

Young, James. (2000) *At Memory's Edge*. New Haven, Conn.: Yale University Press.

Zaharoff, William J. (1978) *Success in Struggle: The Squamish People and Kitsilano Indian Reserve No. 6*. Master's thesis, Department of History, Carleton University.

Index